AF469388

MES11964

SYMBOLS OF SURVIVAL

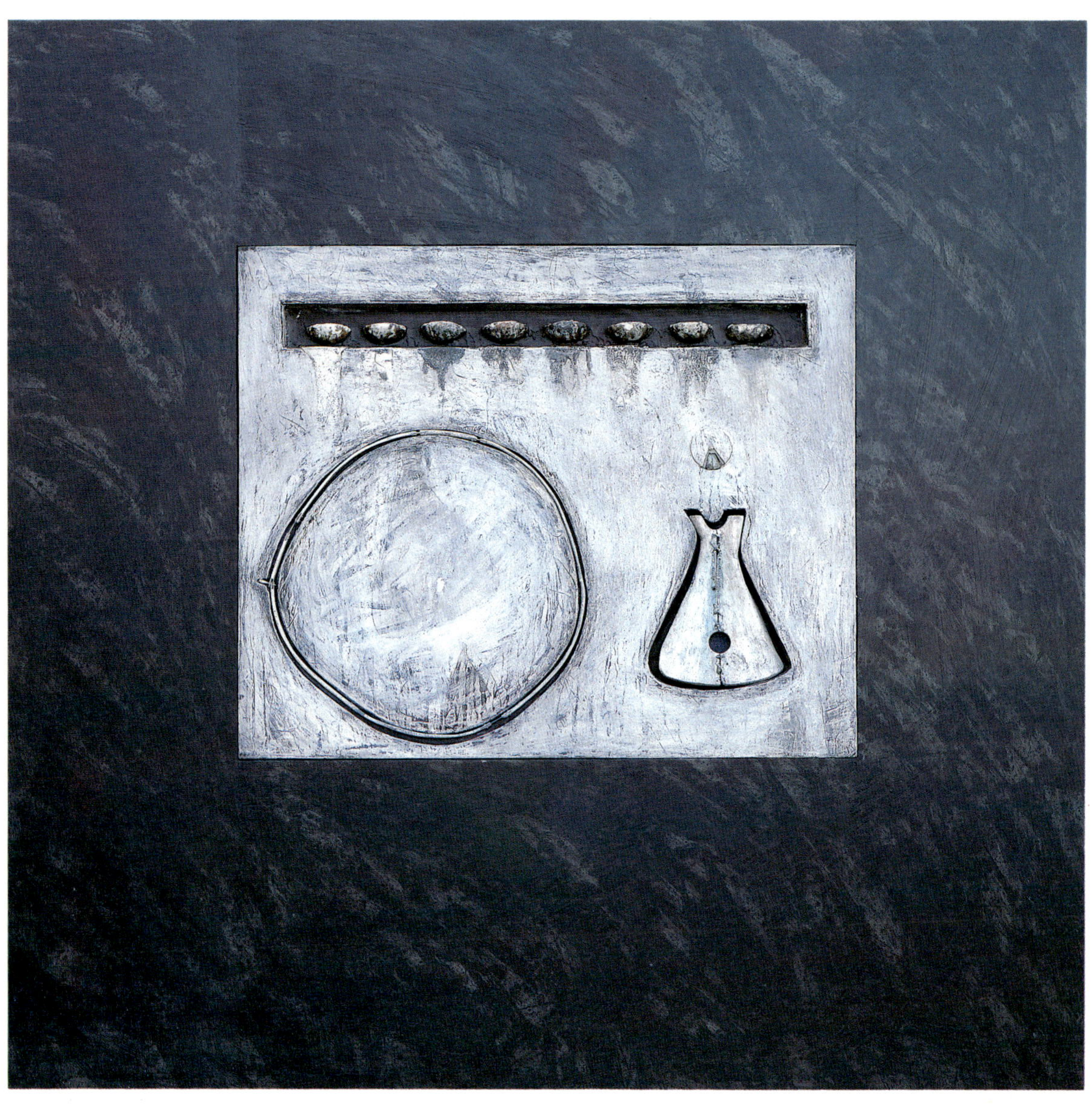

Frontispiece, *Diviner's Wall* (1992) (Cat. 170)

SYMBOLS OF SURVIVAL
The Art of WILL MACLEAN

by DUNCAN MACMILLAN
Foreword by SORLEY MACLEAN

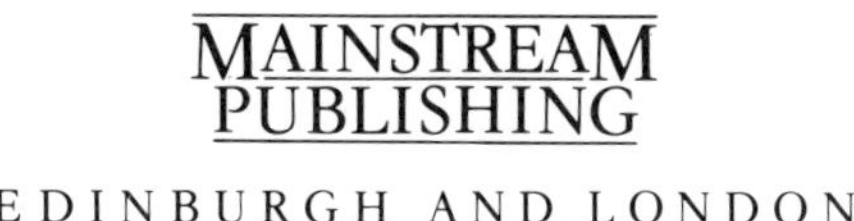

EDINBURGH AND LONDON

First published in Great Britain 1992 by
MAINSTREAM PUBLISHING COMPANY (EDINBURGH) LTD
7 Albany Street
Edinburgh EH1 3UG

ISBN 1 85158 419 6 (cased)
ISBN 1 85158 424 2 (paper)

The publishers wish to acknowledge grateful thanks to the Scottish Arts Council for their financial assistance in the production of this volume.

A catalogue record for this book is available from the British Library

Designed by James Hutcheson and Paul Keir, Edinburgh
Printed in Hong Kong

PHOTOGRAPHIC CREDITS

Prudence Cumming: Plate 43
Joe Rock: Plates 1, 2, 3, 5, 10, 22, 60, 76, 78 and 89
Colin Roscoe: Portrait of the artist, Plates 19, 39, 84 and 86
Tom Scott: Plates 15 and.16
Aberdeen Art Gallery: Plate 58
National Gallery of Scotland: Plate 51
Robert Fleming Holdings Plc: Plate 81

SPONSORS

This publication has been sponsored by Mr Calum Murray, Argyll. It has also been supported by a grant from the Russell Trust.
The Talbot Rice Gallery is supported by the Scottish Arts Council.

CONTENTS

ACKNOWLEDGEMENTS

This book would not have been possible without the generous help of the artist and his wife, Marian, to whom I extend my grateful thanks. The artist himself also wishes to join me in thanking Sorley MacLean for very kindly agreeing to write a foreword. We would also like to thank Michael Hue-Williams and Turske Hue-Williams Fine Art Ltd for their generous help, in kind as well as with the financing of the project. We are also very grateful to Calum Murray and the Russell Trust for their financial assistance. Claus Runkel and Sylvia Stevenson have both been generous with their help and support in preparing the project.

The book will be published on the occasion of the artist's retrospective at the Talbot Rice Gallery. In preparing this exhibition, the artist has been greatly helped by the award of a bursary from the Scottish Arts Council. With the agreement and support of the Duncan of Jordanstone College of Art this has enabled him to take time off from teaching to prepare the exhibition.

Duncan Macmillan

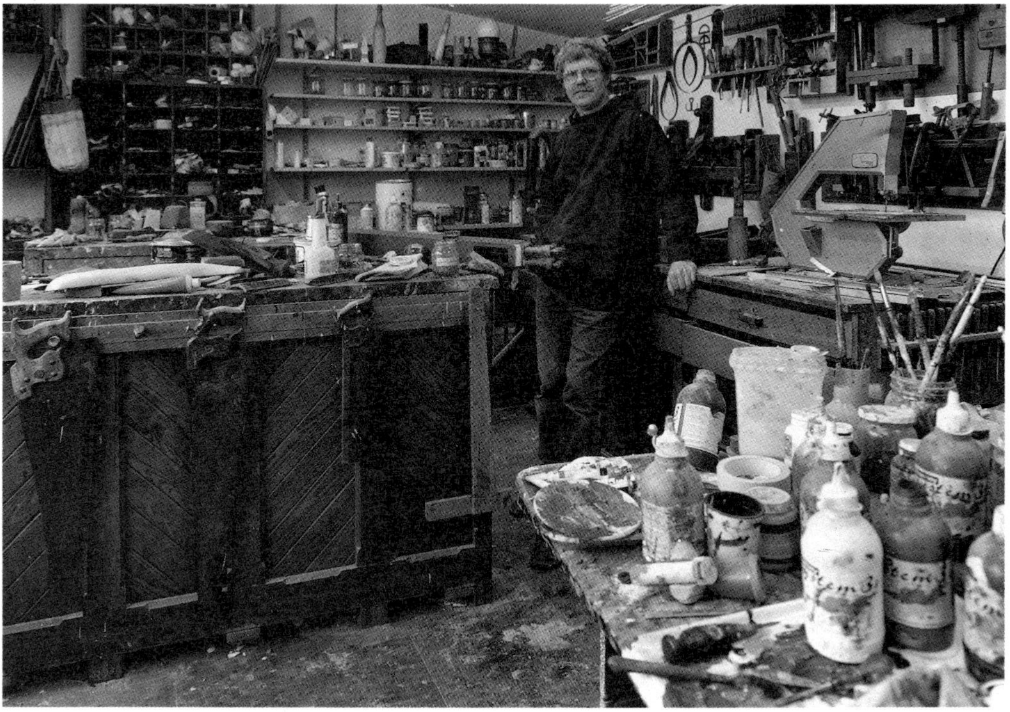

Photograph of the artist in his studio by Colin Ruscoe, 1989

FOREWORD
BY SORLEY MACLEAN

I was greatly honoured to be asked to write a foreword for the admirable book that Duncan Macmillan has written for Will Maclean's exhibition this summer.

The book contains a fascinating account of his own family's influence on Maclean, and especially of his father's influence. Captain John Maclean was a man who impressed me very much on the few occasions that I met him, which was at the Gaelic Society of Inverness. I did know William Reid when he was a pupil at Portree High School before the war and I liked him very much; and from a very early age I heard most favourable opinions of the Reids in general from Raasay and Braes men who were members of the crews of their fishing boats. I vividly remember the (to me) almost legendary *Star of the Sea* putting in during a very high tide at the natural jetty at Osgaig in Raasay. [William Reid was the artist's uncle and is commemorated in *Skye Fisherman: In Memoriam. Star of the Sea* was his grandfather's boat.]

We are fortunate in having Will Maclean, and Will himself is fortunate in having such an able, learned and enthusiastic interpreter as Duncan Macmillan, whose tastes are catholic and who is acutely aware, as Will himself is, that the local and contemporary and the present, and near and very distant past are in many ways continuous, and that the local and parochial are often poignant and universal. Macmillan puts the essential qualities of Maclean's art splendidly very early in his book: 'His art . . . is not nostalgic or self-pitying; rather it draws strength from the qualities and the continuity of Highland culture, while seeking universal and contemporary metaphors from it and from the tragedy of Highland history. He should also be seen in the tradition of the Scots Renascence, however, in the way that his art relates the history and traditions of Scotland to the objectives of modernism', and, again, 'his realisation that art is not a remote, abstract and self-contained entity, but a way of reflecting on life's concerns, both immediate and wider.'

Macmillan's account of his range and development is admirable, not least in the way he brings out the complexity and subtlety of Maclean's work, with its social realism transmuted with immanent religious and surrealist images, sometimes against a background of geology and archaeology, which adds to their universality and timelessness. To make a metaphor or another image a symbol, and to do that unobtrusively or, as it were, unconsciously, is to my mind a mark of great natural power in any art. Among other things, I think of the way it happens, as it were artlessly, in the poetry of Mary MacDonald (Mrs MacPherson), who died in 1898, a woman of great vitality and even *joie de vivre*, who is the most individual of all the Gaelic poets moved by the Clearances and the Land League. Macmillan goes on to say that there came to Maclean the 'realisation that it should be possible to record real experience without curtailing the poetic resonance of an image, or its power to suggest.'

The book is a most perceptive and sympathetic study of the art of a man who is consciously and unconsciously aware of the philosophy, literature and visual art that Scotland has encountered and produced from the Enlightenment and Scottish Renascence to the present day; of a man passionately concerned with the whole history of his country, especially with its tragedy, which is part of the tragedy of the world, and which transcends 'any lines of territorial demarcation of the arts'. Never has a common ground between art and poetry been more necessary than it is today, but that necessity is timeless and universal.

Sorley MacLean
May 1992

SYMBOLS OF SURVIVAL

THE ART OF WILL MACLEAN

William McTaggart was the greatest Scottish artist to come from the Highlands in modern times. He was also one of the very few. The reason for this certainly has nothing to do with talent. The Gaelic poets who have flourished over the same period are witnesses to this. Art is a more urban business than poetry and also, for virtually the whole of the modern period, the period in which art has flourished in the main cities of Scotland, life in the Highlands has been chronically dislocated.

The Celtic tradition in a broader sense has however played a significant part in the inspiration of a good many artists since the eighteenth century. For instance, J. D. Fergusson and William Johnstone, the two key figures in the history of modern art in Scotland, both stressed the importance to them of their identification with the Celtic past. Following Fergusson too, Ian Finlay based his history of art in Scotland on the thesis of racial continuity with the Celts[1] and it was an important element in the Scots Renascence of the 1920s and 1930s. Nor was J. D. Fergusson's identification with the Highland tradition merely whimsical either. It was based on the fact that his father was a Highlander and that there were Gaelic speakers in his family, although he himself was brought up in Leith. It was serious enough to bring him to settle in Glasgow in 1939, which he regarded as a Celtic city, and it led him to take a lively interest in Gaelic tradition.

For all these artists though, except for McTaggart, Celtic or Highland culture was a generalised thing. Their interest was shaped more by their knowledge of the artistic achievement of the ancient Celts than by their understanding and appreciation of the modern Highlanders. McTaggart, on the other hand, came to comment directly on the present Highland situation at the end of his life in his remarkable series of paintings of the *Emigrants* and *The Emigrant Ship*.

Will Maclean is from a Highland background as McTaggart was. His commentary on the Highland situation is first hand too, and although like Fergusson he is not a Gaelic speaker, he has always been close to the present life of the Highlands. Indeed, his art has been shaped by this, though, as with the poetry of Sorley MacLean whom he greatly admires, this is not a limitation. It is not nostalgic or self-pitying; rather it draws strength from the qualities and the continuity of Highland culture, while seeking universal and contemporary metaphors from it and from the tragedy of Highland history. He should also be seen in the tradition of the Scots Renascence, however, in the way that his art relates the history and traditions of Scotland to the objectives of modernism. It should therefore be seen alongside that of Paolozzi, Davie and Bellany.

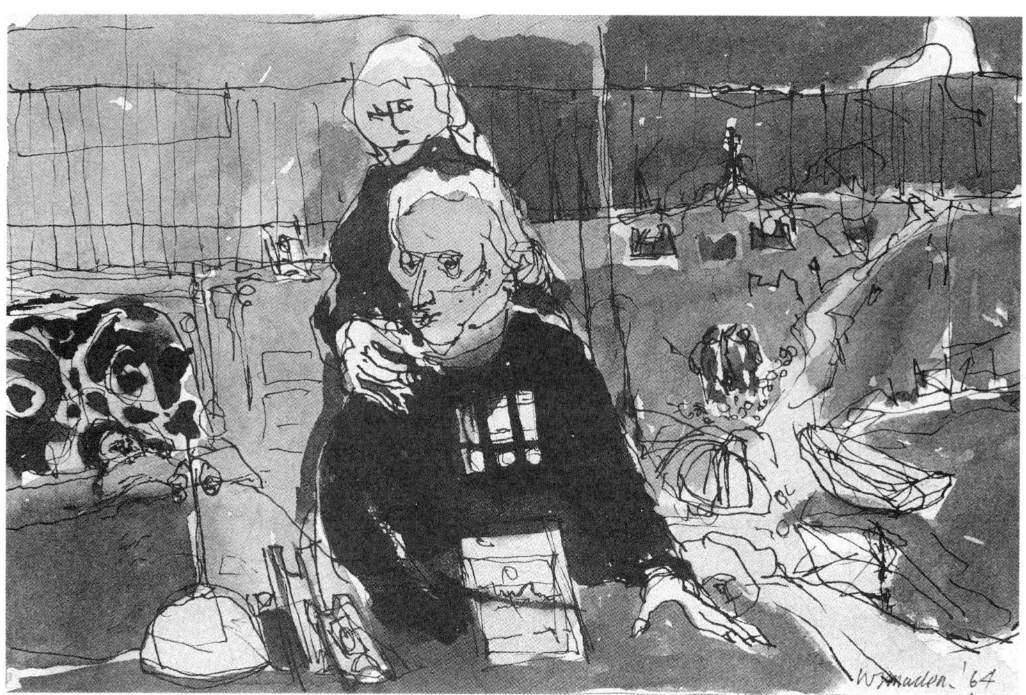

1. Study for painting of the Clearances, pen, 11.8 x 17.5 cms (1964)

It took him a while to reach that position and he had been working for almost ten years before he began to produce work which he now recognises as reflecting his real ambitions as an artist, though as artists often are, he is perhaps a little hard on his early work. Certainly he describes his experience of art training as a little like maths at school. It was something you had to learn. It was difficult, but to do it at all, it had to be done well, or it was simply wrong. In a way, his development as an artist has been the unlearning of that attitude and its replacement by the realisation that art is not a remote, abstract and self-contained entity, but a way of reflecting on life's concerns, both immediate and wider.

Maclean was brought up in Inverness where his father, John Maclean, was harbour master. John Maclean had been brought up in the fishing-crofting community of Polbain in Coigach. It was a Gaelic-speaking world, largely self-sufficient, but the last community to cultivate what is now fallow land. He has left a vivid account of it in a manuscript memoir of his childhood and family history. Like most of his generation there, he only learned English when he went to school and his memoir recalls a world that was vigorous and carefree even though material property was minimal and luxury unknown. It was, too, a world in part still regulated by custom and mutual help. As he looked back on it near the end of his life, it had the quality of a golden age and as such had a powerful effect on his son's imagination.

From Coigach, John Maclean went to sea. He trained as a wireless operator in Glasgow, but later, after a time as a deck-hand, he took his mate's ticket and,

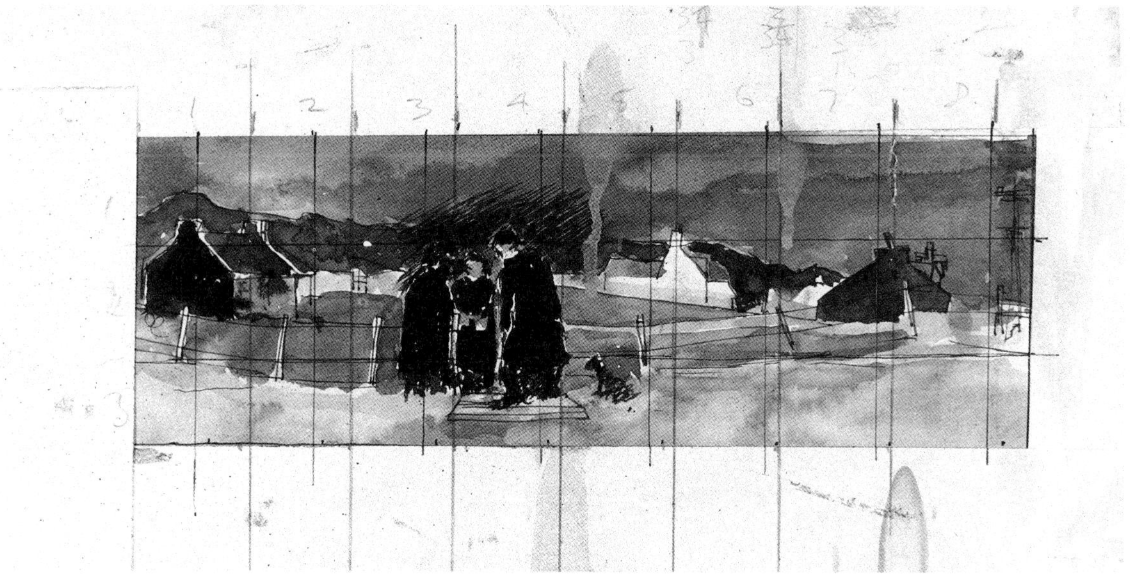

2. Study for a projected painting of the Clearances, pen and wash, squared in pencil, 7.1 x 21 cms, (1964)

by then a Master Mariner, ended up in Inverness in charge of the harbour. John Maclean died in 1962, but his son's memory of him and above all his sense of the link that existed through him, back into the world of Gaelic culture that seemed to pass with his generation, has been a primary motive in his art. It is as though, through it, he could build a bridge back into that disappearing world. Indeed his mature art is informed above all by this and it reflects on the history of the Highlands and the seagoing tradition of his family there. That he has managed to build out of this an art that is of universal relevance is a measure of his stature as an artist.

To follow in his father's footsteps and go to sea himself was Will Maclean's first ambition, however, and he began his career at the age of fifteen when he went to train for the merchant navy at HMS *Conway.* He then became an apprentice with the Blue Funnel Line and spent two years at sea, but his career as a sailor was cut short when he failed an eye-test. He had to think again and returned to Scotland to take Highers, studying for a year in Edinburgh. His choice was between art and gymnastics, the two subjects that had been his best at school, but while he was studying in Edinburgh, he went to evening classes at Edinburgh College of Art and his career as an artist began. When he went for the entrance examination for the Edinburgh College though, he was asked to draw a lady in a crinoline. He had never drawn the draped figure. All he had drawn all year was the nude. He was completely thrown and it was only afterwards that he discovered that he had been in the wrong class all year! However, in spite of this fiasco at Edinburgh, he was accepted at Gray's School of Art in Aberdeen.

As it was at Edinburgh, the curriculum at Gray's was still highly structured. Ian Fleming was Principal, but Henderson Blyth was head of painting and it was reflecting on the situation in the painting school that Maclean produced his com-

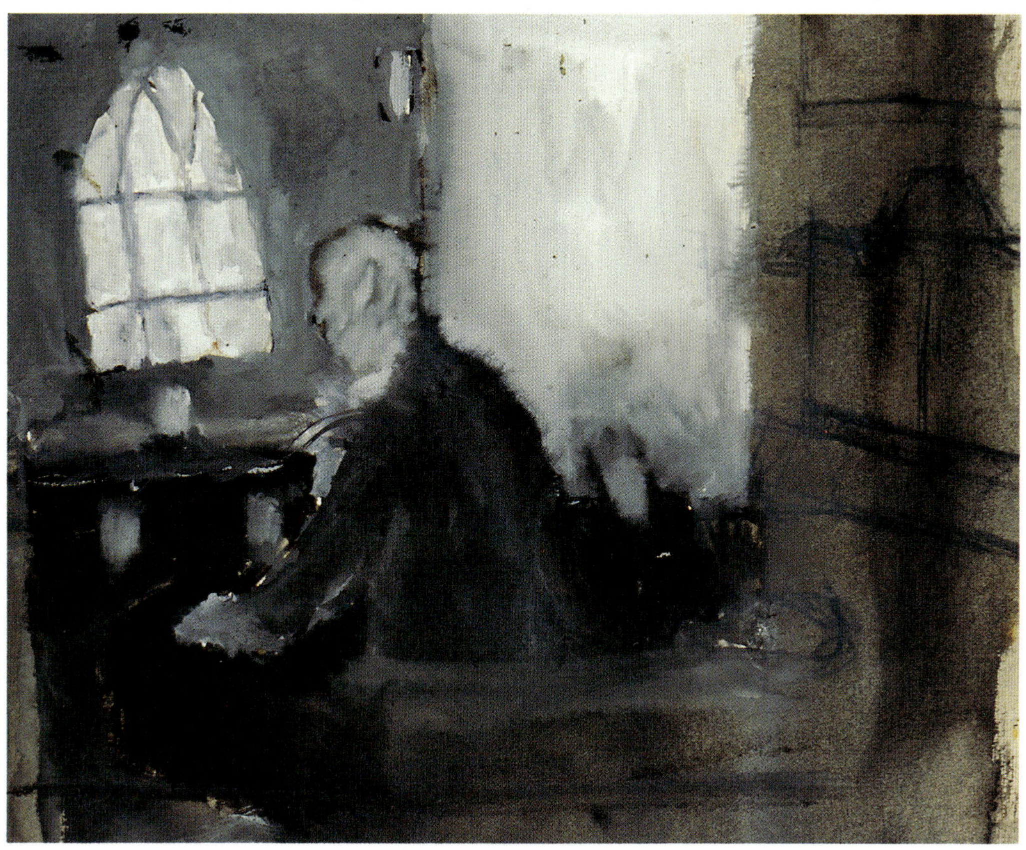

3. *Minister Preaching in the Kirk at Achiltibuie*, pen and wash with Chinese white, 11.8 x 14 cms (1964)

parison between art and maths. Nevertheless, he speaks very warmly of his time at Gray's and of the way that the people who taught him there — Ian Fleming, Frances Walker, George Mackie, David Foulkes, Fred Stiven — supported him and have remained his friends. He remembers still, not only the kindness, but also the experience of seeing the houses of Mackie, Stiven and Foulkes, a new kind of environment to him, filled with art-works and treasured objects as his own house is now.

The school also provided opportunities for students to travel to see exhibitions in Edinburgh, Glasgow or London. In Edinburgh too, he had friends at the College so he was conscious at first hand of the defiance of the establishment by his contemporaries, Sandy Moffat and John Bellany, in their exhibition on the railings outside the National Gallery in 1964. The significance of this was not just in the dramatic gesture. It was in Bellany's proposal that there was a place in painting for social subject-matter of a kind that reflected the reality that the artist shared with his own community. Maclean's own work, though, was shaped by the stimulus of his immediate artistic environment. Surviving landscapes show his affinity to Fleming and Mackie, but also in his later work, he has remained loyal to Fleming's underlying conviction of the social involvement of art, so clearly seen in the older artist's

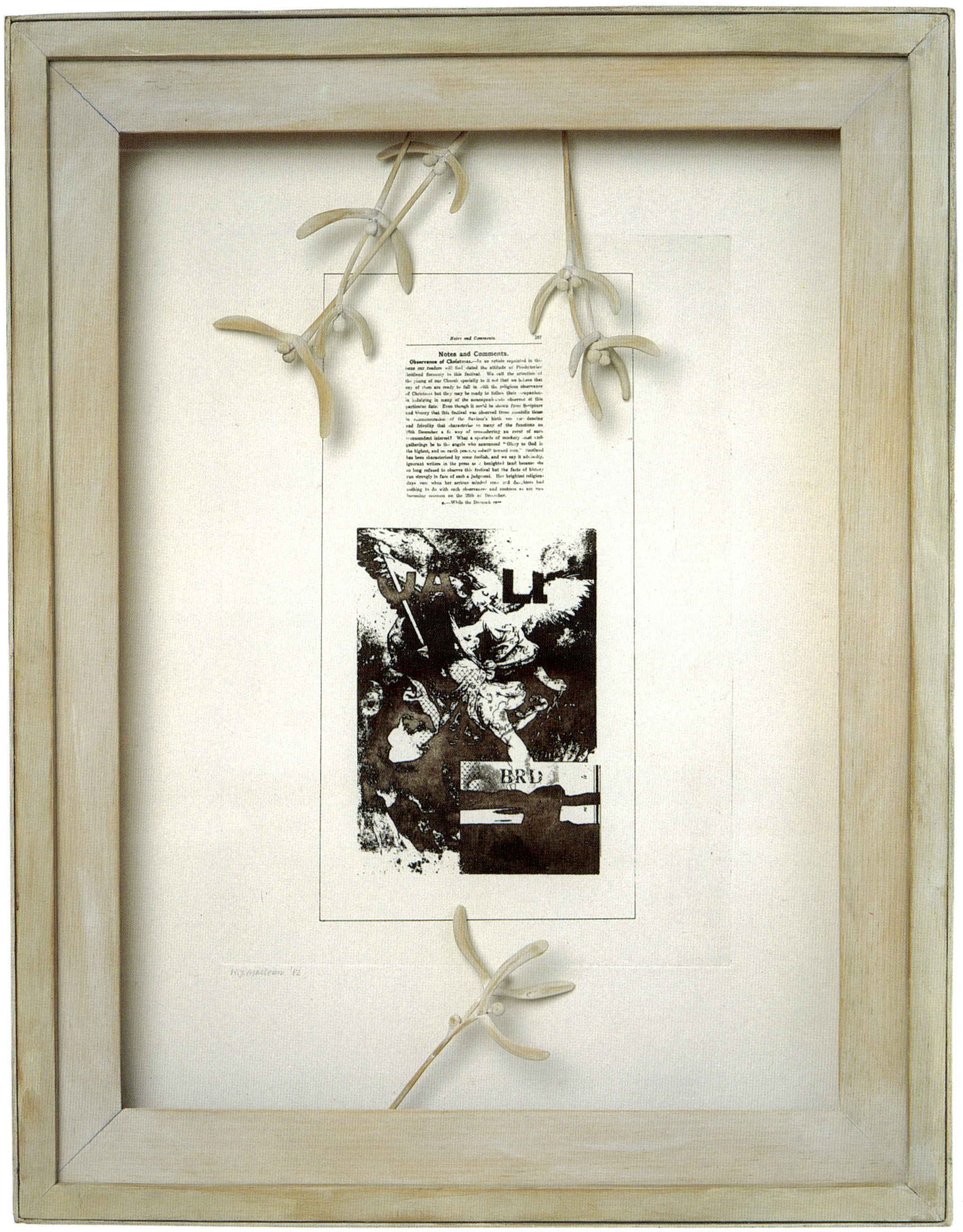

4. *Observation of Christmas* (1982) (Cat. 76)

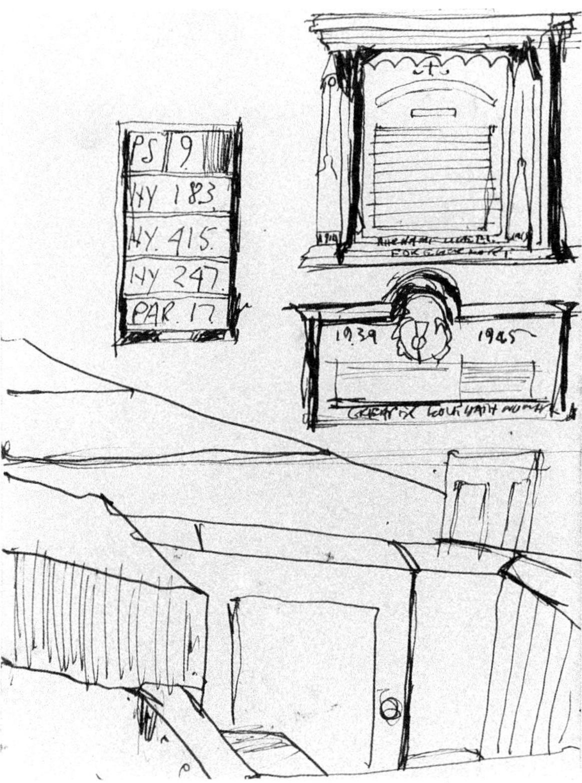

5. Studies of church furnishings, Kyleakin, pen, 253 x 179 mm (1965)

etchings.

Most of Maclean's work at the time was landscape, however, and in a way his art has developed from that premise, for it is still very much concerned with places, with environments and the people in them. Perhaps it is landscape seen in more than just three dimensions and in that respect, though from a different angle, it is comparable to Frances Walker's economical and unsentimental vision of the underlying facts of the landscape of Scotland. Even as a student, however, he already had an interest in Highland issues, though at the time this was expressed in his art in social realism rather than symbolism.

Maclean spent the summer of 1964 at Hospitalfield. Willie Reid was still the teacher there and David McClure was the visitor, but the most important thing was the freedom and the sharing of experience with new friends in the other art schools. For instance, he and George Donald, who was at Edinburgh, taught themselves to etch. To do this they reassembled, by trial and error, E. S. Lumsden's press which was lying dismantled in a shed. At that time, etching was not an approved part of the painting curriculum, but in this and in other ways the experience of Hospitalfield broadened his outlook. He has continued to etch ever since and indeed some of his most important recent work is in that form.

In spite of the example of such people as Fleming and Walker, at Gray's, says Maclean, 'Art was forced to labour in the mines of life-painting,' and in this academic tradition, for their diploma shows students had to produce a large-scale, figure composition with at least three figures. Maclean's painting was prophetic of one of the central themes of his later art, the tragic history of the Highlands. It was a picture of the Clearances. It no longer survives, but its genesis is recorded in a number of drawings (*Pl. 1 & 2*). Stark and monochromatic, these are quite unsentimental.

It is not surprising that he should turn to this sad history for a subject. For in his manuscript family history, his father remarks:

> There are many these days who say that the Clearances should be forgotten and the hatchet buried, but I do not take that view. I think it should be kept alive and every Highlander should have copies of the histories of the Clearances along with the bible in his bookcase. It is not right that the Clearances should ever be forgotten.

True to his father in two ways, Maclean

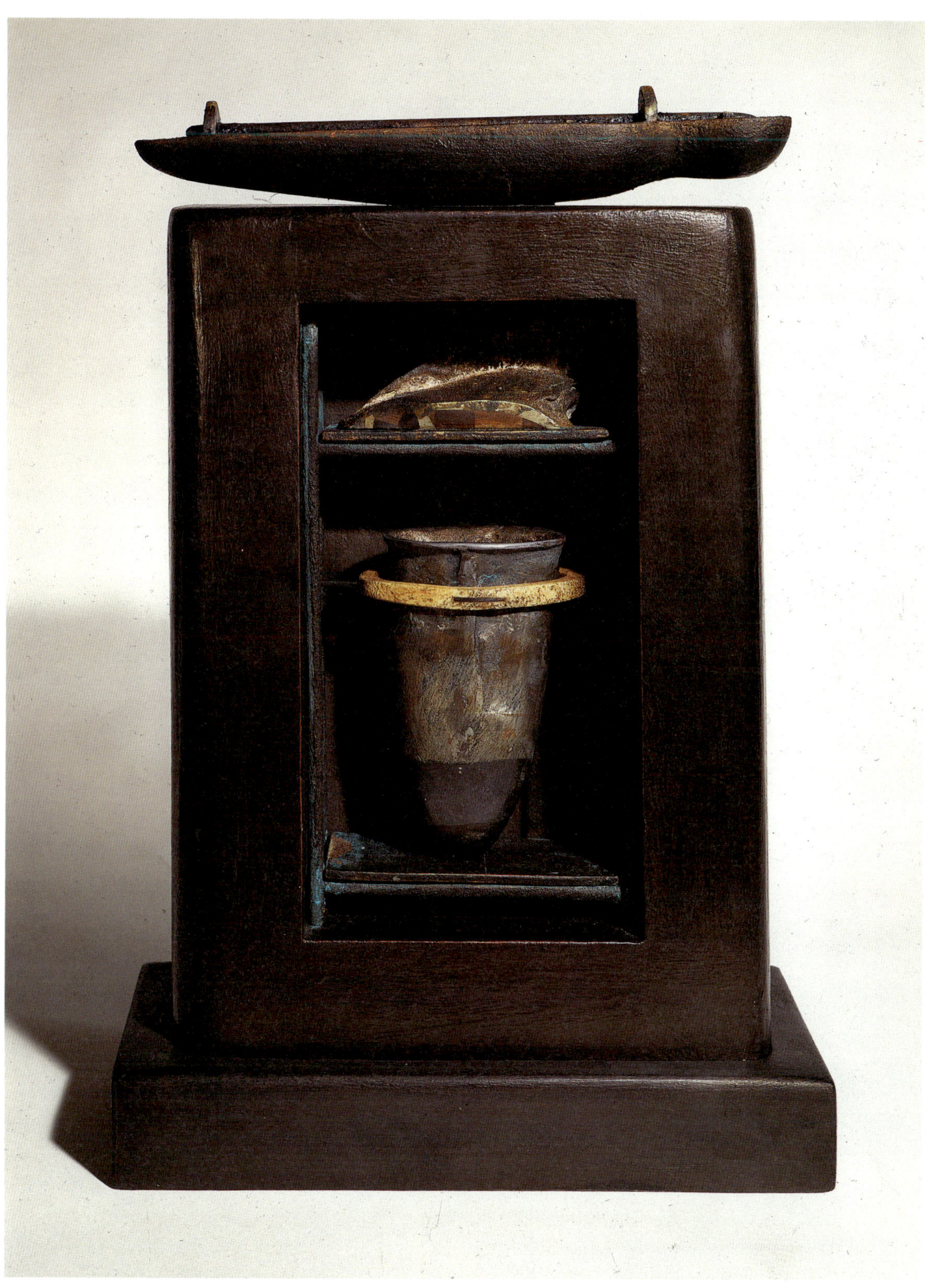

6. *Museum Casket* (1989) (Cat. 155)

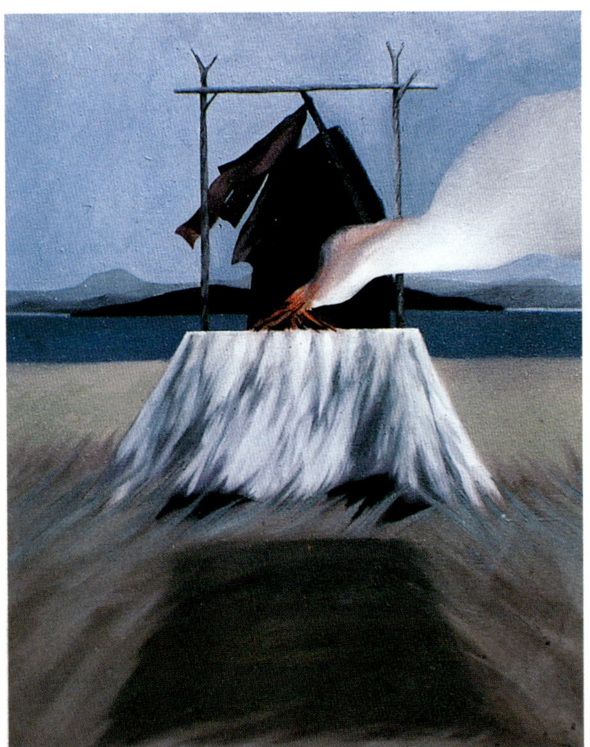

7. *Beach Allegory*, oil on canvas, 50 × 30 cms, Private Collection, Edinburgh (1973)

seems to be contemplating the tragic sense of the loss of a land and its people and the wrong done to them, and at the same time the remarkable way in which the persecuted Highlanders still found dignity even within their diminishing resources, a dignity of which his own art is a continuing assertion.

One of the drawings related to this composition is of the minister preaching in the church at Achiltibuie (*Pl. 3*). It is a drawing worthy of Wilkie in its terseness. The church was leaking and the monochrome washes of the drawing reflect the cold and the damp and, by extension, the fact that there is little comfort in such a religion. Organised religion failed the Highlanders as their ministers betrayed them, but perhaps their religion reflected their reality nevertheless. Recognition of man's ineffectuality in controlling his fate and of God's arbitrariness in dispensing it is the measure of the realism of the Calvinist belief. It is not a creed of false comfort. It matches the harsh reality of a northern existence, just as the brutality of the Clearances is matched by the harshness of the Highland environment. Maclean has never forgiven the life-denying joylessness of the Free Kirk though. Many years later, for instance, he made a work, *Observation of Christmas* (1982, *Pl. 4*). Its centrepiece is a text warning against the celebration of the feast and, summoned by the Kirk's fulminations, an avenging angel is descending on Skye to chastise those foolhardy enough to find pleasure in it.

A constant theme in Maclean's later work is religion, though not always in such a specific and satirical way as in *Observation of Christmas*. It is more often present by implication through the analogy suggested between the objects that he makes and the objects made in the service of religion. He sees continuity from earliest times in a people's spiritual need for some kind of mediation between themselves and the natural world, expressed in a material form. In *Observation of Christmas*, this is present in a piece of carved mistletoe, linking modern Christmas to its pre-Christian origins, and elements of this kind, that are already present in this early drawing with its religious subject, often reappear subsequently.

For instance in the drawing, beyond the minister is the church window. In Maclean's later work, windows became a metaphor for the art work itself, allowing us to move between the real and the imaginative or spiritual, as this church window opens on to the landscape beyond. Behind the minister, too, is a board carrying a text.

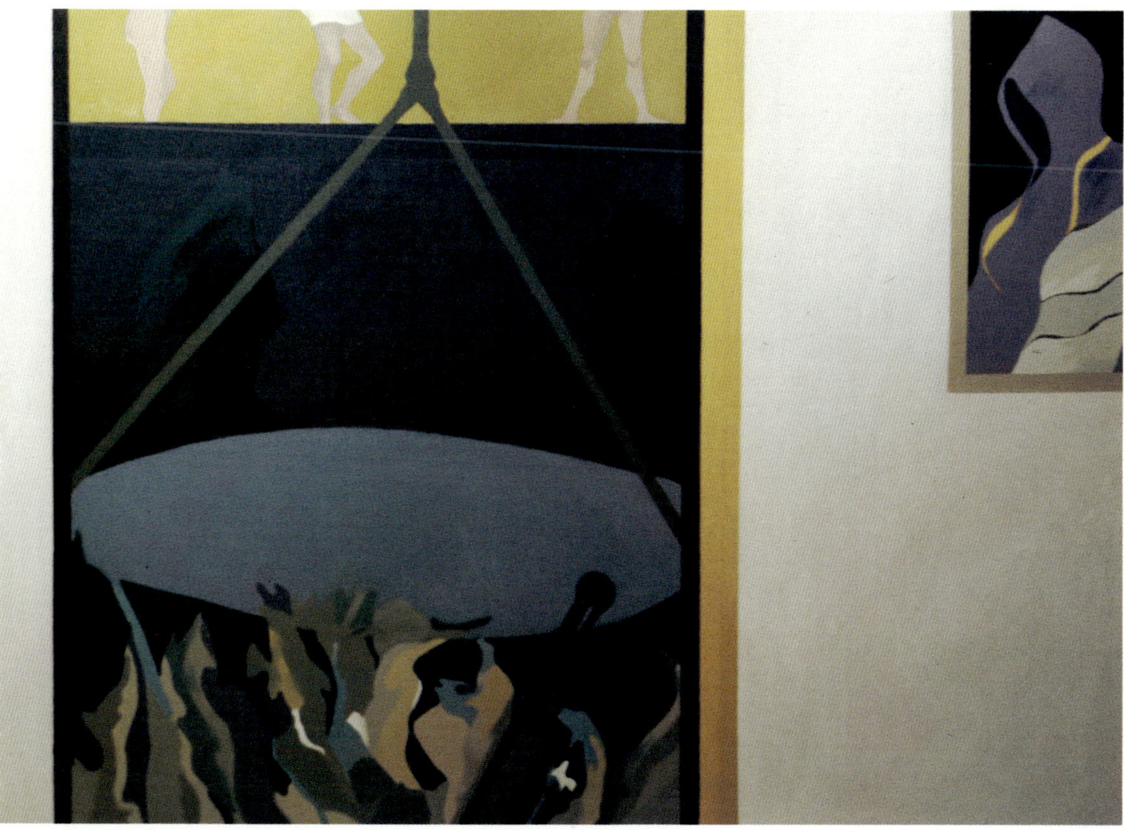

8. *Fisherman with a Broken Arm*, oil on canvas, 152 x 122 cms (1973)

It is not legible, but the fact that it is even minimally carved and shaped identifies it as a religious object in a way that reaches far beyond the severe limitations of the Presbyterian tradition (*Pl. 5*). It is after all only one of many religions that may have prevailed amongst the Highland people. Each in its turn must have met their needs and as he invokes religion, Maclean comments on this underlying continuity even while he implicitly condemns the barrenness of the Free Kirk.

Maclean graduated from Aberdeen in 1965 and spent the following year, 1966-7, on a travelling scholarship which took him to France, Italy and Greece. He himself remarked of his work of this period: 'When you grew up you were expected to become an "abstract" artist.' It sounds a bit like progressing to the wearing of long trousers and a group of paintings done on Mykonos does indeed show him working to develop a more abstract language from an observed scene. The work from this travelling year is still recognisably landscape though, and other surviving works include some beautifully economical drawings of Venice. This work was so much more overtly modern than what he had been doing at Aberdeen, however, that when he returned to Gray's to report on his travels, it met with little approval from Henderson Blyth.

One of the most important things that happened to him during this year abroad,

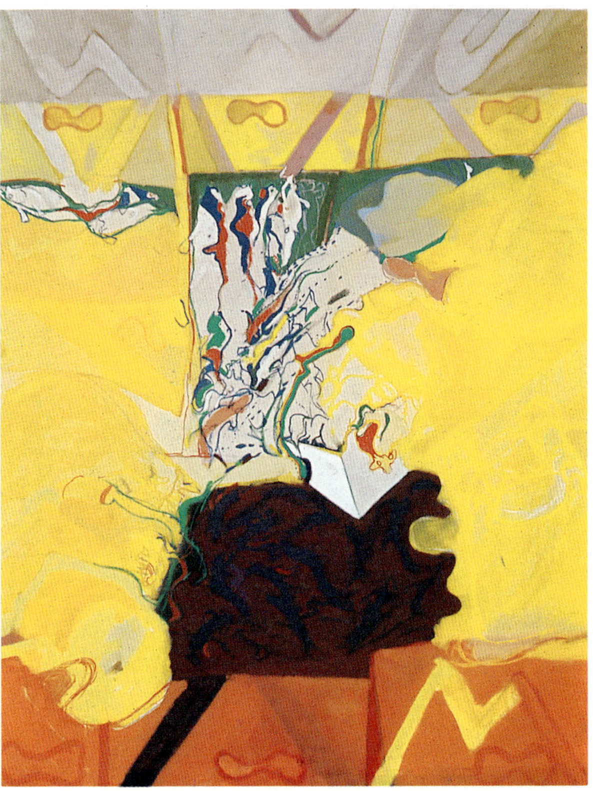

9. *Boarding Herring*, oil on canvas, 122·x 98 cms (1973)

and which has left a lasting impression on his art, was his discovery of archaeology. While he stayed for three months at the British School in Rome, he became friendly with the archaeologists there and was introduced by them to their subject. He visited Etruscan and early Christian sites in their company and learned the basic techniques of investigation. This experience established an interest which has remained part of his inspiration to this day. He is a keen amateur archaeologist and objects still appear in his work whose origin can be traced back to this early stage of his interest in the subject.

His whole method too, at least since he began to make constructions, presents an analogy with archaeology in the way that it depends on buried meaning. In archaeology, objects whose use may originally have been trivial or matter-of-fact assume a significance when seen in context, from which we can read something of a whole culture. His constructions often work in this way and frequently contain references, not only to genuine archaeological objects, but he also invents material and often combines fact and fiction to make a reconstruction, reinvented from his imagination, of something that might have existed — an imaginary museum piece such as *Museum Casket* (1989, *Pl. 6*). He has always been interested in the special imaginative quality of museums. It is an interest that he has in common with Paolozzi and is as much a fascination with the startling and arbitrary associations of heterogeneous objects that museums display, as with the objects themselves. Paolozzi's major print, *Blue-Print*

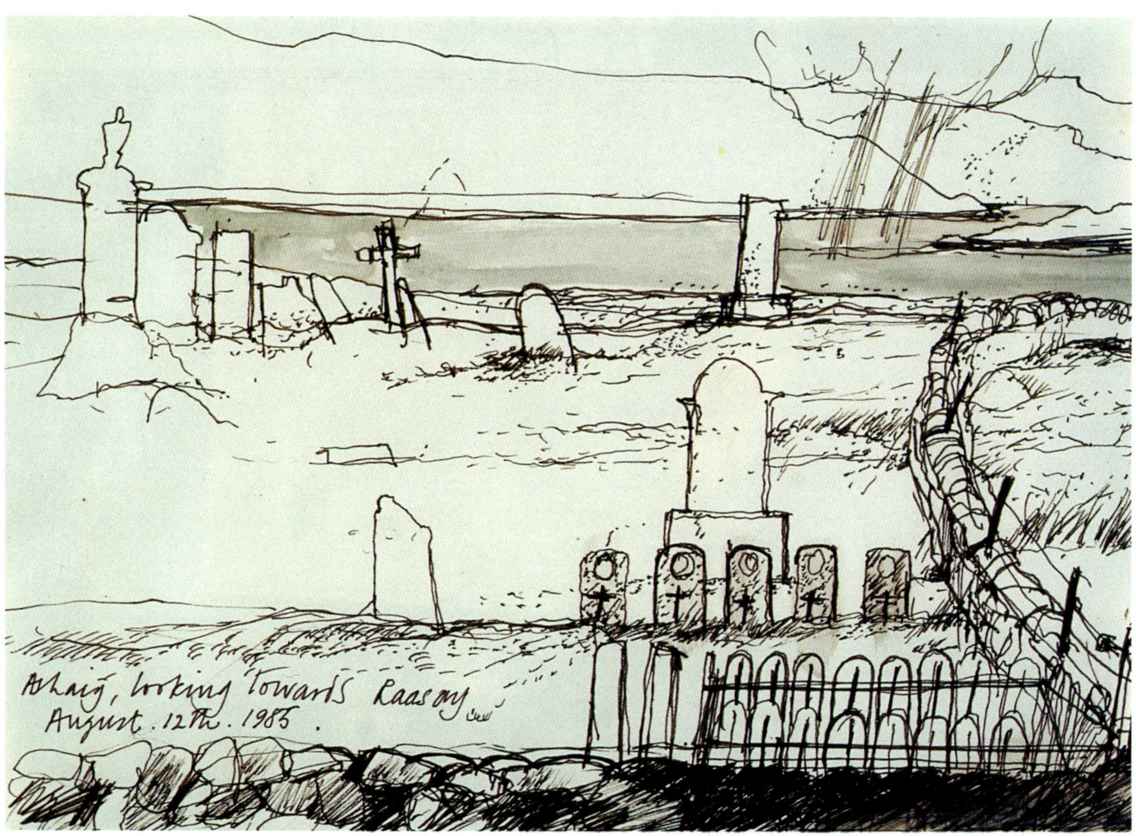

10. *View of Raasay from Ashaig*, page from a sketchbook, pen and wash, 14.4 x 20.8 cms (1985)

for a New Museum, gives expression to this idea.

Maclean's fascination with museums had begun with the little town-museum in Inverness. In Rome, it was the Etruscan museum at the Villa Giulia (which is near the British School) which particularly interested him. It is rich in collections of objects of great beauty, but whose uses record a whole range of the activities of daily life and he spent a lot of time there. Since then, he has transferred the imaginative impact of the mystery of the Etruscans to that of the vanished communities of the Highlands in which his own immediate forebears lived. It is a process of foreshortening similar to that which happened when, through *Ossian*, James MacPherson seemed to make direct contact with the remotest past through the memories of living people.

After returning from his travelling year, Maclean married his wife, Marian. She had a teaching post, while he spent some time working as an uncertificated teacher in schools around Aberdeen, before going on to teacher training in Dundee. For the next few years, he was finding his way artistically. He had inherited from his time at Gray's the idea that in art's stern apprenticeship, a young artist should not expect any recognition for ten years. It was perceived as a kind of period of trial. By this formula, no one should have a one-person show in less than five years from graduation, but Maclean had his first exhibition at the 57 Gallery, Edinburgh, in 1968 and then a bigger one with Ricky Demarco in 1970. His first show was favourably reviewed by Edward Gage and his second by Cordelia Oliver as well. He has always valued this early and continuing critical support and he sees the opportunity offered by these exhibitions as an important stage in his career. He is also one of many Scottish artists of his generation who look back with gratitude to Demarco for giving them the opportunity to establish their names in the public eye much sooner than academic convention would allow.

* * *

The work for this exhibition still reflected the prevailing artistic mood in Europe in the 1960s, however, and the idea that art was a self-contained process, though Maclean was already struggling with the unsatisfactoriness of this idea. The pop art movement was the beginning of a wider protest against such solipsism, but most of what was done in Britain in the name of popular culture was merely nostalgic and camp. It was only with such pioneers as Paolozzi that, by this route, art engaged again with any significant contemporary reality.

Subsequently Maclean's own art certainly linked up with the tradition represented by Paolozzi, and his later use of collected memorabilia and cultural artifacts as things that can be incorporated directly into an art work does perhaps reflect his origins in the art of the 1960s. The severity of Paolozzi's engagement was foreign to most artists, however, and Maclean's own first essays in a more modern idiom reflect rather the stylishness of Hockney and Allen Jones, though perhaps modified by Bellany's rather sterner example. He uses flat colours and semi-abstract shapes in which broad areas of continuous colour are contrasted to more agitated, brushed passages. This kind of art put style before content, even to the point where in Jones's art the extreme stylistic language of the fetishes of sado-masochism became a metaphor for the style of art itself.

In such moral confusion, it is understandable that the problem of style and execution continued to trouble Maclean for a good many years and to stand between him and the realisation of meaning in his work. A different approach was offered by an important exhibition of Belgian Surrealism held in Edinburgh in 1971, however. The work of Magritte and others showed how forceful imagery could be on its own and how it could be used to set up a vivid internal drama without needing to fall back for support on to the still discredited conventions of narrative. This exhibition followed the Magritte retrospective in London, in 1969 and confirmed the importance of the alternative model that he offered.

For Maclean, the surrealist idea of the autonomous world of the imagination was also reinforced by reading Alain-Fournier's novel, *Le Grand Meaulnes* around this time (Meaulnes is the name of the principal character). It is a novel about growing up, told through the eyes of one of the participants and against the changing perspectives of the transition from childhood to adolescence and manhood. It is told so well that it presents the possibility of the adult artist recapturing the vividness of childhood experience. To emulate the vision of children has for long been one of the

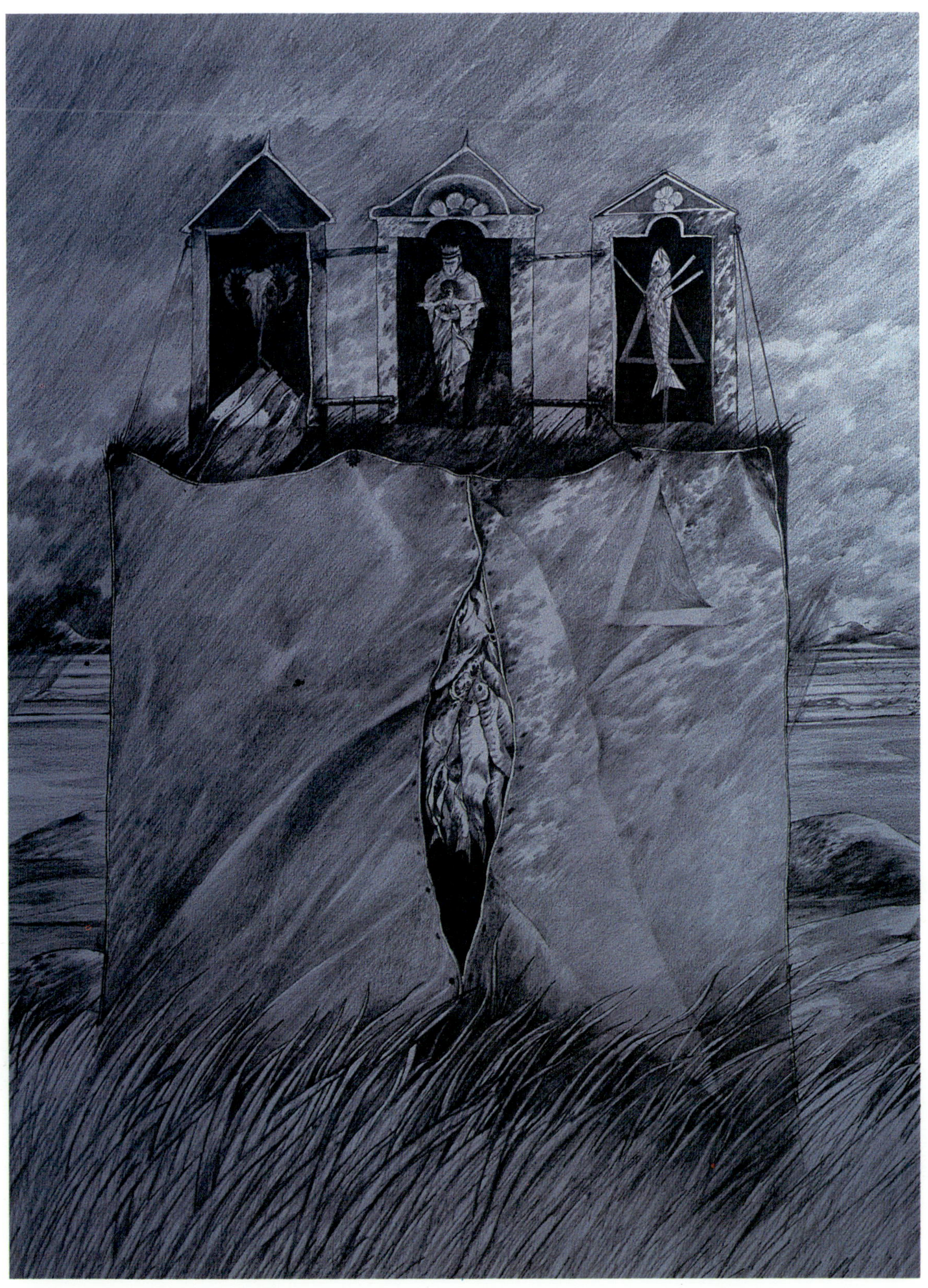

11. *Welcome to South Uist*, pencil, 76 x 50 cms, Private Collection, St Andrews (1981)

objectives of modern art, but it is normally presented as the general idea of childhood. Alain-Fournier's book finds an echo in John Maclean's memoir of his childhood and it suggested to Maclean that, like Wordsworth, he could validly explore his own particular childhood experience. It suggested a way of re-entering its secret garden, an idea that has continued to inspire him as he has sought to recapture something of the imaginative power of the remembered images of his childhood and the mythic character with which memory clothes the people who inhabited it.

The imaginative contemplation of childhood experience can very easily be infused with a profound sense of loss: loss of innocence, loss of security, loss of loved ones; but for Maclean this universal sense of personal loss was compounded with his father's account of the loss of the world of his childhood. In this way it came to be incorporated into a larger sense of the loss entailed in the disappearance of the old way of life in the Highlands whose people and culture were his background. From there he elaborated it into one of the fundamental themes of modern art, the opposition of innocence and experience — though in his later work it becomes increasingly apparent that these two things are inextricably intertwined and that this simple opposition cannot be sustained. Thus he was encouraged to turn again in his work of the early 1970s to the life and landscape of the Highlands which he had already tackled in his diploma picture of the Clearances. His wide and individual reading has always been a source for the inspiration and information of his work. In the early 1970s, he began to collect books about the history and people of the Highlands and a book among these which had as profound an imaginative effect as Alain-Fournier's had done was Sir Archibald Geikie's *Scottish Reminiscences.*

Geikie was one of the pioneers of modern geology. It was he who identified and described the Ice Age, for instance. He produced a geological map of the Highlands and he was also, incidentally, a nephew of the artist Walter Geikie. His *Reminiscences* are a discursive account of his travels as a geologist in the Highlands over a period of sixty years, from the 1840s to the beginning of the twentieth century, the closing decades of the old Highlands.

He writes as a scientist should, in a way that is quite free either of pomposity or of patronage, and his book is informed by the same sympathetic sharpness of observation as his uncle's art, but this observation also has an extraordinary depth. He sees the beleaguered people of the Highlands in the foreground, their life and language threatened by changes that they cannot control. He sees their gaiety and humour even in the face of impending tragedy and in spite of the dourness of their Church; beyond them he sees their ancient traditions, the memories of the greatness of their past and the extraordinary continuity of their culture preserved in popular memory. But beyond that too, his observation is informed by his understanding as a geologist of an even greater continuity, the immense antiquity of the landscape itself, the framework of their history.

At one point in his *Reminiscences,* Geikie describes the pathetic scene of a village being cleared. It was a re-enactment of Wilkie's *Distraining for Rent* in its explicit injustice, for the clearance was in the interest of 'improvement' to redeem a

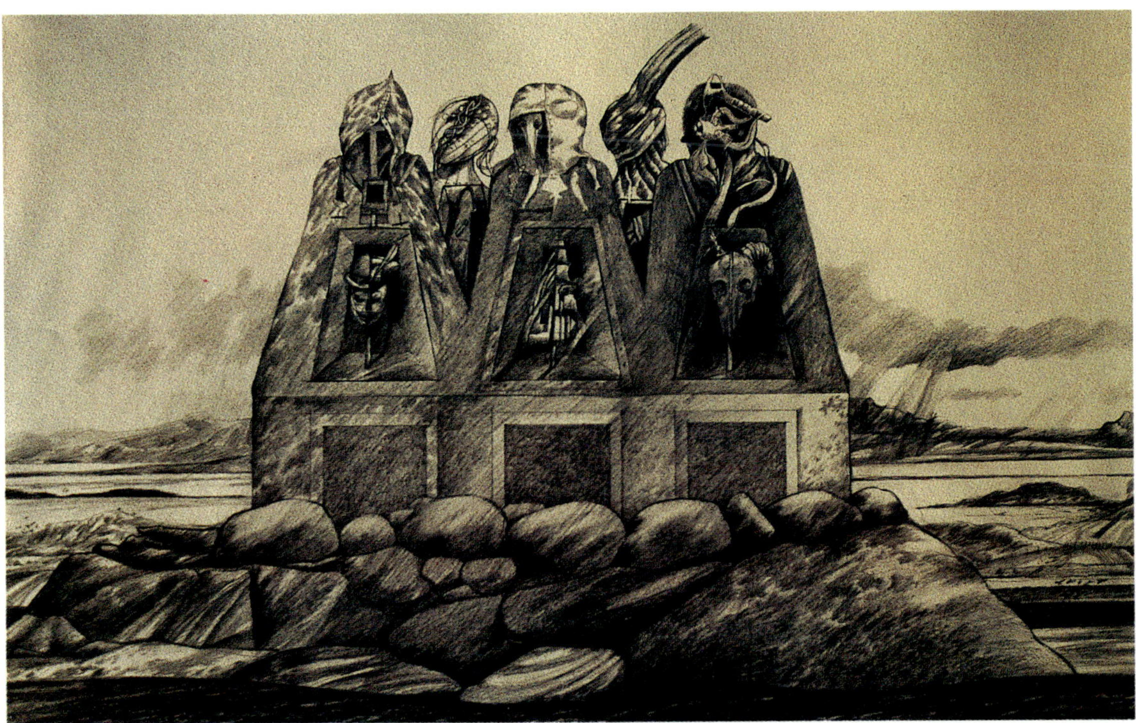

12. *Memorial to the Glendale Martyrs*, study for the etching, pencil. Private Collection (1981)

wastrel landlord's debts. Geikie came across the scene by accident:

> One afternoon as I was returning from my ramble, a strange wailing sound reached my ears at intervals on the breeze from the west. On gaining the top of one of the hills on the south side of the valley, I could see a long and motley procession winding along the road that led north from Suisnish . . . There were old men and women, too feeble to walk, who were placed in carts; the younger members of the community on foot were carrying their bundles of clothes and household effects, while the children, with looks of alarm, walked alongside. There was a pause in the notes of woe as the last words were exchanged with the family of Kilbride . . . When they set forth once more, a cry of grief went up to heaven, the long plaintive wail, like a funeral coronach was resumed, and after the last of the emigrants had disappeared behind the hill, the sound seemed to re-echo through the whole wide valley of the Strath in one prolonged note of desolation. The people were on their way to be shipped to Canada. I have often wandered since over their solitary ground at Suisnish. Not a soul is to be seen there now, but the greener patches of field and the crumbling walls mark where an active and happy community once lived. [2]

He then goes on to recall his experience of the island of Raasay, already depopulated when he had first visited it:

> When I paid my first visit . . . the crofters had only recently been removed; many of their cottages still retained their roofs, and in one of these deserted homes I found on a shelf a copy of the Bible wanting the boards and some outer pages. When I revisited the place a few years ago, only ruined walls and stripes of brighter herbage showed where the crofts had been.[3]

The way that Geikie reports these images of desolation without embroidering them is very moving. In one man's lifetime, what is at first an eye-witness's account of a terrible spectacle of human suffering becomes history and then archaeology. One is reminded of Eliot's classic invocation of time in a landscape near the beginning of 'East Coker':

> Houses live and die: there is a time for building
> And a time for living and for generation
> And a time for the wind to break the
> loosened pane
> And to shake the wainscot where the
> field-mouse trots
> And to shake the tattered arras woven with a
> silent motto.

Maclean did not need Geikie in order to understand the history of the Clearances, but Geikie's writing has an imaginative immediacy whose inspiration reinforced his own interests. He began to produce paintings in which a new vision of the Highland landscape can be seen, in which he has managed to achieve the same unsentimental sense of tragedy and a similar sense of time. Geikie's account of the dispossession of the people of Suisnish directly inspired the painting, *Beach Allegory* (1973, *Pl. 7*), one of the first in a series of works to follow his diploma picture and which continues to the present day with the Clearances for their theme. Maclean's picture is an elegy. A fire is burning on a kind of altar against a background of a dark, deserted landscape, a view of Borreraig. It is a spiritual fire, still burning in a land bereft of its people. In *Highland River*, Neil Gunn wrote about a heath fire:

> The scent of a heath fire has in it something quite definitely primordial. Involuntarily it invokes immense perspectives in human time: tribes hunting and trekking through lands beyond the horizons of history. [4]

This is such a fire, though it is on an altar and is not the heather burning. Maclean has discovered and recreated a land peopled by ghosts. The altar is within a kind of open frame of wood, like a drying frame for fishing nets, and on this is something resembling an Etruscan funerary banner, a frequent motif in his later art, suggesting some kind of funerary rite. The way that the composition is roughly symmetrical round a central axis endorses this. It suggests that the arrangement is deliberate and formal as rituals are. The objects, too, suggest forgotten uses. It is as though the Bronze-Age people had returned, or never fully left; but perhaps also it is the artist performing a ritual of lamentation.

Significantly, Sorley MacLean had also found inspiration in Geikie's account of the clearance of Suisnish and had interpreted it in verse:

> Bha mi latha an Srath Shuardail
> agus thànaig gaior gu m'chluasan:
> chuala mi corronach nan truaghan
> a bha am Morair a'ruagadh
> á Boraraig is Suidhisnis uaine
> gu taobh eile nan cuantan.
> Thug mi sùil air Dùis Mhicleòid
> 's cha do mheall a'bhriag mo bhròn.

> *I was one day in Strath Swordale*
> *and a sore cry came to my ear:*
> *I heard the coronach of the poor ones whom the*
> *Baron was driving*
> *from Borreraig and green Suisnish*
> *to the other side of the oceans*
> *I looked at the land of MacLeod*
> *and the lie did not deceive my grief*
> (*The Cuillin*, VI)[5]

This parallel was the first reflection in Maclean's work of his feeling for Sorley

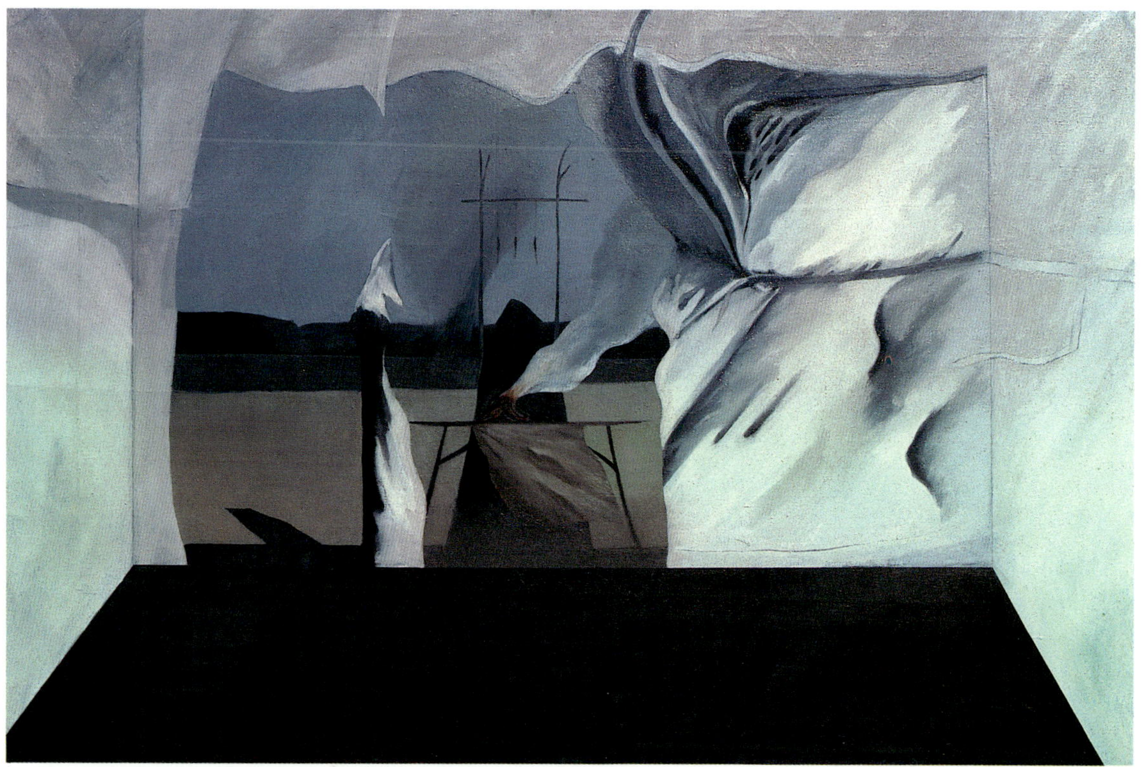

13. *Eskimo Summer*, oil on canvas, 90 x 125 cms approx., Private Collection (1975)

MacLean's poetry which was to be both directly and indirectly a major influence on his art as it developed. Sorley MacLean's status as a Gaelic poet has remained an example for him in his own aspiration to create an art true to the Highland trad-ition. Indeed, one could compare Will Maclean's mature ambition as an artist to Sorley MacLean's account of his own intention in undertaking in 1938 his long poem, *The Cuillin*:

> I conceived the idea of writing a long poem . . . on the human condition, radiating from the history of Skye and the West Highlands to Europe and what I knew of the rest of the world. [6]

* * *

It took the artist some time to formulate this kind of ambition though, and he drew not only on the past, but also on his own present experience of life in the Highlands. In the early 1970s, for instance, he worked on the fishing boats on the west coast during the summers and he recorded this directly in paintings such as *Fisherman with a Broken Arm* (1973 , *Pl. 8*) and *Boarding Herring* (1973, *Pl. 9*). The first is a memory of Ullapool. The boat tied up at the pier after a long period at sea; the artist, tired and unwashed, is looking up from the dark and stinking hold to the light and the freshness of the girls on the pier.

This internal contrast, which is also a contrast between the sexes, suggests an affinity with the contemporary work of Neil Dallas Brown with whom Maclean became friendly at this time. He acknowledges the importance to him of Dallas Brown's facility as a draughtsman and Maclean's own works are based closely on drawing. These drawings can be simply notes in sketchbooks and diaries (*Pl. 10*), but from this time he also regularly produced highly finished drawings with a complex iconography. These finished drawings are also closely related to his etchings such as *Memorial to the Glendale Martyrs* of 1983 (*Pl. 11 & 12*).

The fisherman with a broken arm was an individual whose arm was crushed between his boat and the pier and whose reaction to the incident was stoic indifference worthy of the legends of ancient Sparta or the American Indians — heroism among modern fishermen is not different in kind from that of the most ancient times. It is an image of a man silhouetted by the cape and hood of his yellow oilskin, an image that recurred almost twenty years later in the collage, *Skye Fisherman: In Memoriam* (1989, *Pl. 39*), a memorial to the artist's uncle, William Reid. Another heroic image to appear in his painting at this time, and to recur much later, was that of the ship *San Demetrio*. Torpedoed in the war, terribly damaged and abandoned, she was rejoined by her crew who came up with her again after they had rowed in a circle and they managed to bring her into port. Maclean saw a film of her on his first visit to the cinema, taken there by his father. In a painting called *Eskimo Summer* (1975, *Pl. 13*), the torn metal of her damaged bow frames a landscape. (The title was made up by a friend because of this white, igloo-shape when it was sent to exhibition untitled.)

The direct use of the people and the incidental details of the artist's own experience of the world of fishing and the sea is a link to John Bellany's work of the 1960s and 1970s. Bellany built on the experience of his own boyhood and family in Port Seton, an iconography capable of suggesting universal themes. Within Maclean's own work though, this subject matter, dependent on his own first-hand experience, was still separated from the more generalised poetry of his Highland landscapes. The will to bring these two things together reflected the realisation that it should be possible to record real experience without curtailing the poetic resonance of an image, or its power to suggest.

An important step in this direction was the *Ring-Net* project. This began in 1973 with a promise of funding from the Scottish Educational Trust through Ricky Demarco. For Maclean, the prospect of a year's release from teaching was something to leap at. Originally his intention was a fairly loosely focused enquiry into the practice of ring-net fishing and its initial, artistic inspiration was the example of the historical use of drawing as a vehicle for the recording and transmission of information. He had seen this in the way that the early explorers, like Captain Cook, took an artist with them for the recording of visual information. The worries about style and expression which had plagued Maclean since he was a student had no part in such a use of the skill which, however, was paradoxically also still the principal objective of the same teaching that had been the source of the problem. Use of art as a documentary instrument therefore suggested a release from the burden of inherited, unsatisfactory aesthetic objectives while exploiting the same learned skill from which they were derived.

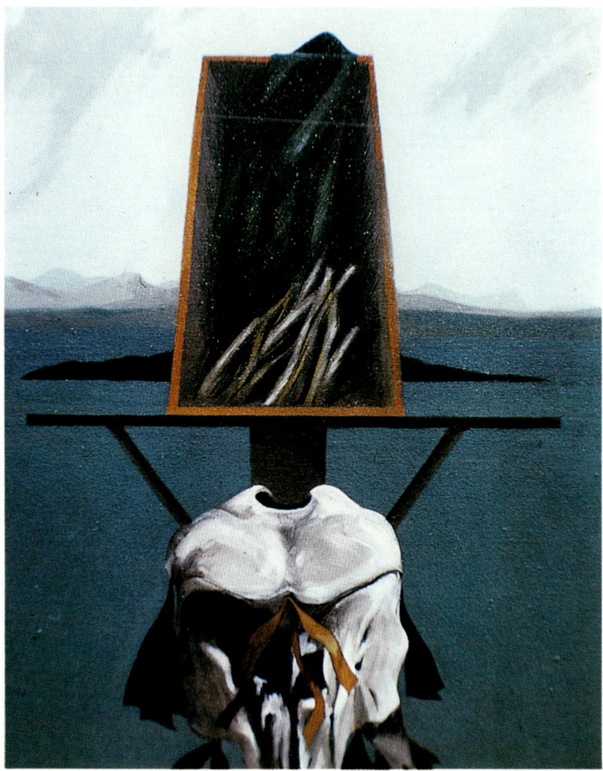

14. *Skye Totem*, oil on canvas, 60 x 40 cms approx. (1975)

Maclean's eventual objective was a documentary exhibition, one of the fashionable modes of conceptual art at the time. It was through this means especially that one of the most important legacies of the conceptual art movement was to bring content back into art in a form that could present a complex commentary on a given area of subject matter. In Scotland, Glen Onwin's *Saltmarsh*, 1974/5, and his *The Recovery of Dissolved Substances*, 1978, are just two contemporary examples of this. They did not have a sociological dimension as Maclean's did, but they had the same assumption of almost scientific objectivity and they were also shaped by the idea that an exhibition itself can be a single work of art.

Onwin's projects also had a marine theme and this was another important area of common ground that Maclean had and still has with others of his contemporaries in Scotland — for example with Liz Ogilvie, Bob Callender and John Bellany, and also with Ian Hamilton Finlay. Finlay had developed an iconography of fishing and fishing boats which ranged from diagrammatic drawings and concrete poems using the serial numbers of boats, to works like *Star Steer* (first version 1966) in which he suggests a cosmic reflection on the whole business of navigation. Maclean's later work, too, has some affinity with the poetic complexity of meaning and exploration of history which are characteristic of Finlay.

Maclean's *Ring-Net* project, working

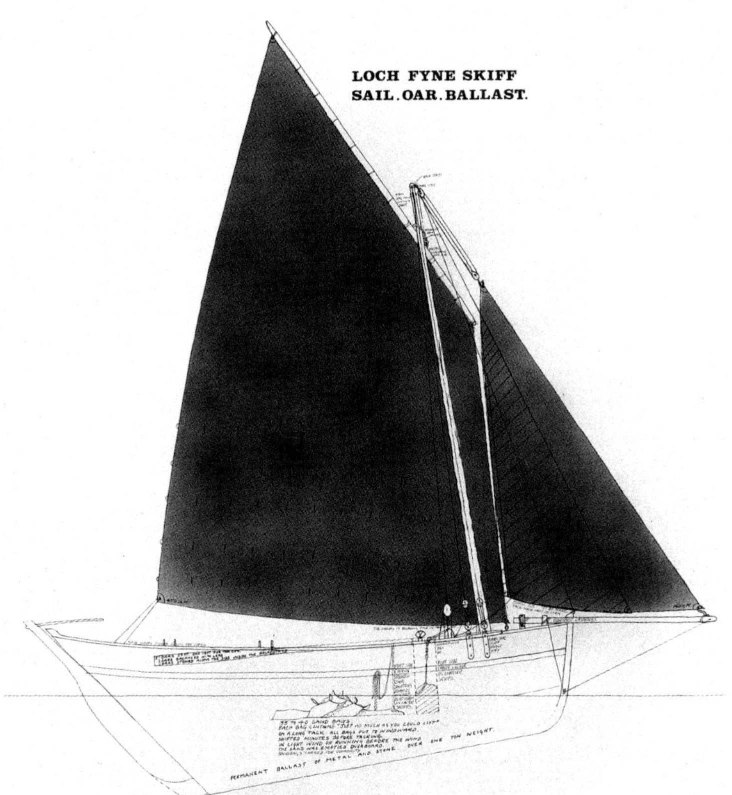

15. *Loch Fyne Skiff*, drawing from the *Ring-Net*, pen and wash, Scottish National Gallery of Modern Art (1973-4)

closely with Angus Martin from Campbeltown, developed into a full-scale research undertaking of extraordinary detail and thoroughness. His uncle, William Reid, was a ring-net fisherman and so his involvement was first-hand. The ring-net was a method of fishing that had evolved on the west coast following the Clearances and the forcible move into fishing of Highland farming people, the move that is recorded in Neil Gunn's saga, *The Silver Darlings* and which both Maclean's father's family in Coigach and his mother's family in Skye had experienced at first hand. The *Ring-Net* project eventually consisted of some 400 drawings (*Pl. 15 & 16*), as well as notes, photographs, press-cuttings and other documents. Some of the drawings of boats, winches and other pieces of equipment are of a very high standard of accuracy and Maclean was fascinated, not just by the single — and as it turned out final state of the industry — but by its development; ingenuity in the solving of problems and the dead-ends that followed wrong turnings both form part of his survey.

The project was first exhibited at the Third Eye Centre in 1978 and eventually ended up in the Scottish National Gallery of Modern Art, though for a very small sum. This comprehensive study of a culture through its tools and its artifacts was almost a paradigm of archaeology which is, after all, the interpretation of society through its artifacts and its material record. The whole

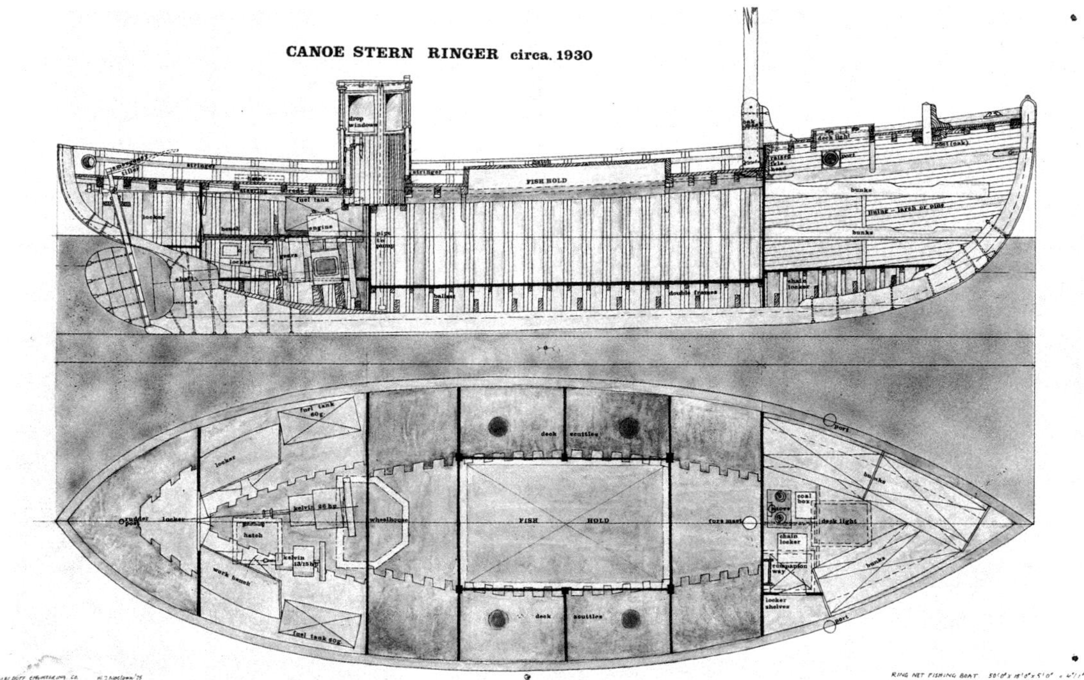

16. *Canoe Stern Ringer*, drawing from the *Ring-Net*, pen and wash, Scottish National Gallery of Modern Art (1973-4)

collection records a culture and technology that had evolved over little more than a hundred years and which, by historical accident, suddenly declined and disappeared almost as Maclean finished his project. It thus became an important piece of documentary history.

Angus Martin wrote a poem, 'Dancers', about the end of ring-net fishing. The poem is dedicated to the artist:

> And I wished that I could dance
> in a yellow oilskin suit,
> dance on the dancing water
> to the slap of an old thigh boot.
>
> They were the champions of some greater dance
> performed in a night of islands. [7]

Maclean took the title for his set of ten prints to Gaelic poetry made in 1991, *A Night of Islands*, from this poem. One print also reworks his image, *Skye Fisherman: In Memoriam* as a specific illustration to the poem and so it too becomes a memorial to the passing of ring-net fishing.

What distinguishes Maclean's art in the *Ring-Net* from other contemporary examples of the documentary exhibition is his thoroughness, together with his historical sense and his insistence on information rather than personal interpretation. These are the qualities that underlie the distinction of his later work too. It is often constructed around complex and precise information about fishing, whaling or Highland history and myth. Its continuity with the *Ring-Net* is therefore much more than just a question of subject matter.

The *Ring-Net* project represented a watershed in his career and, alongside the almost obsessive work on it, Maclean continued to paint. He developed the imagery

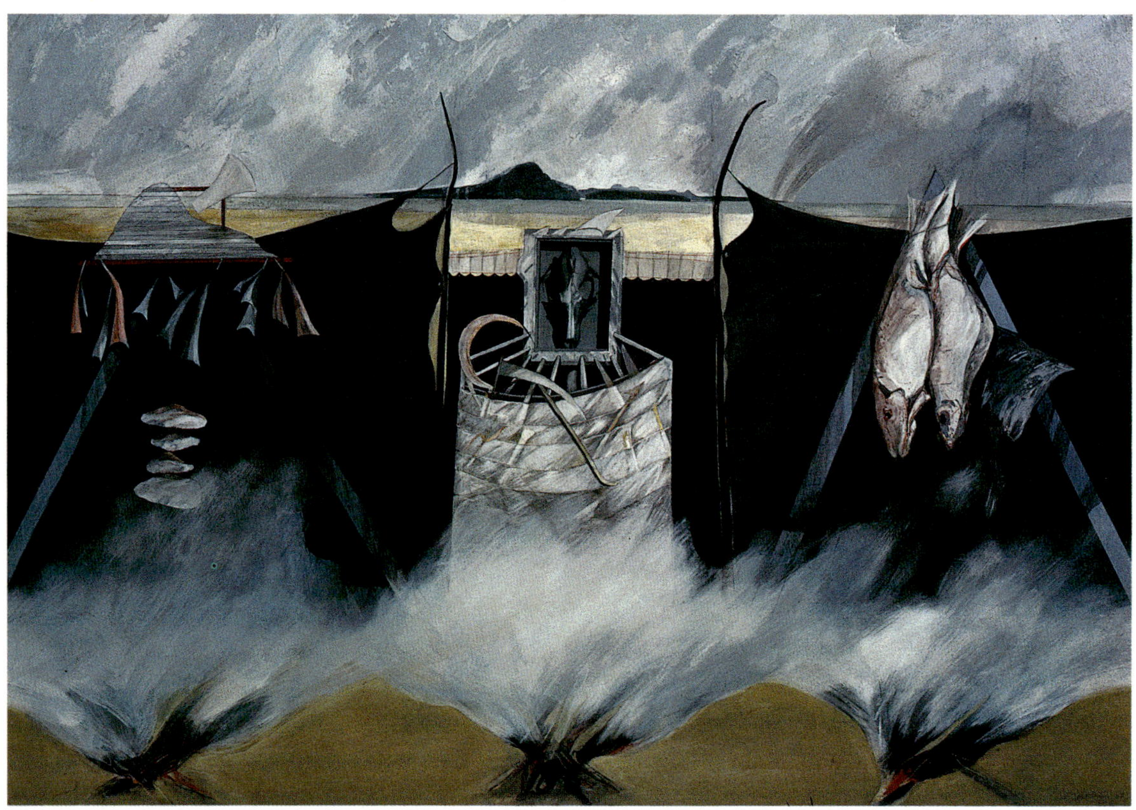

17. *Three Fires, Achnahaird*, oil on canvas, 120 x 184 cms, Private Collection, London (1975)

of the Highlands as he had first formulated it in *Beach Allegory* and related works such as *Skye Totem* (1975, *Pl. 14*). In this mode, a key picture in his development was *Three Fires, Achnahaird* (*Pl. 17*), painted in 1975, but now lost. This takes the fire and altar image of *Beach Allegory* and repeats it three times symmetrically. The setting is a Bronze-Age site at Achnahaird which is also the subject of a number of drawings (*Pl. 18*). The background is a dark and sombre view of Achiltibuie. In the smoke of the altars, fish and hides are curing as though they have just been left by some Bronze-Age inhabitants. Etruscan funerary banners reappear as fish-driving lines, lines with rags attached to them that are dragged through the water to drive the shoals towards the shore. This is a detail that makes a visible reference to the continuity of the ancient technology of fishing, as though in a temporal sense the substitution for the Etruscan image was insignificant. The history of the place represents an archaeology in which the Bronze Age and the age of the Clearances are indistinguishable. Time is foreshortened just as it was by William Johnstone in his key painting, *A Point in Time*, painted almost fifty years before; a painting which the artist described as 'a primordial landscape' — the word that Neil Gunn also used in the quotation given above — and which is based on the landscape of his childhood in the Borders with echoes running through it of the earlier peoples who had inhabited it.

In the centre of Maclean's composition,

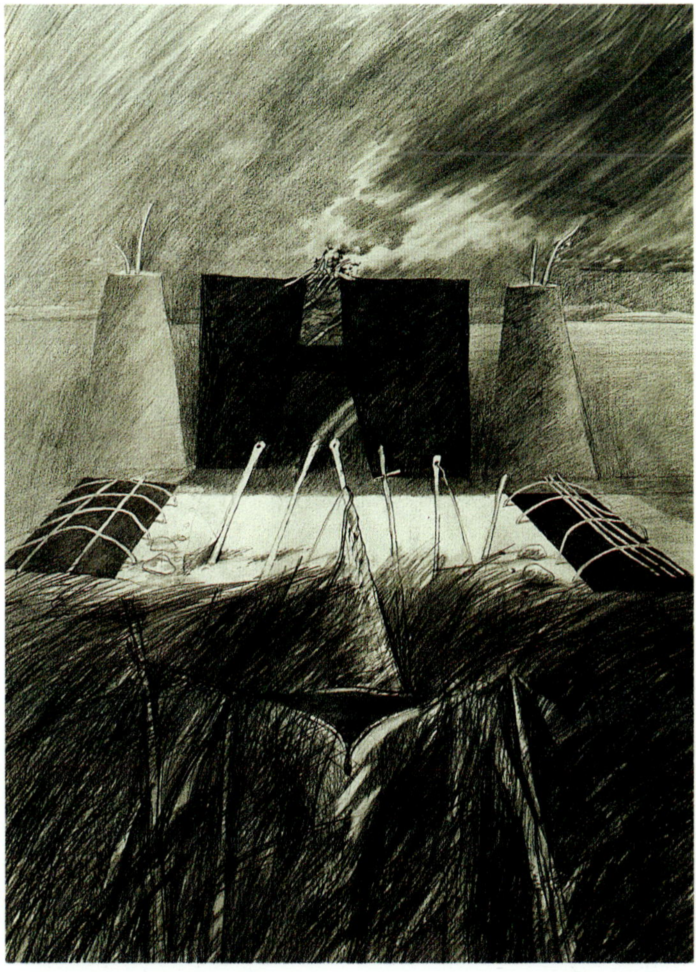

18. *Ceremony Site, Achnahaird*, pencil, 48 x 76 cms (1975)

the skull of an animal has been mounted in a recess in the panel. This is the first step towards the constructions that have been central to his art since shortly after this picture was painted, and such a skull, or that of a fish, a bird or a small whale is a frequent motif in them. It is a macabre touch which has a parallel in John Bellany's current work, but Maclean makes it his own. The skull is a real presence, a ghost and a memorial to all the inhabitants of the place, human and animal, an image of the people's livelihood; perhaps a totemic sacrifice of their forgotten religion, but a symbol, too, of their own sacrifice upon the altar of a stranger's greed.

The way this real object is set in the fictive space of the painting is a solution to a pictorial problem too, focusing the essential shift from the real to the imaginary level of the image. Technical problems still preoccupied Maclean at this time and the question was how to get beyond the aesthetic enclosure of an art in which style and form seemed to be self-sufficient, to be the only objective of the painter to the rigorous exclusion of all other content. This device which achieves an exchange between the

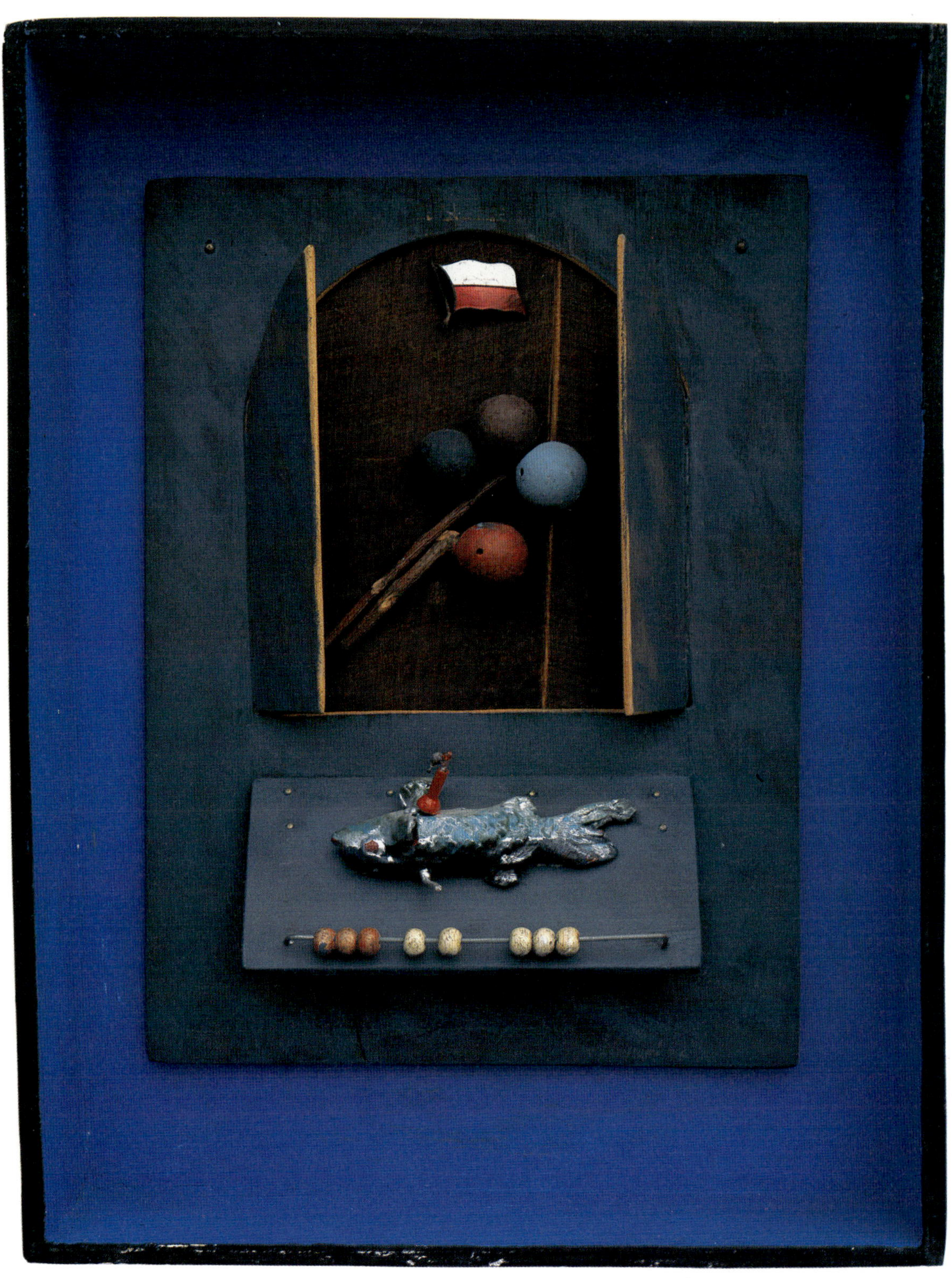

19. *Requiem Construction (John Maclean)* (1974) (Cat. 1)

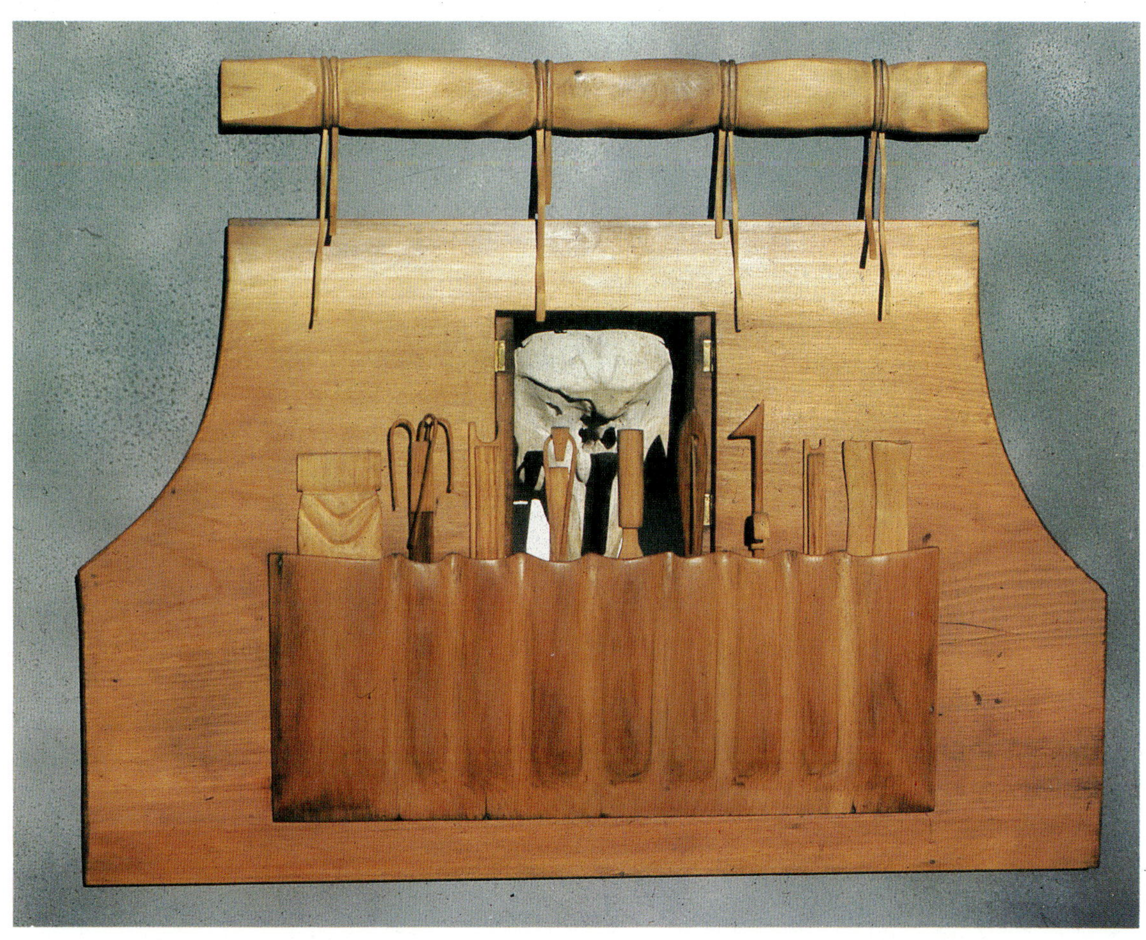

20. *Symbols of Survival* (1976) (Cat. 13)

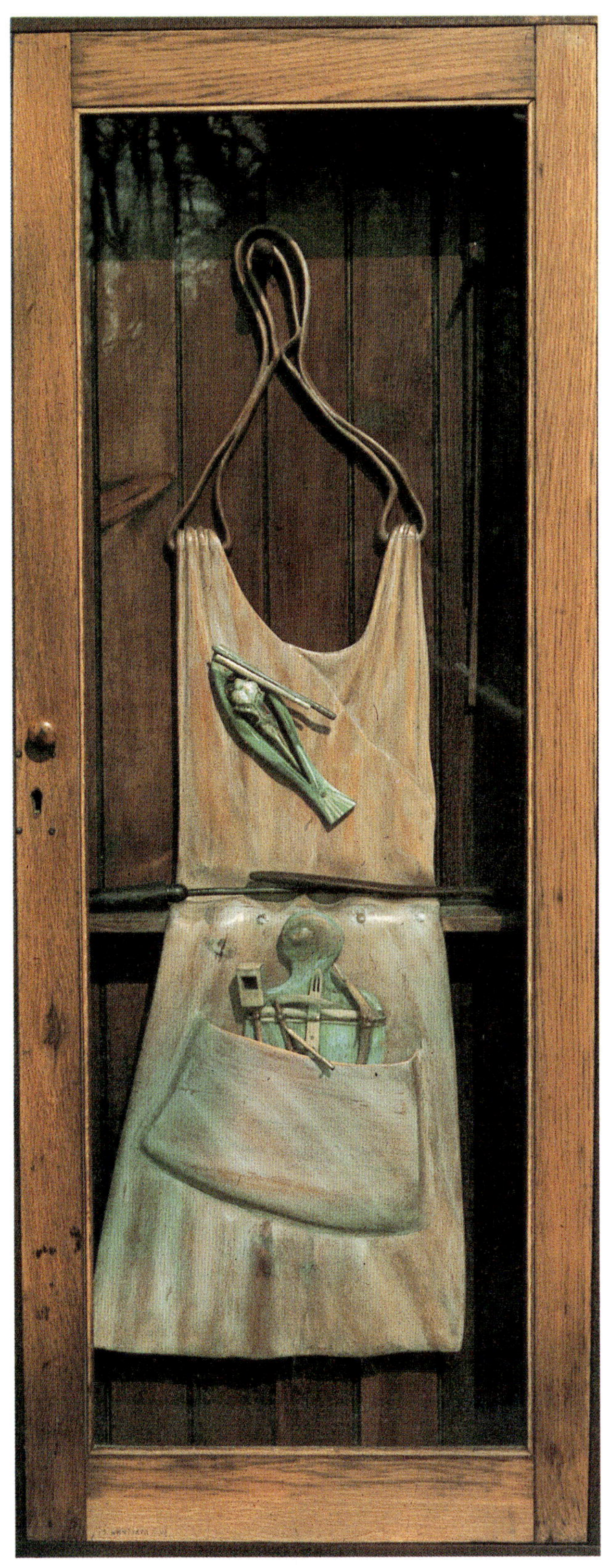

21. *Abigail's Apron* (1980) (Cat. 49)

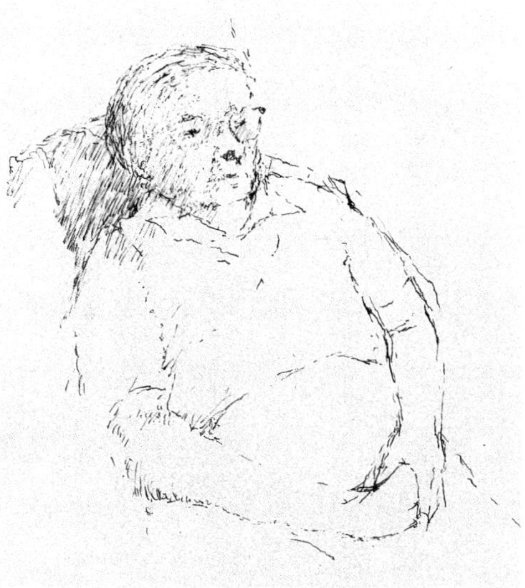

22. Sketch of the artist's aunt, Abigail Mackenzie, pen, 25.3 x 17.9 cms (1966)

enclosed object and its painted environment breaks out of that constraint and, as it does so, it becomes a metaphor for a new kind of poetic resonance; the real object functions in the imagination's space. Maclean had brought together the objectives of his painting with those of the constructions that he had begun to make the previous year.

* * *

The Surrealists had developed collage, assemblage and the use of found objects as the basis of a poetry of association. They had recognised that these new vehicles made it possible to bring together into a single image, things that could carry with them from their previous existence memories and associations, even as they became part of something new. This way of working became a metaphor for the way that in our experience present perception, memory, dreams and reality can all coexist and intercut. Following the surrealists, the greatest British exponent of this has been Paolozzi, though a number of the pop artists had also used it, notably Peter Blake. Maclean followed in this tradition and had made his first true assemblage or construction in 1974, *Requiem Construction (John Maclean)* (*Pl. 19*). It followed on from model-making undertaken for the *Ring-Net* and was made almost casually as a relaxation, but it involved a vital change in focus. Instead of trying to make a statement with a consciously general application, the artist worked from a starting point that was so particular that it involved using the objects themselves. It was also at first very personal.

The requiem in this construction was for his father. The work consists of a group of objects framed in a church window. Its gothic shape seems appropriately to suggest a requiem, but it also recalls the childhood experience of the kirk. Within the window are his father's pilot's capbadge — a symbol of his professional career — some abacus beads and a twig with painted oak-apples on it. The abacus

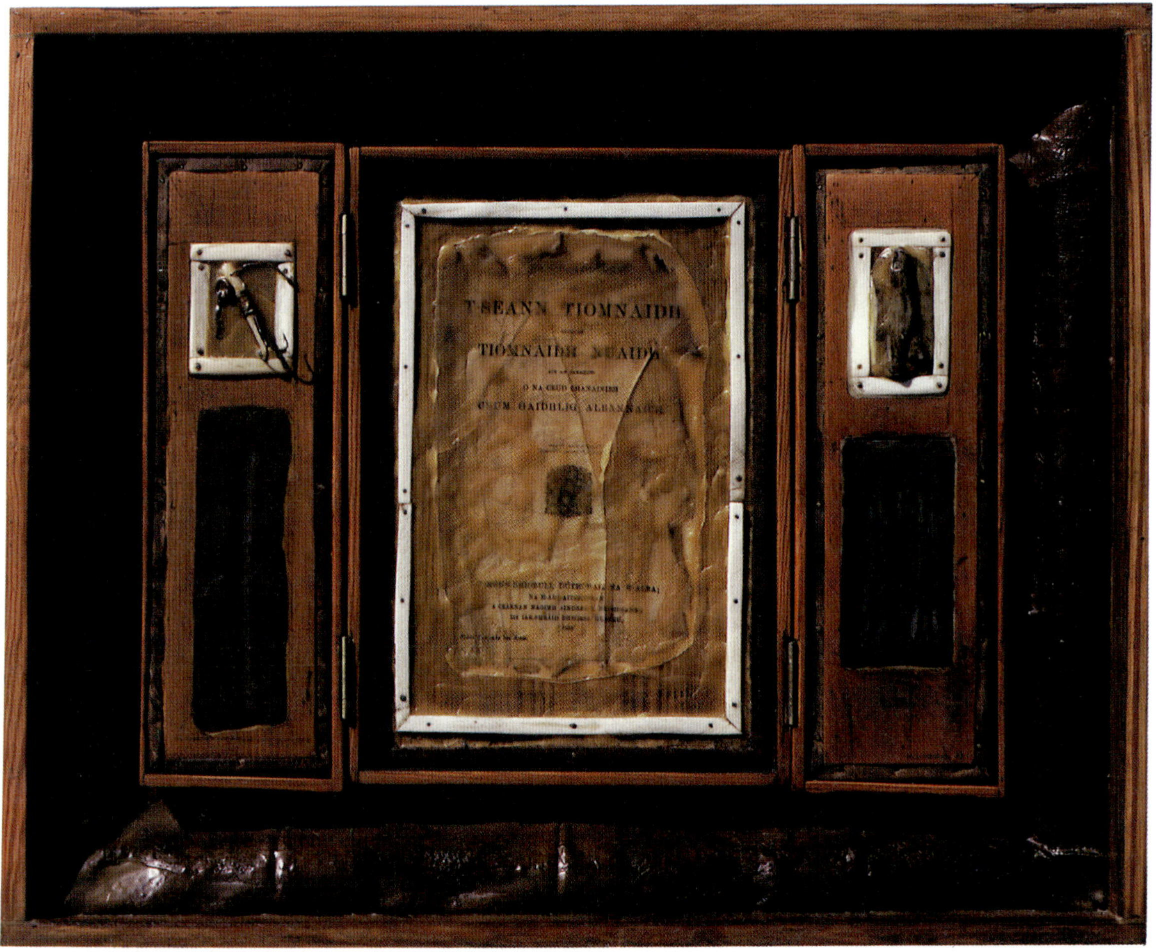

23. *Portrait of Angus Mackenzie* (1982) (Cat. 70)

beads are a relic of primary school, but they might also represent the mathematical calculation which is the basis of navigation. The oak-apples are a natural form. They have heroic, even druidic associations, but in a double image typical of the artist, they also represent the model ship's lights used by his father in teaching navigation.

Maclean was teaching in Fife when he made these first constructions. He found that he could take bits of them in his pocket to carve or polish while he was at school. He could do nothing like this with painting and his whole approach could be more casual. This way of working was almost craft rather than art and so he did not really need to think of what he was doing as carrying the burdens of the 'serious' business of painting. That way, he bypassed the aesthetic impasse in which he still felt he was trapped, but he did not fully realise that he had done so until 1975. He had already made nine or ten of these assemblages, when in that year Jack Knox came to select some work for what was to be the opening show at the Scottish Arts Council's new Fruitmarket Gallery. Instead of selecting paintings, Knox became excited about the assemblages and rather to the artist's surprise, he chose them for the exhibition.

It was the turning point in Maclean's career. He had finally broken out of the aesthetic constraints imposed upon him by his art-school training and he had done this by turning to the concrete and specific. Now he was incorporating actual objects into the artwork. He had left the artificiality of paint on canvas in favour of the simple pleasures of making, of cutting, carving and assembling; imitating the traditional sailor's forms of scrimshaw, model-making and whittling. It is the quality of the concrete and the care and skill in the artist's touch that gives their character to these assemblages. Although the themes of his paintings are continued in them, the paintings seem unfocused beside the assemblages, which were carefully planned and whose imagery is consequently often very precise. They are also extremely beautiful. Indeed, it is a feature of Maclean's constructions from this time forward that it is their beauty that makes them persuasive.

These constructions can be read as poems and in a way that is more common in poetry than in visual art, the starting point, especially of the earlier ones, is frequently some childhood memory. One consequence of working in this way with the concrete and particular is, too, that in these early constructions, his work is not generic. Because the objects from which they are composed have a quite specific set of associations and because of the way they were carefully planned, though later it became more fluid, his work at this time is not a set of variations on given motifs within the general parameters of a personal style. There is a clearly identifiable group of themes running through it and there are recurrent motifs, but the works themselves are each individual. As in Alan Davie's painting which he admires, the symbols that he uses function at a level of suggestion that is intended to be less precise than conscious meaning, but each also has its own set of references and so repays separate exegesis.

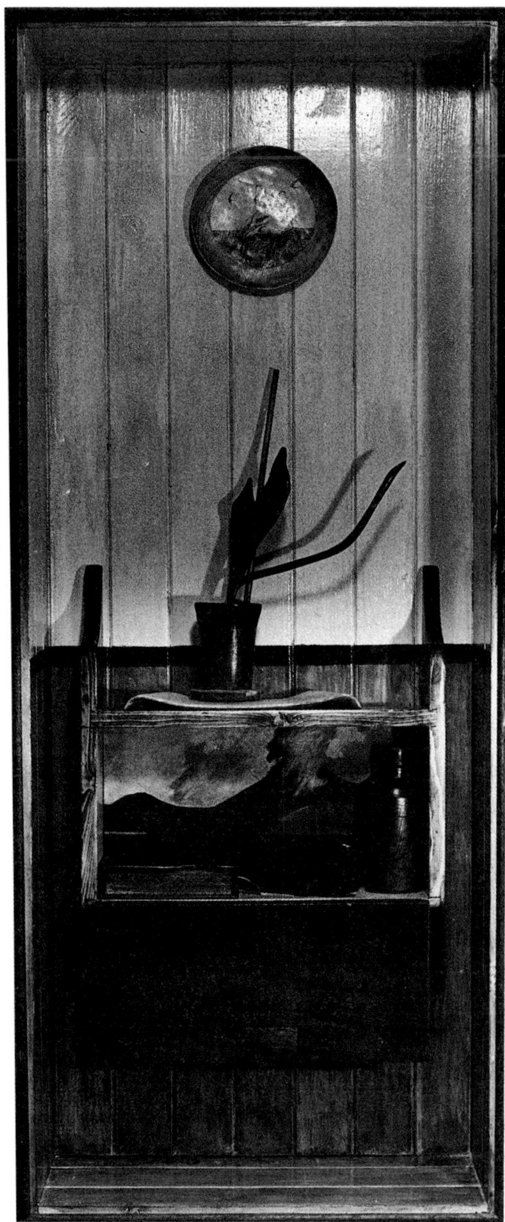

24. *Interior Wester Ross* (1980) (Cat. 53)

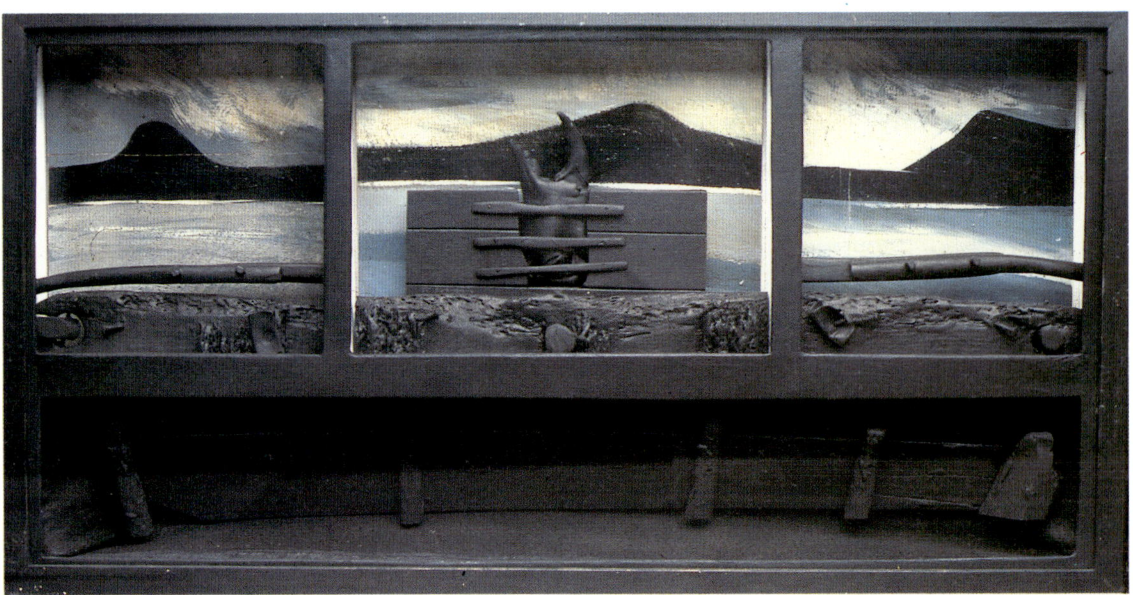

25. *Sabbath of the Dead* (1978) (Cat. 26)

One of the most beautiful of this early group, *Symbols of Survival* (1976, *Pl. 20*), illustrates this precisely. It was in the Fruitmarket exhibition and, bought from the exhibition, became Maclean's first major sale. Its inspiration is a wartime, US Navy survival kit, given to the artist by an uncle when he was a boy. One of those wartime souvenirs which to a boy at the time were invested with an extraordinary glamour, to the adult artist it is an object as potent with mystery in his own personal archaeology of childhood as an Etruscan bronze. He has it still. The kit is in a canvas apron with pockets. It is the epitome of life at sea and contains fishing gear, harpoons, even pork-rind for bait, but also rather improbably detailed, printed instructions on how to use these things.

Made of carved and polished pine, in the assemblage — or perhaps it is a still-life sculpture — the kit is seen both open and rolled. The open apron is suspended from the rolled one. Each of the tools is faithfully reproduced with the same care as he had used in the drawings for the *Ring-Net*, but set in the centre in a window, like a window to the imagination, is a porpoise skull, a reminder of the stark simplicity of the sailor's alternative to survival — death. At the same time, Maclean's own childhood response to the magic of this strange, exotic kit is present in the finished work. The beauty of the wood and the way it has been lovingly carved and polished suggest how as the imagination handles such a memory, it becomes a cherished thing.

Another beautiful work from these years which follows directly on the theme of childhood memory and which uses the same technique of imitating real objects in carved and polished wood, is *Abigail's Apron* (1980, *Pl. 21 & 22*). It is a work which in a remarkable way also opens from the memory of a specific individual towards the whole theme of Highland history and culture and the artist's perception of it. It is an oblique portrait, a marvellous, still-life memorial to

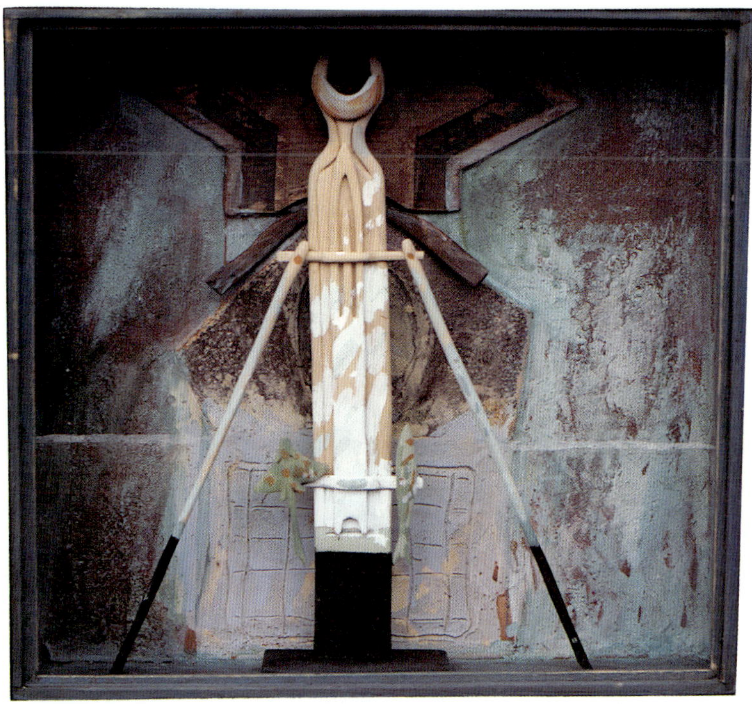

26. *Star of the Sea* (1983) (Cat. 77)

the artist's aunt Abie, his father's sister Abigail Mackenzie who had stayed in Coigach. Her apron, a garment which was typical of the Highland women of her generation, itself carved in pine, is hanging on a peg against the tongue-and-grooved, pine lining of her kitchen.

In her apron pocket is a group of mysterious objects, half-recognisable as kitchen utensils. One of them looks like a wooden spoon, but it has a strange lump on it. Johnny Allie Mackenzie, one of the men in Polbain, had such a lump on his head. It was some kind of benign growth. It is not included here to mock him, but is a reference to the community in which Abigail belonged and to the characteristic of the Highlands, which is perhaps common to all small, relatively isolated communities as it also is to children, of giving a very high definition to individuals, accepting their peculiarities in relief as it were, not glossing over them. In the Highlands, this characteristic is typified by the use of nicknames and here, while with gentle irony it puts this individual in her pocket, it is a way of conveying her own strength of personality.

This strength is implicit too in the bold simplicity with which the wood is carved, just as the artist's affection for her memory is implicit in the careful beauty of the finish. That we are dealing with memory is suggested by the way that the whole assemblage is set behind a glass cupboard-door. This has a keyhole and handle and forms part of the work, so it is a handy way of presenting it, but it also means that we are looking in, into the mind, the imagination, or the memory. It also suggests that the shallow space of the relief is actually the space of a picture. This is a reminder that the artist began as a painter, but at the same time it is also a way of cutting through all the confused mythology and mumbo-jumbo of modernism surrounding the significance of the picture plane. Here it is what it has always been, simply a transparent boundary between the contingent world of experience and the world of the imagination.

On the apron, too, is pinned what seems to be an outsize brooch. It is a herring with a bird's skull contained within it, which together suggest both the tragic recent history of the Highlands and the extension of memory back into remote prehistory where perhaps she would have been a priestess of some forgotten cult. It was only later that evidence in a collection of eagle-skeletons of just such a Bronze-Age cult was unearthed in Orkney.

In keeping with this suggestion, like the requiem for his father, its enclosure gives to *Abigail's Apron* the quality of a shrine or a reliquary, though it contains no actual relics. It is a memorial to someone who, alive, was vividly individual, but it also invokes, if only by this detail, what she stood for, a whole way of life that seemed to be ending after millennia of continuity. Its companion portrait of her brother-in-law, *Portrait of Angus Mackenzie* (1982, *Pl. 23*), makes this point equally clearly. It was made two years later and its central element is a page from a Gaelic bible, coated with transparent resin and then waxed so that it looks like a fly in amber, suspended in time. This central element is edged with bone. Angus Mackenzie was a sternly religious man, but he taught his nephew to fish and made him model boats. In the work these appear together with the whet-stones that he used to sharpen his tools. In the Iron Age, whet-stones, with their power over metal, were a symbol of kingship, reflecting the stature of such an individual in a child's eyes.

In Maclean's art as a whole, the natural sense of loss in the memory of childhood is enrolled into the much more tragic sense of loss at the passing of Gaelic culture, and this is nowhere clearer than here in these intensely personal works. To illuminate history by personalising it in this way is in the tradition of Walter Scott. It reflects the essential understanding of history which Scott himself derived from the thinkers of the Enlightenment, that we can only reach the general through the particular. This is not something nostalgic or sentimental, but is central to modern philosophy and is at the basis of modern art. It reflects the arguments put forward by Hume and Reid which had a far-reaching impact on European art, about the nature of experience and our perception of it. The basis of all knowledge and understanding, they argued, must be in experience and so it is only through the imagination that we can transcend this limitation to the subjective. In just this way, Maclean himself approached the wider themes suggested by Highland history through his own immediate, subjective perception of it and first of all through his memory of those close to him like his aunt Abigail Mackenzie.

His attempt to create a meticulous account of the perceived world as a means to a wider, imaginative perception such as he used in *Abigail's Apron* reaches its most elaborate form in *Interior Wester Ross* (*1980, Pl. 24*). This is a view of a domestic interior with a plant on a bookshelf, a bible and other details of ordinary life, all of them made of carved, or turned wood. Within the bookshelf, though, is a painted landscape and so even as he was striving to reach some kind of hyper-realism by craft

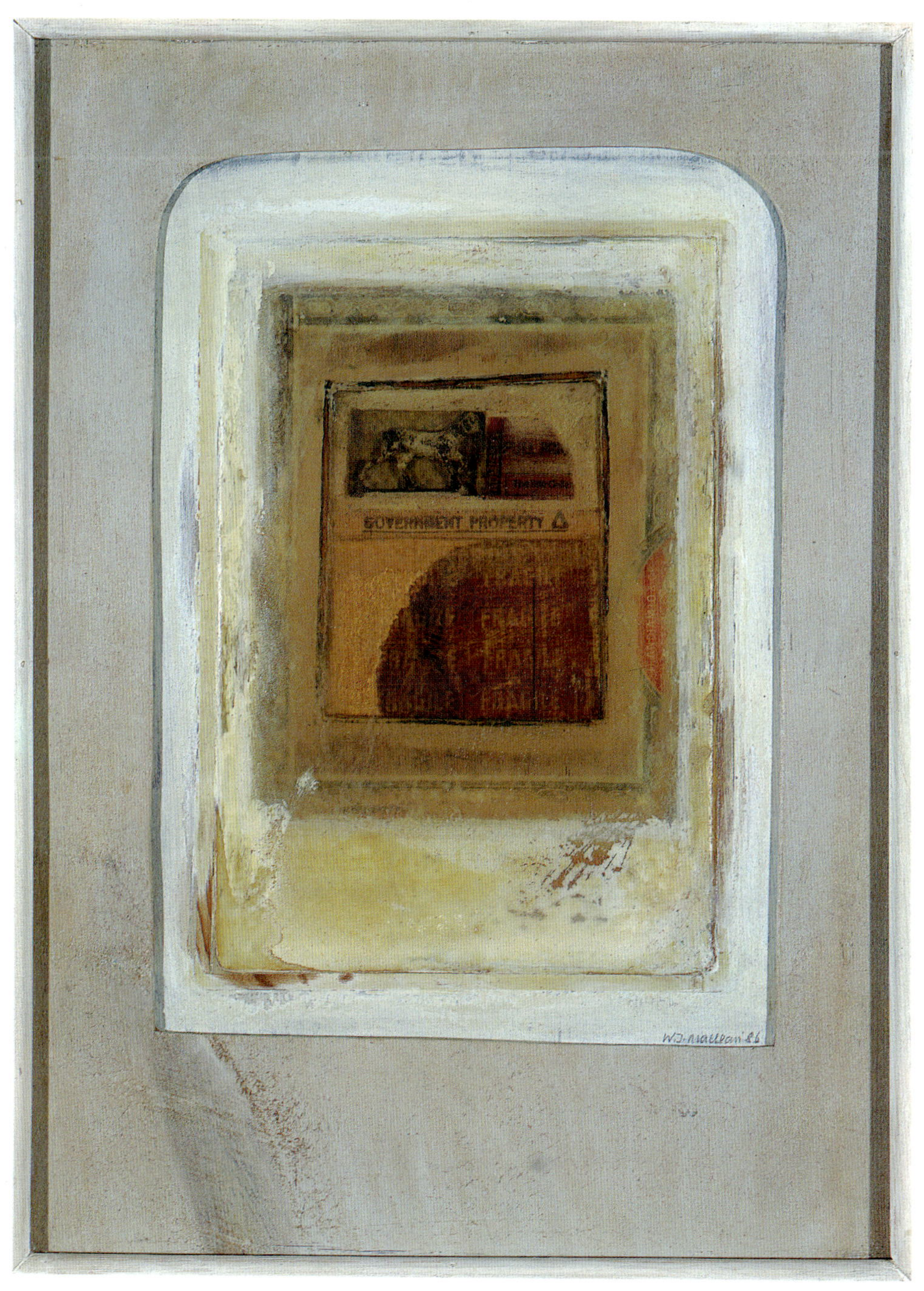

27. *Calotype for Schwitters* (1986) (Cat. 113)

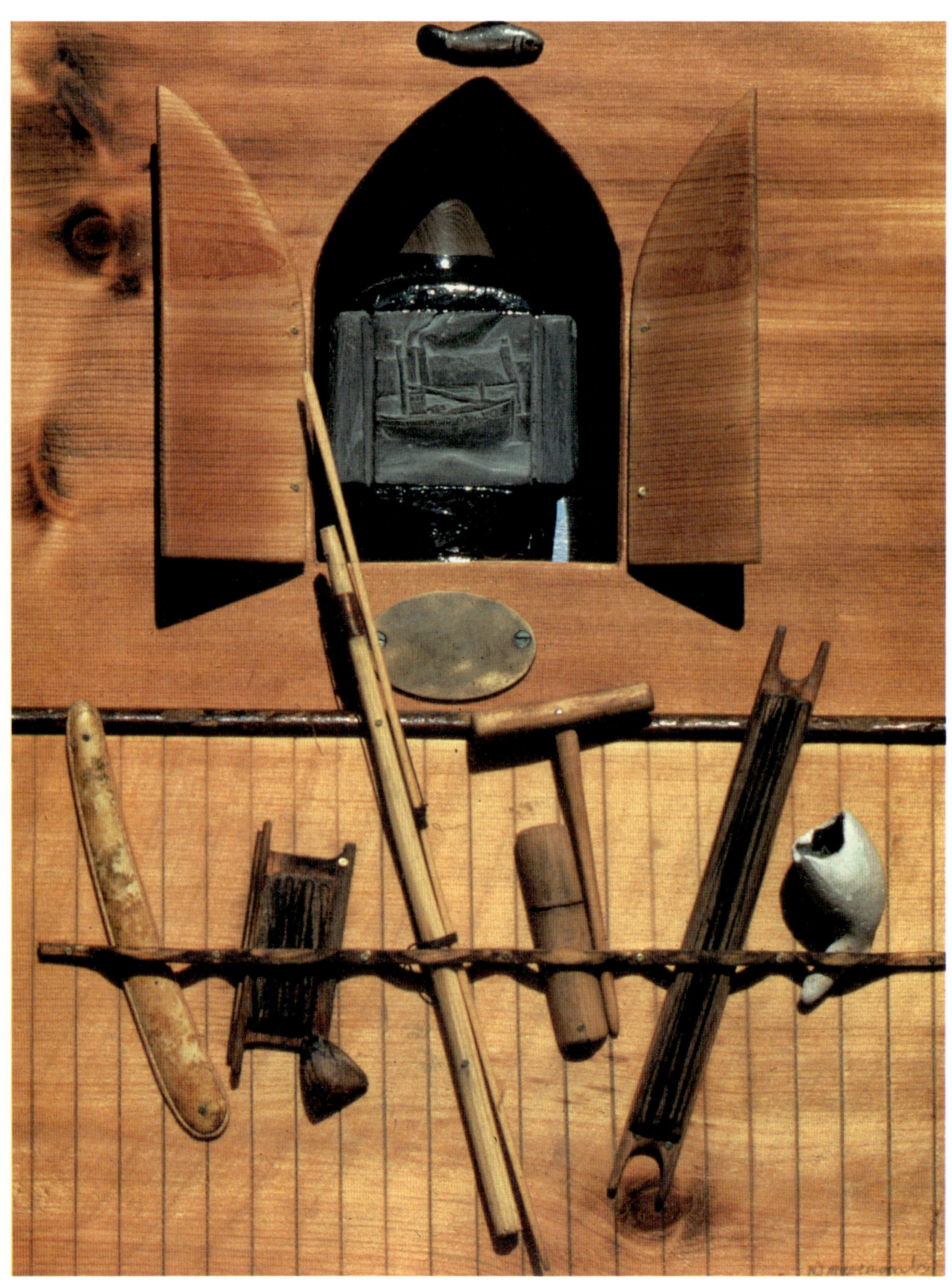

28. *Memories of a Northern Childhood* (1977) (Cat. 20)

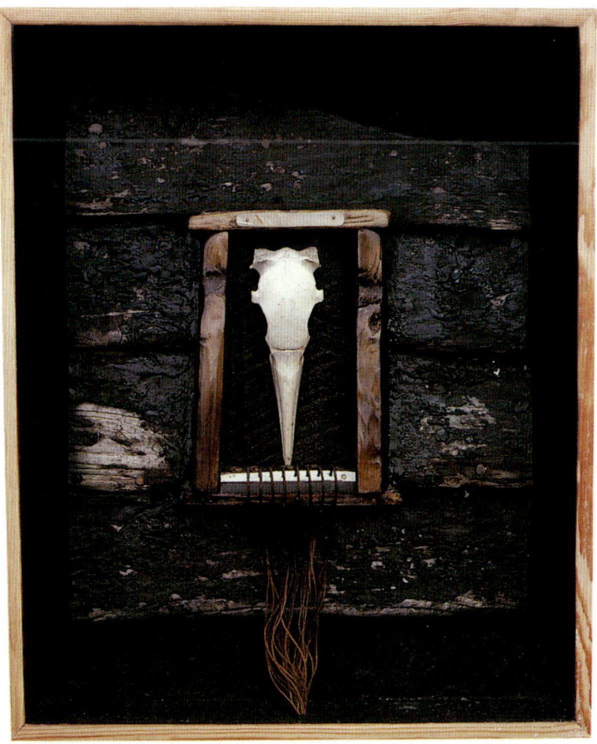

29. *Fladday Reliquary* (1978) (Cat. 29)

methods, he was also thinking still about painting. Indeed, in 1978, in *Sabbath of the Dead* (*Pl. 25*), he had already returned directly to the imagery of his paintings of five years before of the desolation of the Highlands and the ghosts of the Clearances.

Sabbath of the Dead was inspired by 'Hallaig' by Sorley MacLean. It is a poem of loss, a poignant lament for the vanished people of an empty place:

Mura tig's ann theàrnas mi a Hallaig
a dh'ionnsaigh sàbaid nam marbh,
far a bheil an sluagh a'tathaich,
gach aon ghinealach a dh'fhalb.

Tha iad fhathast ann a Hallaig,
Clann Ghill-Eain's Clann Mhicleòid,
na bh'ann ri linn Mhic Ghille-Chaluim:
Chunnacas na mairbh beò.

Na fir'nan laighe air an lianaig
aig ceann gach taighe a bh'ann,
na h-igheanan 'nan coillie bheithe,
dìreach an druim, crom an ceann.

Eadar an Leac is na Feàrnaibh
tha 'n rathad mór fo chóinnich chiùin,
's na h-igheanan 'nam badan sàmhach
a' dol a Chlachan mar o thùs.

Agus a'tilleadh as a'Clachan,
á Suidhisnis's á tir anm beò;
a chuile té òg uallach
gun bhristeadh cridhe an sgeòil.

If it does not, I will go down to Hallaig,
to the Sabbath of the dead,
Where the people are frequenting,
every single generation gone.

They are still in Hallaig,
MacLeans and MacLeods,
all who were there in the time of
Mac Ghille Chaluim
the dead have been seen alive.

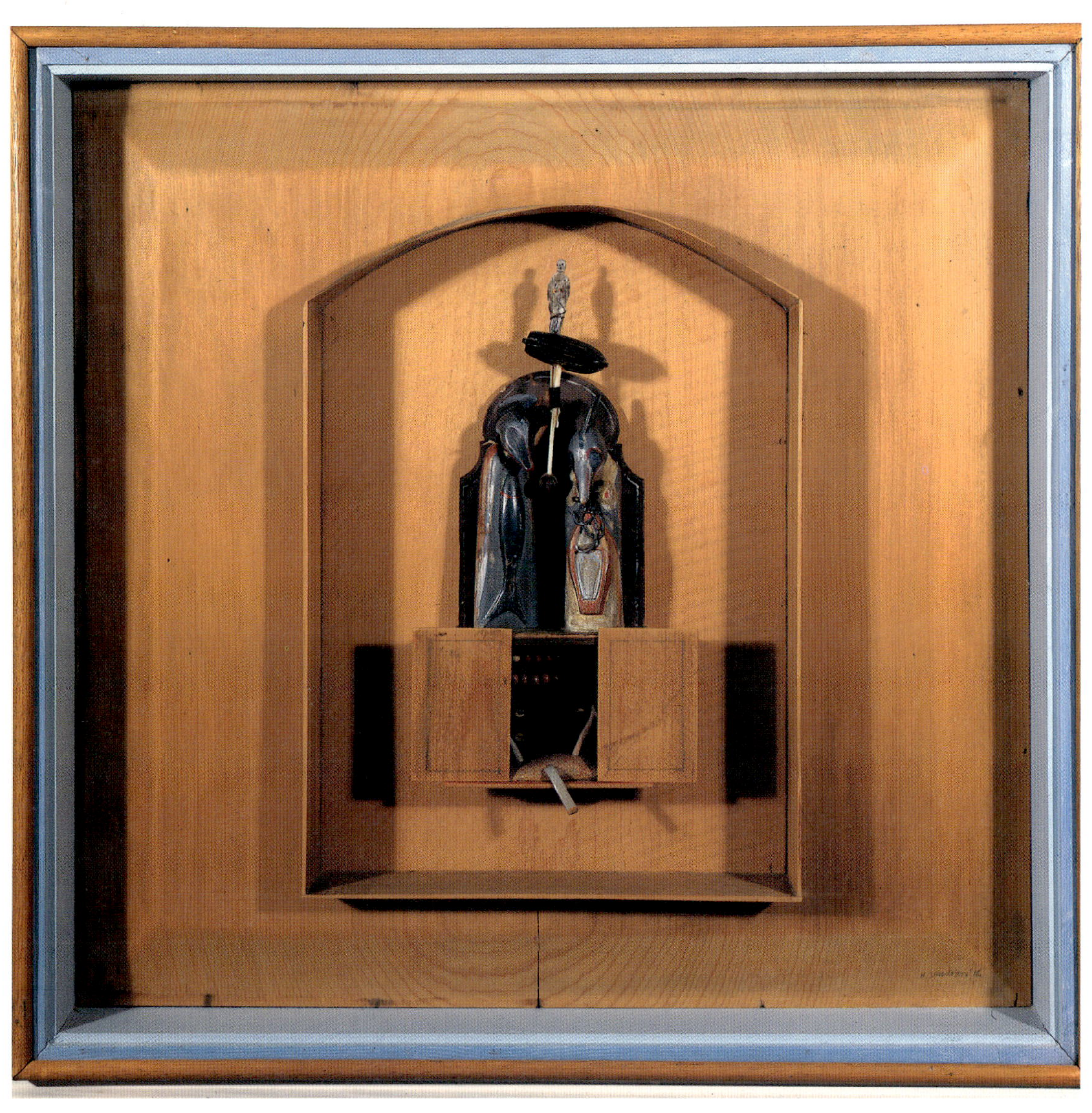

30. *Icon for a Fisherman* (1978) (Cat. 30)

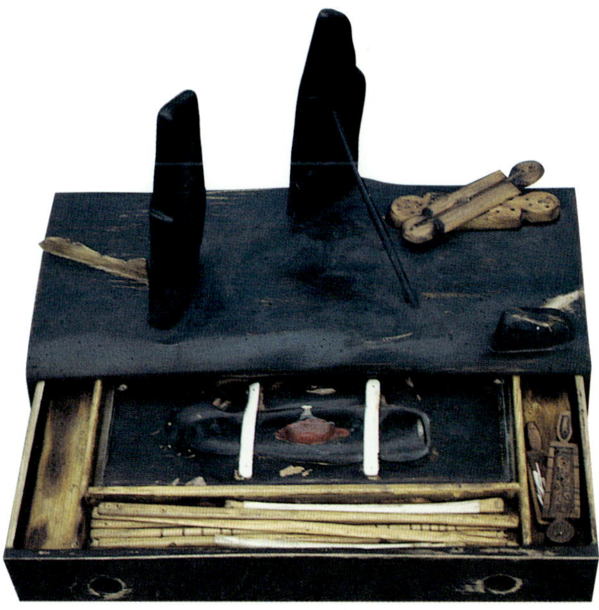

31. *Black Priest's Box* (1982) (Cat. 64)

The men lying on the green
at the end of every house that was,
the girls a wood of birches
straight their backs, bent their heads.

Between the Leac and Fearns
the road is under mild moss
and the girls in silent bands
go to Clachan as in the beginning,

and return from Clachan
from Suisnish and the land of the living;
each one young and light-stepping,
without the heartbreak of the tale.[8]

It is a congregation of ghosts, of absences in an empty land. Maclean's response is a painted construction in four sections. Its main features are its dark, sombre colour, only relieved by the stark light in three separate views of the hills of Raasay seen across the water. Beneath these, in a single compartment spanning the whole work, is a piece of driftwood; a plank from a boat, black-painted, but a natural material once turned into a human artifact, now wasted and reclaimed by nature like the empty, once populous island of Raasay itself. In the foreground of each of the landscapes is a dark section of beach, reminiscent of the raised beach mentioned in a later verse of the poem. Against the central section, held in a wooden cage, a black-painted crab's claw stretches to heaven like the hand of a drowning man, suggesting a powerful presence in the landscape and expressing both anguish and anger.

Sabbath of the Dead is a construction, but it is also a painting and in the early 1980s, Maclean's constructions tended more and more to have a painted finish. Painting was a language that lent itself more readily to a wider frame of reference than constructions of polished wood could do. Maclean has always been conscious of this and, conversely, of the risk of identifying his own art with the very different, craft tradition. In 1981 he was appointed to the painting school at Dundee College of Art by Alberto Morrocco. In the company of painters once more, he began to explore again the language of painting in the painted surface of his constructions. *Star of the Sea* (1983, *Pl. 26*), for instance, is an assemblage which is called after his grandfather's boat and pays homage to it. It is made of various elements to suggest a totem figure, but its character depends on the rubbed and splashed blue paint which manages to suggest at the same time the space against which the totem is standing and the worn paintwork of a working boat.

This use of the texture of rubbed paint led directly to experimentation with the surfaces that can be achieved with resin and plaster so that later works somehow succeed in being both more sculptural and more painterly. Certainly formal concerns have always been part of his art and their subordination to delight in the possibilities of *trompe l'oeil* was a short phase in his development.

A further stage in the evolution of Maclean's confidence in his new way of working had already come in 1977. His work was selected by Paul Overy for a Scottish Arts Council exhibition held that year, *Inscape*. It was an important exhibition and it explored in the work of a group of six Scottish artists, just those areas that interested Maclean himself. The other five were Ian Hamilton Finlay, Glen Onwin, Eileen Lawrence, Fred Stiven and Ainslie Yule. Amongst these, the work of several in particular had common ground with what Maclean himself was doing. Eileen Lawrence for instance was making fastidious drawings of collections of natural objects, not unlike some of Maclean's *Ring-Net* drawings. Ainslie Yule was making drawings for sculpture of mysterious, surreal objects which suggest the same kind of pseudo-archaeological mystery that Maclean was exploring in some of his constructions. Fred Stiven was making boxes, but their use of a formal aesthetic also underlined the distinctiveness of Maclean's approach. Finlay was also using imagery of ships and fishing in a way that opened up its poetic and metaphoric possibilities, linking past and present.

In his introduction to the catalogue of *Inscape*, Overy remarks that there were no painted canvasses in the show, that this was not by design, but that it simply reflected the current concerns of some of the most thoughtful artists then working in Scotland. A few years later, in 1982, Overy again selected Maclean for an exhibition, *Inner Worlds*, on a similar theme. It was drawn from a more international group of artists, but also included Finlay and Bellany. It is interesting that in this context, the preoccupations of the Scots did seem distinctive.

Internationally, in the mid-1970s there was a reaction against painting, but in Scotland this found a focus in the rejection of the particular, subjective, painterly ethos that prevailed in the art schools. Individuals in the older generation had always stood out against this as Fleming and Walker did in Aberdeen. With Finlay, too, this rejection had happened much earlier and it had taken him out of art altogether for a while, to return to it via poetry. Several of the younger artists in the group shared this kind of interest, though not going so far as to make concrete poetry themselves, as Finlay had done.

The title, *Inscape*, came from Gerard Manley Hopkins. It means the inner landscape of the mind and in his introduction to an exhibition of the work of Ken Dingwall the same year, Overy made a specific

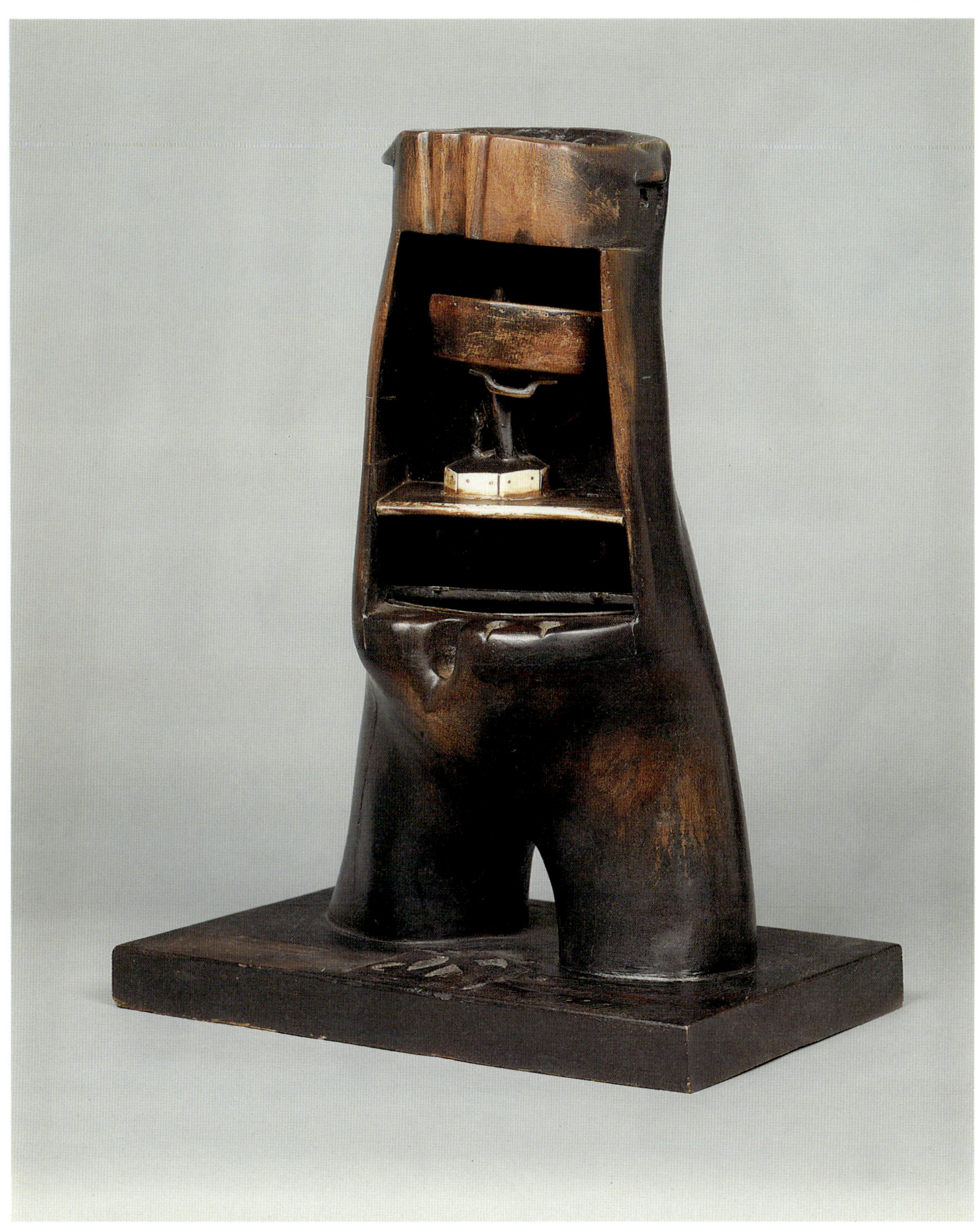

32. *Fire Figure* (1985) (Cat.103)

comparison between contemporary art and poetry. He suggested that art, like poetry, had to withdraw from the grand statement into more intimate and private territory:

> The nearest analogy to painting would be, I think, poetry. It will not have a wide audience. But it will have a density of meaning, a seriousness, and allusiveness (and also an illusiveness) which the best contemporary poetry has.[9]

This may in part be true, but the recognition of significant common ground between art and poetry was also a reflection of the opposite truth; of the way that these artists were moving away from the highly specialised preoccupation with the formal language of art which had been dominant in the post-war years in parallel to logical positivism in philosophy. Instead, they were turning back, or rediscovering the traditions of the Scottish Renascence (and some like Finlay had never left them) and finding inspiration in areas of experience for which, because they were real and actual, the lines of demarcation between the art forms used to describe them were irrelevant. It was a shift in which the exchange once again became possible between the concrete and the metaphysical, of which Hopkins's poetry, like Sorley MacLean's, was a conspicuous example. This had been one of the objectives of progressive painting since the eighteenth century. Recently in Scotland, it had been a characteristic objective of the work of James Cowie and William Johnstone and it was also currently the distinctive characteristic of Finlay's work, but it ultimately derived from the central concern of Scottish empirical philosophy, the relationship between the mind, morality and the external world.

Reviewing *Inscape*, Marina Vaizey compared Maclean's work to the box constructions of Joseph Cornell,[10] one of the masters of this kind of intimate narrative, at the same time semi-private and based on the actual. Cornell's work was a revelation to Maclean who had not known it before. He had of course been familiar with the Dada and Surrealist use of collage and assemblage, his own starting point, and years later he acknowledged this directly when he paid homage to Kurt Schwitters in *Calotype for Schwitters* (1986, *Pl. 27*). It is a collage in Schwitters's manner with a ticket to an exhibition of his work as its centrepiece. Maclean was obviously familiar, too, with the work in the 1960s of artists like Peter Blake who had learnt from Americans like Cornell and Rauschenberg. There were also contemporaries like Fred Stiven, who had taught him at Gray's, or Barry Cooke, who both made boxes of a rather similar character, but apart from the obvious abstract-expressionist painters and the pop artists, American art was still not well known in Britain. It is not surprising that he should not have been aware of Cornell.

Cornell's work was distinctive because he used the technique of assemblage, or rather what Paul Overy calls 'bricolage'[11] (an assemblage made from found objects which preserve something of their original identity) in a novel way. He had made it a vehicle for a kind of narrative. In Cornell's boxes therefore, Maclean found justification for the kind of narrative based on the collection and fastidious arrangement of objects that he himself had begun to explore independently. This helped him to realise how great the potential was of this way of working.

The influence of Cornell was more one of general encouragement, rather than of specific indebtedness and Maclean's own iconography and formal language continued to evolve along lines that were already established. The latter depended on the wider surrealist tradition as well as on those nearer his own generation, but in the former he also came increasingly close to the indigenous, Scottish tradition which had evolved from the work of the Scots Renascence poets and artists and their successors.

Maclean's art represents an interweaving of themes. Through his own childhood, it reflects the history of the Highlands and the life of sailors and the sea and then draws from these wider metaphors. Perhaps by its title alone, the key work in this period is *Memories of a Northern Childhood* of 1977(*Pl. 28*). It still shows his interest in *trompe l'oeil* and is in fact actually organised like a particular kind of seventeenth-century, *trompe l'oeil* still-life of which in Scotland the best known example is Thomas Warrender's painting in the National Gallery of Scotland. Though this particular one was unknown in the 1970s, it is a common type, representing an arrangement of objects held by straps or bands to a board or wall. These objects, which include things like playing cards, quill pens and clay pipes, often seem to have a personal, or even autobiographical significance for the artist, though this is not always explicit.

In *Memories of a Northern Childhood*, there is such a set of objects: a clay pipe, fishing and net-making gear and a cut-throat razor. These are arranged against the wainscot of a Highland cottage. Above them is a tabernacle, its gothic doors opening on to a dark interior. Inside is visible a slate relief of a ring-net fishing boat, a votive image on an altar, carved like a Pictish stone. The title and the objects together suggest a boy's perception of manhood in a fishing community. It is once again the archaeology of the artist's childhood, but the dark tabernacle with its open doors also distinctly recalls the opening plate of Blake's *Jerusalem*. There, the artist stands in front of just such a darkened, gothic doorway. It is the gate of perception and he has a lantern in his hand as he prepares to enter and bring light where there is darkness.

Maclean's gate is the gate of the memory of childhood, but childhood is one of what Paolozzi called 'the Lost Magic Kingdoms', the title of an exhibition that he selected in the Museum of Mankind in 1985. In it, he brought together the artifacts of 'primitive' peoples and his own art works. He was making a double point: an ecological one in which he demonstrated how we are all impoverished by the destruction of such cultures and also how this destruction in itself mirrors our ignorance of our own 'primitive' needs; needs which we still cater for in unrecognised ways, creating totems, fetishes and structures of magical belief. These are the needs which both Paolozzi and Alan Davie see their art as serving and in this way, they demonstrate our community with those whom we mistakenly regard as different because we regard them as 'primitive'.

Paolozzi was also interested in survival and adaptation as non-western people took over the materials and the artifacts of technological society. As they did so they invested them with new imaginative power, as he himself sought to do and just as Maclean had done for instance with a US Navy survival kit in *Symbols of Survival*. Though Duchamp had led the way, it was Paolozzi who had first argued explicitly that we have to take into account all the products of our visual culture if we are to

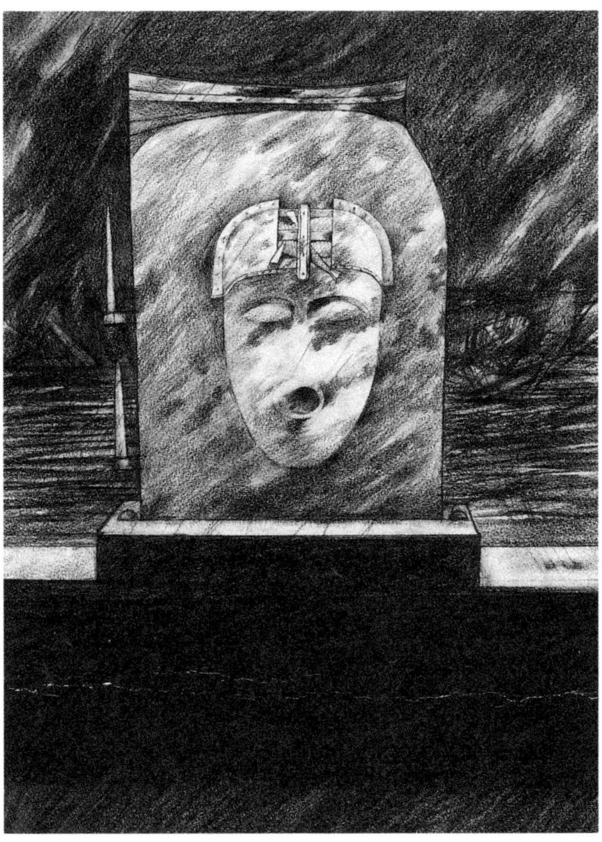

33. Study for *Rudder Requiem*, pencil, 50 x 38 cms, Private Collection (1987)

understand it, not just those sanctified as 'fine art'. In the Dada tradition, he aimed to break down the barriers which isolated art from reality and which emasculated it as it confined it to 'the Fine Arts'. In so doing, he sought to realise the actual, imaginative potential locked in so much of what we regard as trivial, especially in the imagery with which we surround ourselves. In *Lost Magic Kingdoms*, he extended this to explore the continuity between cultures, whether or not they are technologically advanced, and thus the common ground, the ground in which our shared humanity resides.

Maclean was pursuing a similar line independently, exploring through the traditions of the Highlands actual contact with the primitive in our own culture. On the one hand, he uses specific imagery and found objects in a way that Paolozzi does, combining them in non-linear structures including, but not simply dependent on, narrative techniques. On the other hand, like Davie whose exploration of Jungian symbolism closely parallels the way Paolozzi — often literally — cuts through the surface of the conventional reading of an image to other potential meanings, Maclean is deeply interested in the symbolic value of imagery and its ability to resonate in the unconscious areas of the mind. In the way he does this, Davie identifies himself with the shamans of

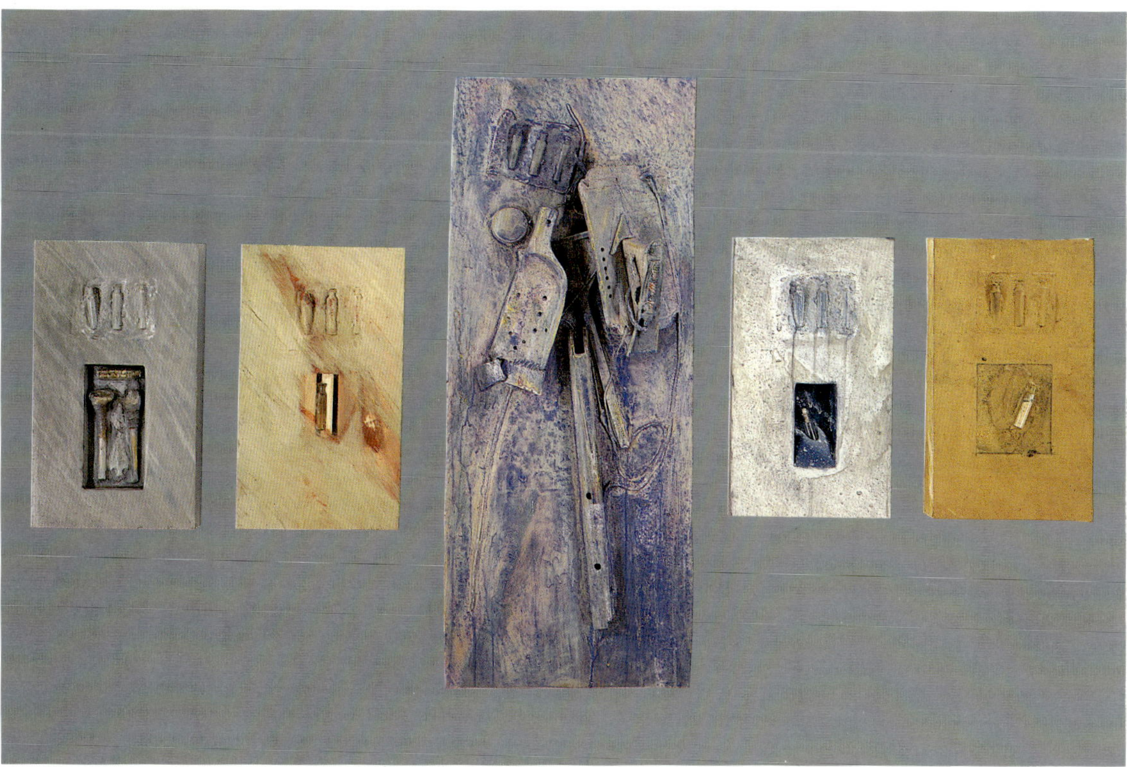

34. *Bottle Beach Settlement, Part II* (1988) (Cat.130)

primitive religion. He proposes that his art mediates between the conscious and the unconscious, or between the material and the spiritual. In a primitive context, this could be between the living and the dead, a subject that is implicit in Maclean's images of the Clearances.

As the very first of them, *Requiem Construction (John Maclean)*, made clear, Maclean's constructions were formally reliquaries. Historically, reliquaries are of course containers for the relics of the saints. Their contents were objects hallowed by association which could act as mediators between the spectator and the saint. His works continued to have this form as long as he continued to incorporate actual objects in his constructions, but even recently when he has come to use casts and other methods of reproducing the significant, collected elements in a construction, he has often still used the idea of the reliquary. Of course, Maclean does not use this in a simple, religious way, but he does use it to mediate between the spectator and the subject of his work which is invoked by association. The religious overtones are often there too though, as they are here both in the gothic window and in the word requiem. Sometimes the works are actually called reliquaries as in *Fladda Reliquary* (1978, *Pl. 29*). At other times, he will use some associated religious word in the title like ex-voto, offertory, tabernacle, shrine, or icon, as in *Icon for a Fisherman* (1978, *Pl. 30*), and moving out of the Christian tradition altogether, his later works are frequently called totems.

There are also more playful images though. *Black Priest's Box* (*1982, Pl. 31*), for instance, is a kind of imaginary tool-kit for a travelling Bronze-Age priest. It contains all the equipment that such a priest might need to set up an alignment of standing stones; a cord measuring a megalithic yard contained in a bone tube, cords for setting straight lines such as gardeners use, even model standing stones. Similarly, *Fire Figure* (1985, *Pl. 32*) is a torso made from the fork of a laburnum tree, hollowed out to contain pseudo-religious fire-making equipment.

These are the kind of thing that one can imagine Naomi Mitchison describing in a novel set in Bronze-Age Orkney and this whole imaginary side to his art presents a literary analogy that illuminates Maclean's exploration of the past, for it extends the parallel with Johnstone's painting *A Point in Time* and Maclean's links with the Scots Renascence. For instance, Johnstone's interest in time and the presence in the landscape of history and prehistory simultaneously with our continuing present experience has close parallels in the novels of Neil Gunn and Lewis Grassic Gibbon. Like Maclean, Grassic Gibbon was fascinated by archaeology and in the *Scots Quair*, he constantly reaches back from the narrative present to the remote past. For instance in *Sunset Song*, in moments of crisis Chris always goes to find comfort in the standing stones on the moor above Blaweary. In his essays, following a lead given by Patrick Geddes, he sought to make sense of the present in Scotland by opening the enclosed perspective of modern history to include the much longer perspective of the prehistoric past — it is as though the conscious mind was represented by history and prehistory was the subconscious. Civilisation originated in Scotland from Ancient Egypt, he argued in his essay, 'The Antique Scene':

> And from that central focal point . . . the first civilisers spread abroad the globe the beliefs and practices, the diggings and plantings . . . of the Ancient Civilisation. They reached Scotland in some age we do not know, coming to the Islands of Mist in search of copper and gold and pearls, Givers of Life in the fantastic theology that followed the practice of agriculture. [12]

Then in 'The Land', he sets out the same thesis and concludes:

> They are so tenuous and yet so real, those folk . . . The ancient men haunted those woods and hills for me, and do so still.[13]

Maclean comes even closer to Neil Gunn than to Grassic Gibbon, though. Gunn's themes of fishing and the Clearances in novels such as *The Silver Darlings*, *Morning Tide* and *Butcher's Broom* suggest an obvious analogy, but it is Gunn's masterpiece, *Highland River*, which best illuminates the symbolism and the underlying themes as well as the subject matter of Maclean's art. It is an extraordinary book, its narrative built up with all the intricate, layered convolutions of Celtic interlace.

The hero, Kenn, an adult revisiting his Highland home, recalls his childhood during the course of a single journey from his birthplace at the mouth of the river there to its source. Thus the novel interweaves simultaneously time and space in

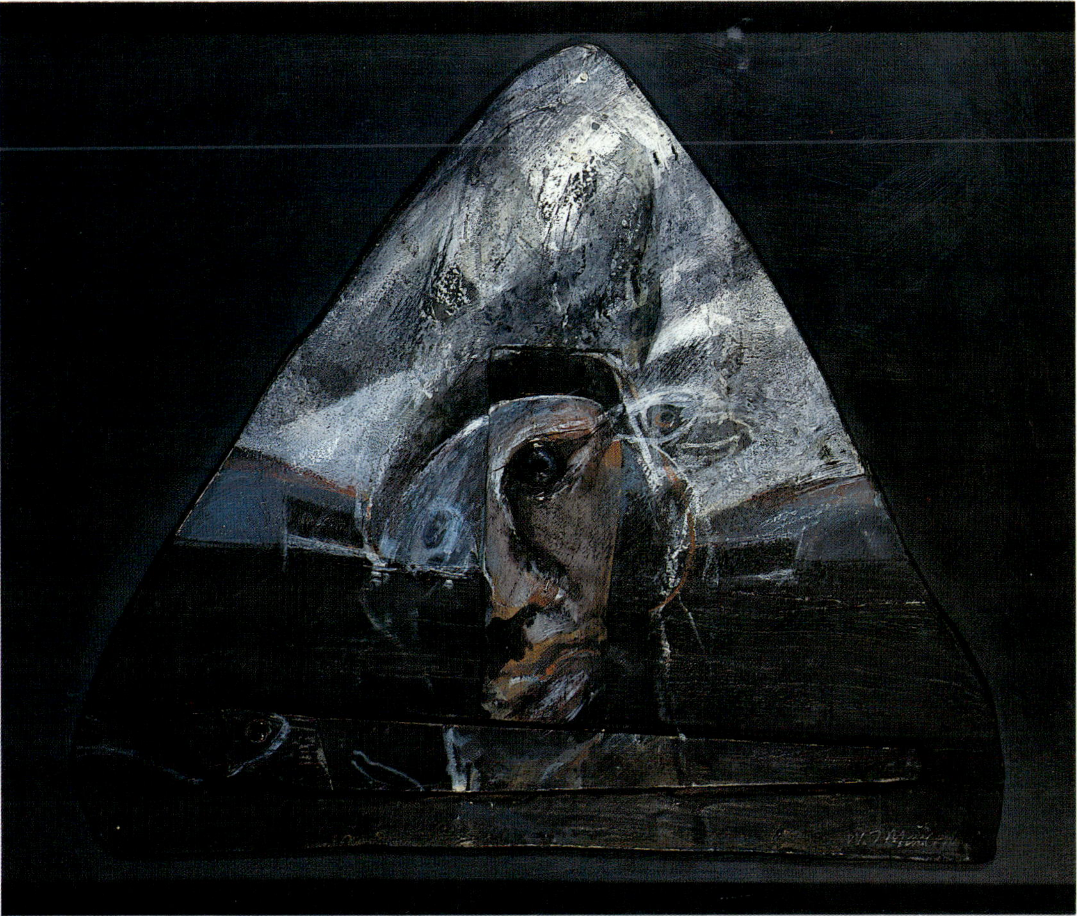

35. *Fisherman Listening for Herring* (1989) (Cat. 138)

the geological and historical dimensions of the landscape, with time and space as we experience them in an individual life and at the present moment. Within these complexities is further interwoven a quest. It is like the quest for the Grail, but it has two forms, the adult hero's search for the source of the river and the boyhood story of his pursuit of a fish. The fish is a salmon. Obliquely, the author identifies it as the salmon of wisdom, the legendary salmon 'the tasting of whose flesh confers all knowledge', [14] while the hero, Kenn, just like a salmon, travels up the river to find at its source, the source of himself.

In the end, as in Johnstone's painting, these things become simultaneous as the novel brings together in a single moment of experience, the present and the primeval. The hero passes through a wasteland, reminiscent both of the wasteland of the Grail myth and of the battlefields he had known in the first war, 'a primeval no-man's land of outspewings like water-logged shell holes', to reach his grail in a pure and virginal loch and 'a moment in which all conflict is reconciled, in which a timeless harmony is achieved'.[15] Kenn has left home and is a scientist. His father was a Highland herring fisherman and at one

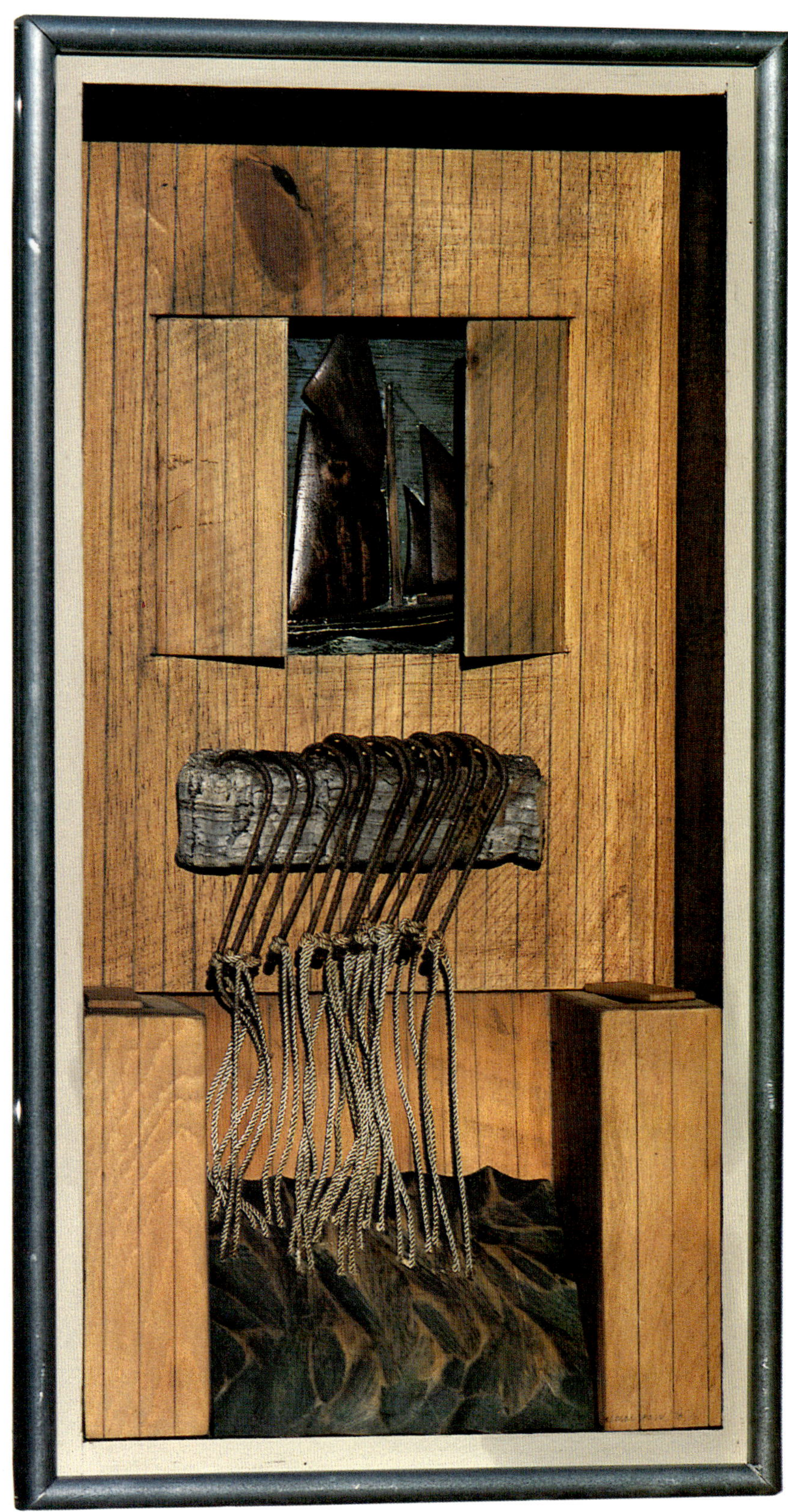

36. *Nostalgic Locker* (1976) (Cat. 16)

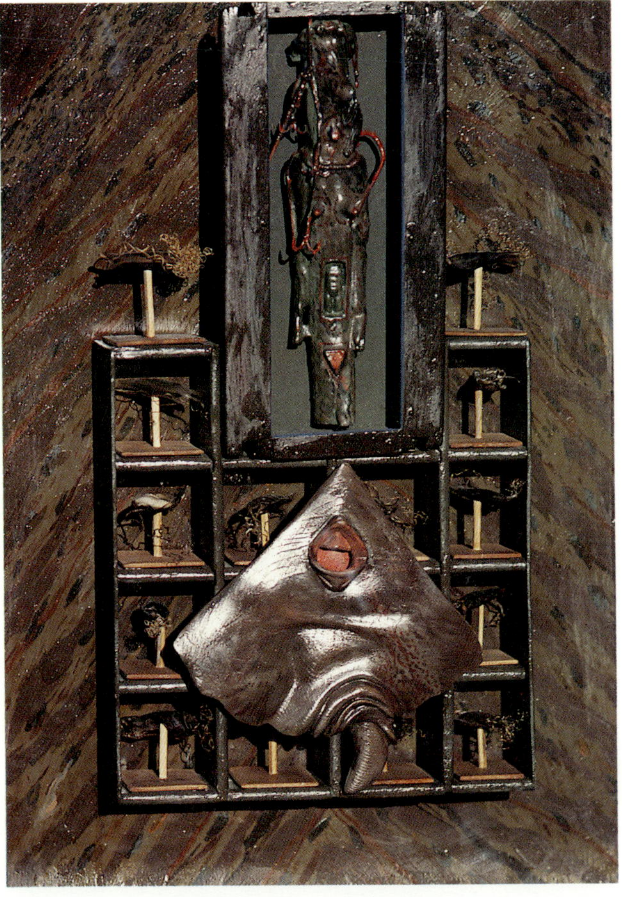

37. *Ray Fish Shrine* (1976) (Cat. 14)

point Gunn amplifies the significance that he sees in the archetypal business of hunting fish as the restless search for knowledge, linking it to Kenn's own pursuit of science:

> Galileo, Tycho Brahe, Kepler, the great Newton, Cavendish, Faraday, Roentgen . . . They were the men who stood behind the fishermen in Kenn's growing mind. From fishermen to them was a natural progression. [16]

In *A Drunk Man Looks at the Thistle*, MacDiarmid uses the figure of Melville and Captain Ahab's pursuit of the white whale in a similar way as a symbol of the quest for knowledge:

> 'Melville, sea compelling man,
> Before whose wand, Leviathan
> Rose hoary-white upon the deep,'
> What thou hast sown I fain 'ud reap
> O' knowledge yont the human mind. [17]

Later, in his whaling imagery, Maclean too comes close to Melville's contemplation of the ambiguousness of this pursuit, but in his themes of time, childhood and dispossession in the Highlands and in the way that he uses the imagery of fishing too, he is here closest to Neil Gunn. His personal link with the tradition of the Scots

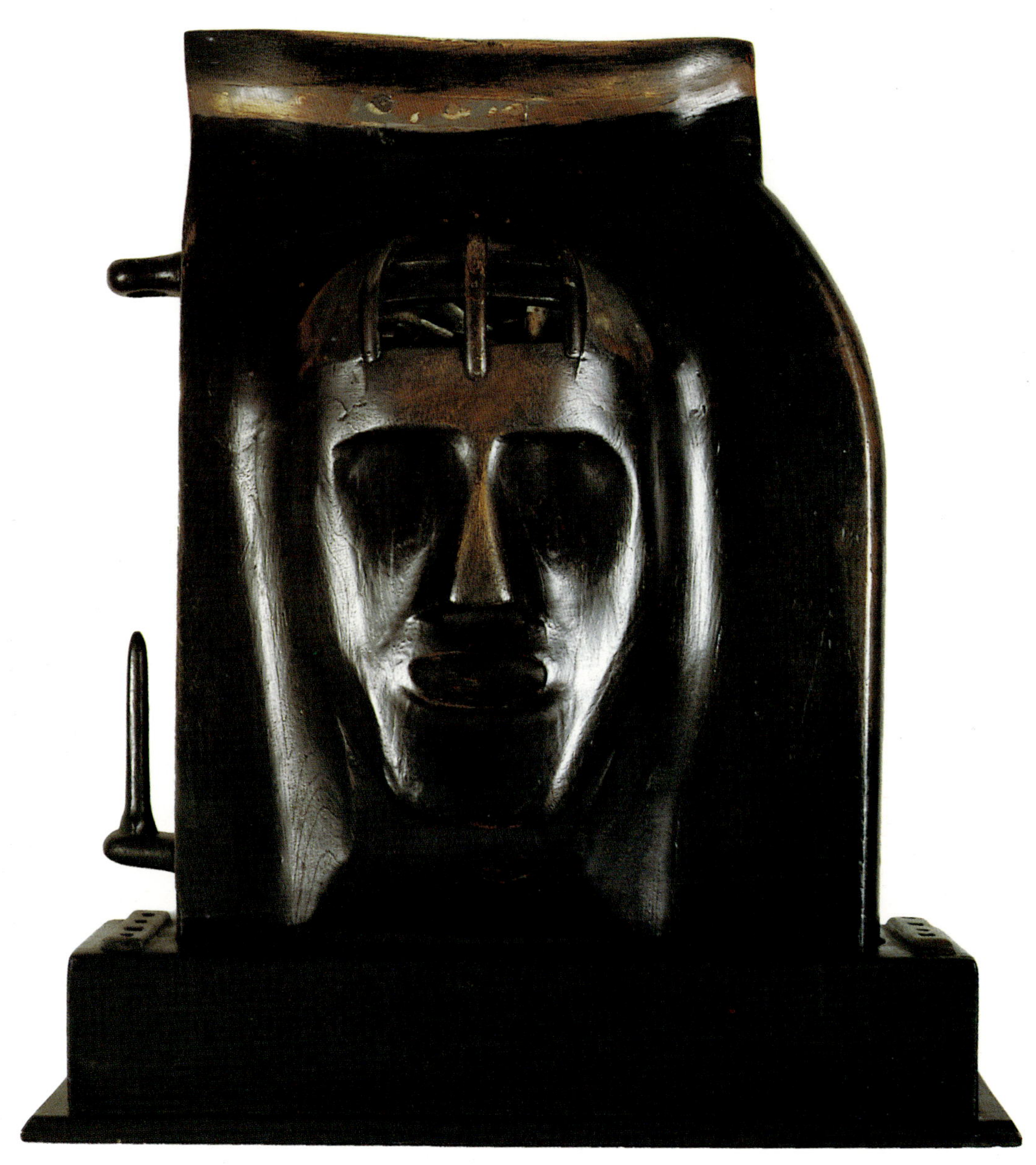

38. *Rudder Requiem* (1985) (Cat. 101)

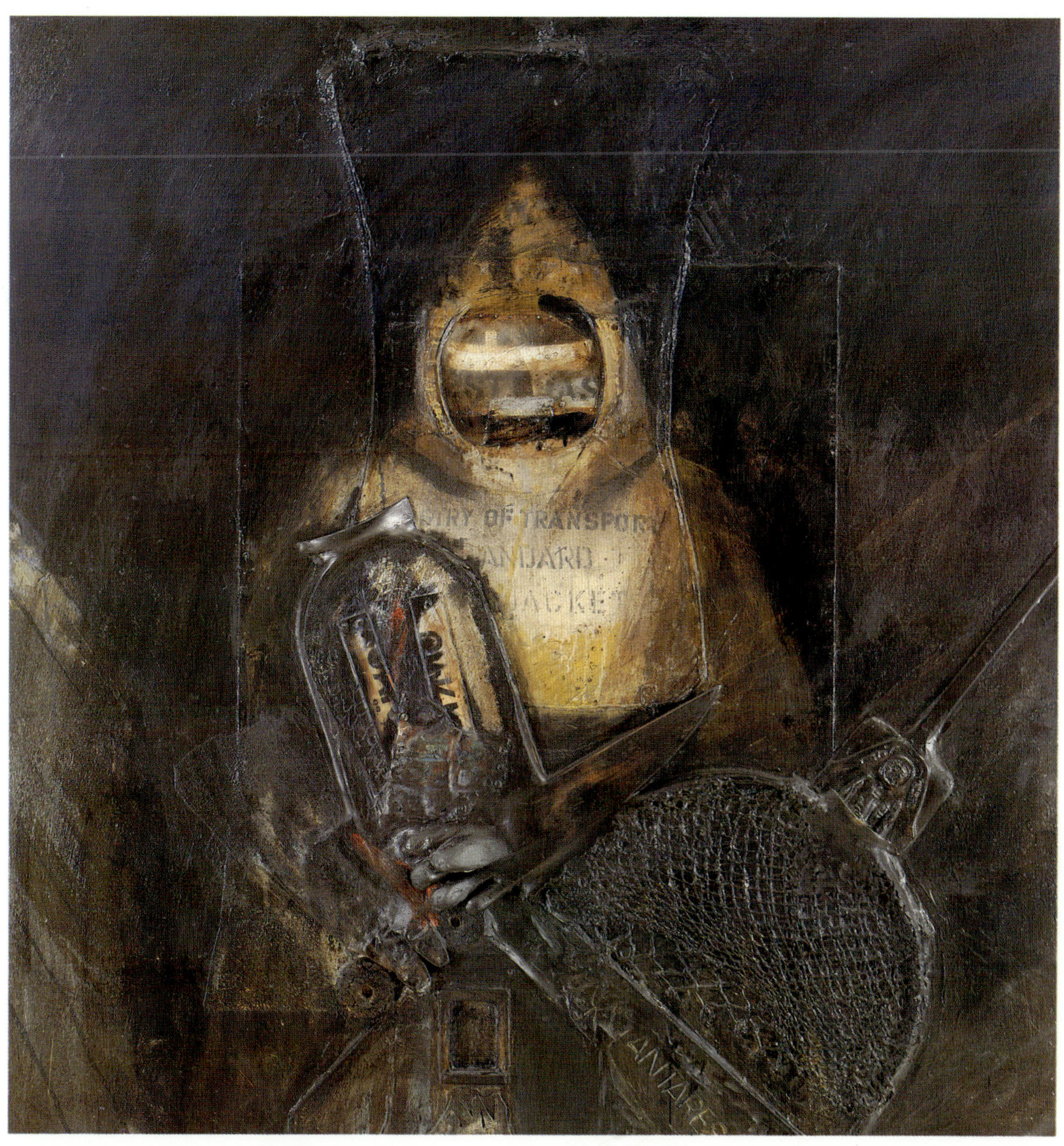

39. *Skye Fisherman: In Memoriam* (1989) (Cat. 143)

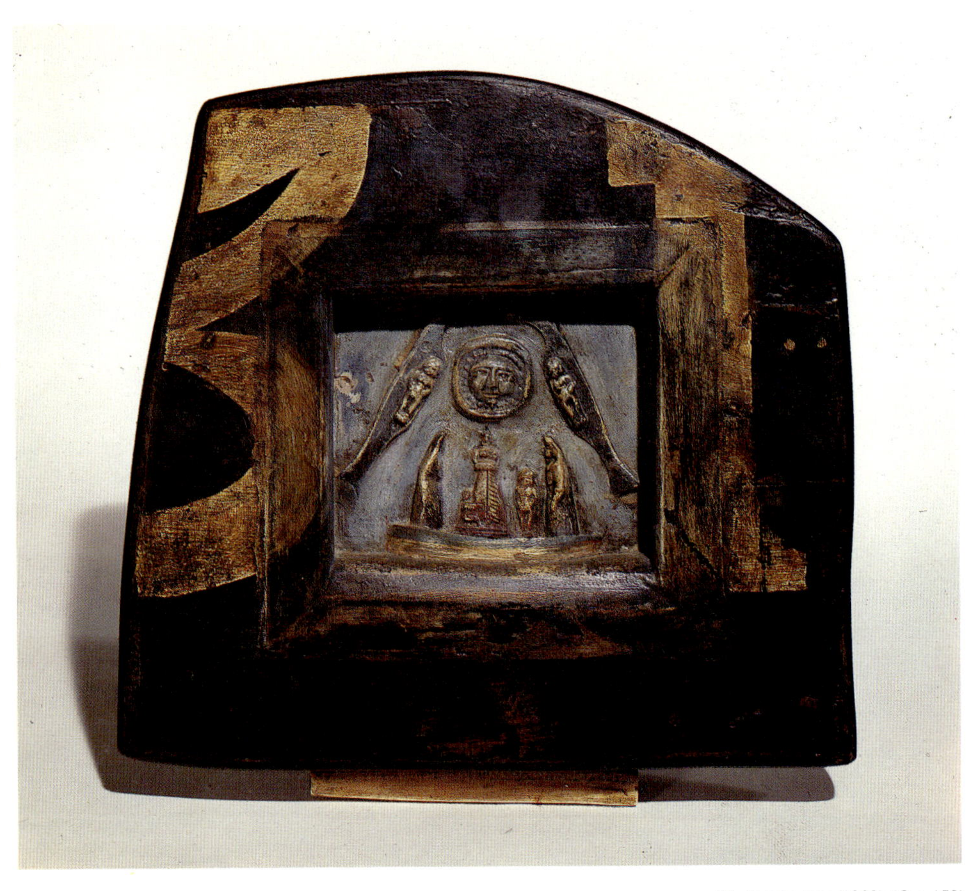

40. *Sea Lectern* (1989) (Cat. 153)

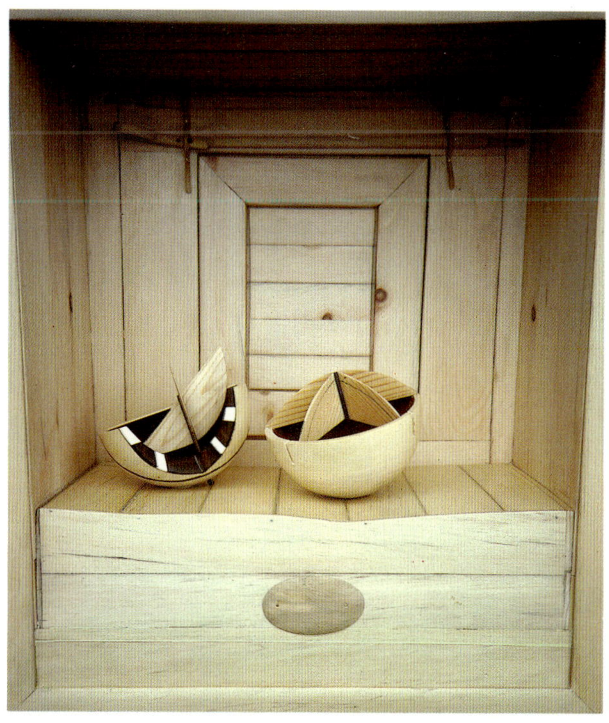

41. *Navigator's Locker* (1982) (Cat. 65)

Renascence, however, is not through Gunn, but through his association with Sorley MacLean in whose poetry of course these same themes occur. It is an important link, for in this tradition the search for identity in the fusion of history and locality, that began with Scott, was developed to incorporate new ideas of time and relativity and the extension of history itself, to include remote prehistory and our subconscious memory of it. For as the surrealists pursued the possibility of drawing images from the unconscious, Jung enlarged this further to suggest that such imagery itself might be drawn from the reservoir of a collective consciousness, shaped by human experience over that vast tract of time. Early in the century too, anthropologists like Frazer and literary critics like Jessie Weston, were enormously influential as they began to argue for similar continuity in the actual survival of memories from prehistory within the present in our own society in both folk custom and literature.

It was this shift that helped to bring the ancient Celtic tradition forward as an inspiration to modern art and literature. In Scotland, this had begun with Patrick Geddes. He is often misrepresented as a revivalist, lost in an imaginary Celtic twilight, but what he actually argued for was a modern culture so well integrated with a sense of national identity that it could draw on these deeper springs of consciousness while dealing on equal terms as a partner in the culture of the wider world. It is in keeping with this ambition that the inspiration of the Scots Renascence was diverse. In the English-speaking world, to say nothing of Continental Europe, Geddes himself was closely in touch with nationalist culture in Ireland, and Yeats and Joyce

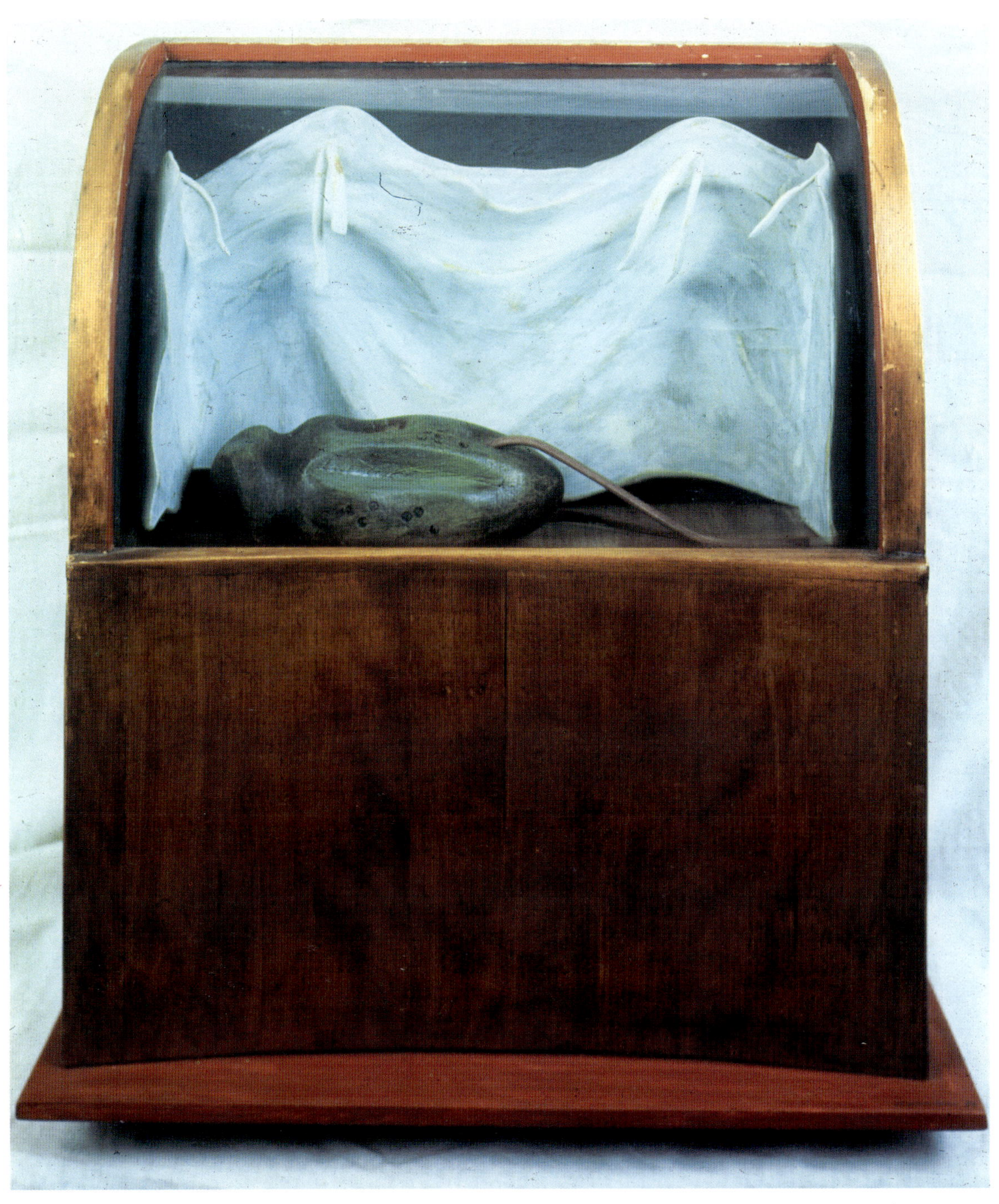

42. *Museum for a Seer* (1983) (Cat. 79)

were important for the Scots (similarly for Maclean, Seamus Heany has been an important inspiration), but to novelists like Gunn, so were Hardy and especially Lawrence from England. Like Lawrence too, Wyndham Lewis tried to break with the prevailing gentility of English culture and he was an important influence on MacDiarmid as well as on Fergusson, McCance and Johnstone. There was also inspiration from America through Eliot and Pound, and among the artists, William Johnstone was clearly influenced by Arthur Dove and Georgia O'Keefe, who were asking similar questions about identity, history and place in an American context. Johnstone was, however, an important advocate of surrealism and of a Jungian view of imagery, a view which in his later life became closer to that of Zen.

An independent, though equally important figure was James Cowie whose highly personal interpretation of surrealism was a distinctive contribution to Scottish art in the 1930s and 1940s. Although Cowie's iconography is otherwise very different from that of Johnstone for instance, and for him history's continuity is to be seen in the specific continuity of western art rather than in anything more diffuse. It is interesting, nevertheless, that the farm that was his birthplace constantly appears in the background of Cowie's paintings and in a similar vein, Johnstone once remarked that it was the landscape of his boyhood that made him a painter.

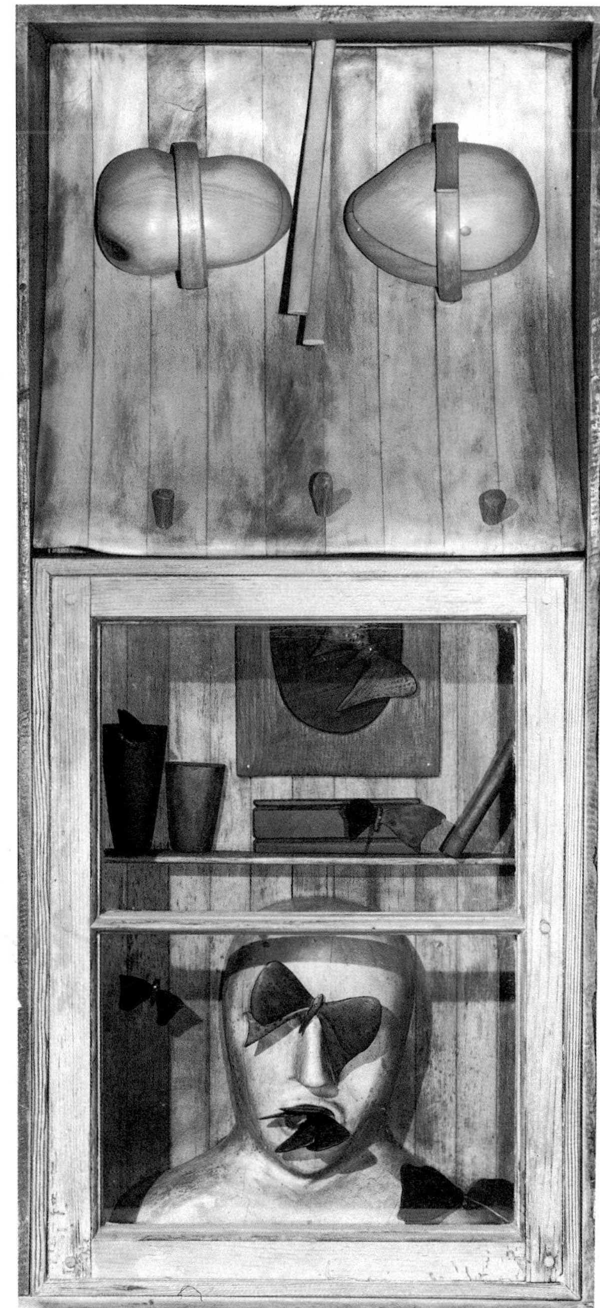

43. *Window Visitation, North Uist* (1980) (Cat. 48)

In fact, the Scots Renascence developed very much as Geddes proposed and as MacDiarmid sought to realise it, on a strong national base, but drawing on a wide international culture. It developed a distinctive character and was given an urgent, social and political dimension by MacDiarmid. In the person of Sorley MacLean though and losing none of its political urgency, the evolving Renascence

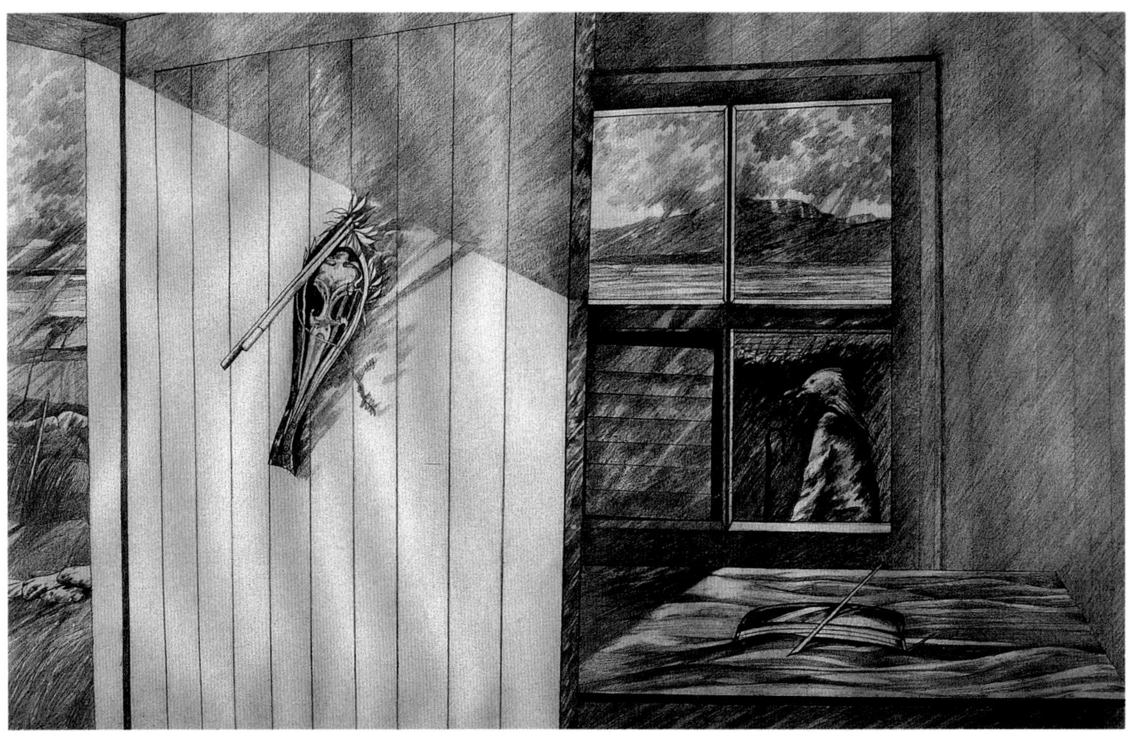

44. *Two Sights of the Sea*, pencil, 48 x 75 cms approx., Private Collection (1982)

converged with the living tradition of Gaelic culture.

This background, still central to Scottish culture in the late twentieth century, was a key factor in the emergence of Joan Eardley, Eduardo Paolozzi, Ian Hamilton Finlay and Alan Davie, as a group of outstanding artists from Scotland in the 1940s and 1950s. These four either had links with the circle of J. D. Fergusson in Glasgow, or with William Johnstone in London. In turn in the 1960s, John Bellany was directly inspired by MacDiarmid and all this was not just a matter of some kind of mystic laying on of hands. These individuals all represented a clear and articulate tradition which went back at least to Geddes. They were, too, in the best sense profoundly serious. For them, art and literature had a social function and were essential tools of imaginative understanding. They were not a pastime, but a forum in which values are forged and the basic questions of history and identity examined and debated. Sorley MacLean writes of 'A poet struggling with the world's condition,' [18] and MacDiarmid says of poetry:

> . . . [it] wins to a miraculously calm, assured,
> Awareness o'the hidden motives o'man's mind
> Noch't else daur seek. [19]

Will Maclean follows in this tradition. Of the painters of the older generation, though, in many ways he is closest to Cowie whose metaphysical still-lifes often work in the same way as his constructions. When Maclean's drawings are considered this parallel seems even closer too (*Pl. 33*), but in a wider sense the search to express the temporal and psychological unities that characterised the novels of Neil Gunn and the paintings

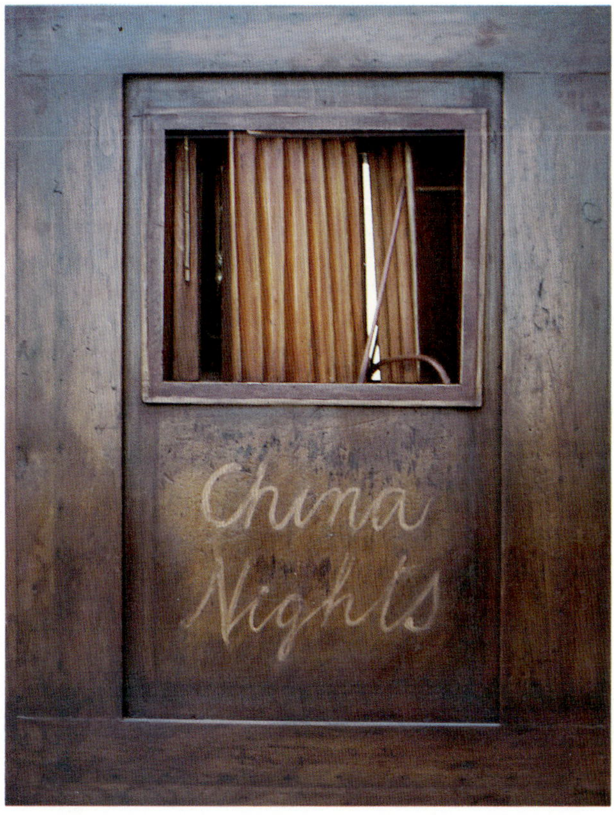

45. *China Nights* (1983) (Cat. 81)

of William Johnstone is also still very much part of his art. It is implicit in his interest in archaeology and it is directly invoked in one of his most elaborate works, *Bottle Beach Settlement* (1988, *Pl. 34*). Here he presents an archaeological find of his own as a still-life with his own commentary. It is a fifteen-piece work which records the discovery on a beach of a buried cache of nineteenth-century bottles, but, documenting time and place, he has developed this prosaic fact into a poem that celebrates the qualities that give archaeology meaning.

Each element in the piece represents an aspect of the context of the find, the elements of the sea and the shore, but too, of time and history. It is this confrontation with time and continuity which is the imaginative dimension of all archaeology. Maclean brilliantly sets this out in the shift from light to dark which extends over the whole sequence of the fifteen separate pieces of this work. It is the diurnal transition, the basic unit of our awareness of time that rolls on so far beyond our comprehension. The passage of time from the moment of burial of this cache to the moment of its discovery has been measured by the succession of night and day, like the ticking of a clock in indifferent regularity and numberless progression.

* * *

These bottles are a memory of whoever buried them. Apart from the diurnal succession which measures our lives, it is only through memory that we can move in time's dimension, whether it is with the individual or with the race. Time is implicit in the images from the artist's own memory and in his historic images from the Clearances that are such a central feature of his art, but it is also implicit in the imagery of fishing which he so often uses to unite these. In a beautiful image in *Comus*, Milton wrote of the movement of the tides, for instance:

> The Sounds, and Seas with all their finny drove,
> Now to the moon in wavering Morrice move. [20]

As Milton saw it, the tidal dances of the sea are dances to the music of time itself; dances in which men join as fishermen more than they do in any other condition, as in Angus Martin's poem they are dancers, dancing between the tide and eternity. Perceived in this temporal dimension, fishing is an activity that links us to our earliest ancestors, to the hunter-gatherers and the state of nature. As Neil Gunn wrote of the fishermen in *Highland River*:

> They were hunters, hunting the northern and western seas as their remote ancestors had hunted the forests and the grasslands.[21]

Even in a technological age, fishing still preserves this link with our remotest past. Those who practise it are in immediate contact with, and unqualified dependence on nature herself. No more than a generation ago, they made many of their tools from wood and bone in ways and in forms that were visibly reminiscent of the artifacts of our neolithic ancestors. They were, too, as close to nature and as dependent upon her. In an extraordinary image *Fisherman Listening for Herring* (1989, *Pl. 35*), Maclean records the practice of the ring-net fishermen of listening for the sound of the fish, identifying the herring by the quality of the noise they make leaping from the water. It is an image that suggests a communion with the natural world as intimate as that of the Australian aborigines, and the artist has caught that analogy in the style of the work.

As Maclean knew it as a boy, fishing was on the edge of a technological revolution, but at that time there were still such links to the most ancient traditions in the items of equipment that were hand-made that so often appear in his work and in the dependence of the fishermen on inherited skill and personal courage. *Nostalgic Locker* of 1976 (*Pl. 36*) reflects on just these characteristics in an arrangement very similar to *Memories of a Northern Childhood*, with a tall, brown-sailed fishing-boat in the half-open tabernacle and a row of iron fishing-hooks above a carved, wooden sea. In the same year, *Ray Fish Shrine* (*Pl. 37*) is a work which, on the one hand, links this imagery directly to the *Ring-Net*, for its inspiration is an old photograph collected for the *Ring-Net* project of a group of fishermen standing with a giant ray that they have caught. On the other hand though, this real image is transformed into a votive altar for some forgotten religion, perhaps for one of the rites of the 'Fisher King', for the idea of the fisherman as the archetype of 'natural man' has an impressive pedigree.

Jessie Weston had identified the Fisher King — *le Roi Pêcheur* — as at the heart of the story of the quest for the Grail. She argued that in that story, the whole symbolism of Fish and Fisher are central symbols surviving from the earliest nature rituals:

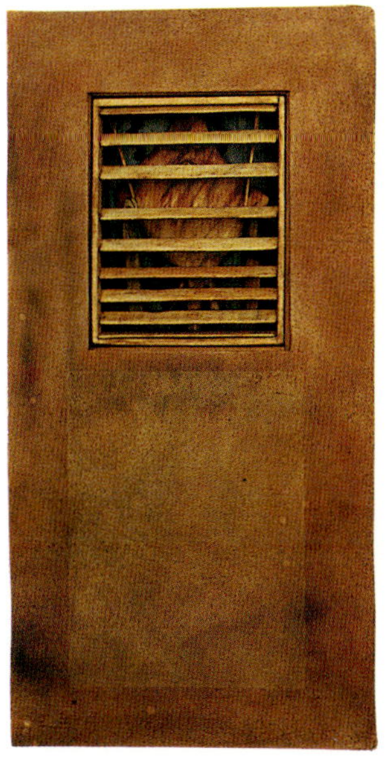
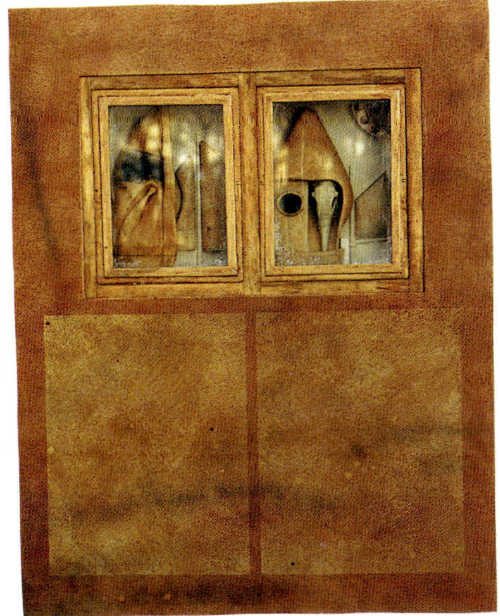
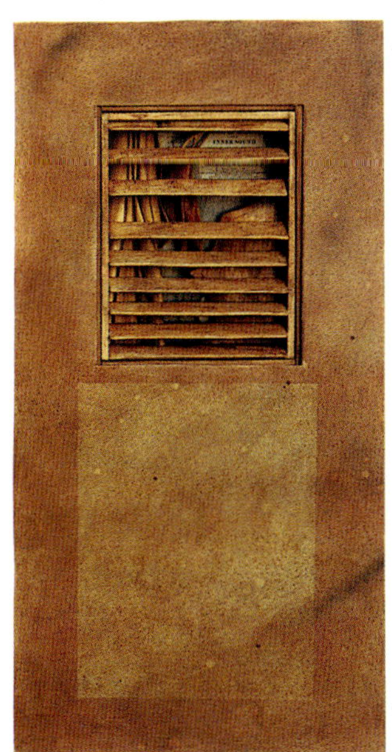

46. *Wheelhouse Triptych* (1981) (Cat. 55)

> The fish is a life symbol of immemorial antiquity . . . the title of fisher has from earliest ages been associated with Deities who were held to be specially connected with the origin and preservation of life. [22]

In the legend of the Grail too, according to her interpretation, it is because of his catching a fish that Brons, brother of Joseph of Aramathea, came to be called the Fisher King and the fish that he caught was identified by some authorities with the salmon of wisdom of Celtic legend,[23] an identification that is imaginatively potent, no matter whether it be authentic. Because of T. S. Eliot's poetic interpretation in *The Waste Land* — one of the best-known poems of the twentieth century — of Jessie Weston's theory of the origin of the story of the Grail in ancient nature ritual, it has been a familiar topic in modern literature. It was clearly an important element in Neil Gunn's *Highland River*, for instance, and it would not be surprising if Maclean's iconography should draw on this kind of symbolism.

He sees it, though, through the immediate example of fishing in the present, but here the immemorial intimacy of the relationship of the fisherman and his prey is being disrupted by technological change. *Rudder Requiem* (1985, *Pl. 33 & 38*), for instance, is a requiem for fishing in its ancient form. The work is in the shape of a rudder, but shaped from the end of a church pew and decorated with carving rather as a Polynesian steering oar might be. On it is the image of a man, his head full of fish, an image both of his dedication and of his skill. It is also, though, a memorial to the particular individual who inspired it and so it is a colloquial image too, for he was described by his friends as having 'his head full of fish'.

Rudder Requiem is therefore an emblematic portrait of the kind that began with *Abigail's Apron*, or even with *Requiem*

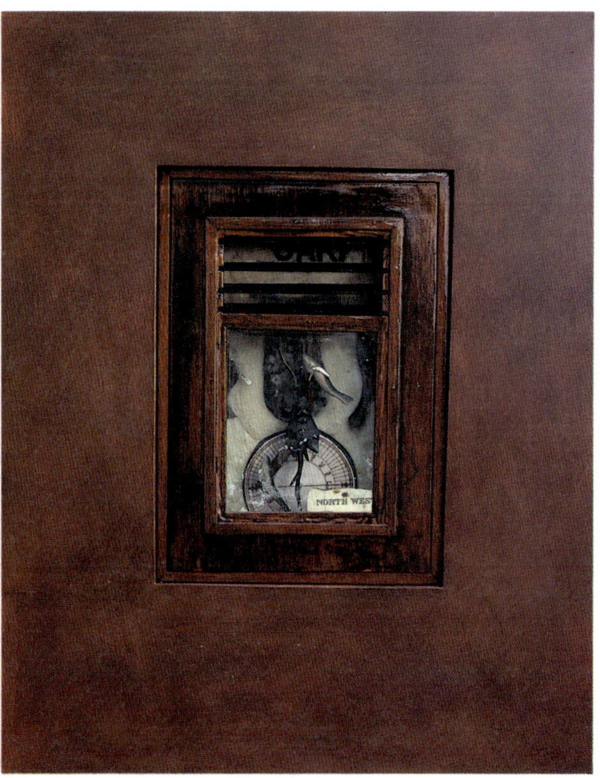

47. *Wheelhouse Study II* (1981) (Cat. 56)

Construction (John Maclean) and which continued in *Portrait of Angus Mackenzie.* The most moving of these is also an image of fishing and it too is both personal and archetypal. This is *Skye Fisherman: In Memoriam* (1989, *Pl. 39*). A yellow life-jacket, heavy rubber gloves and other paraphernalia of the fisherman are combined in a painted relief. It has a powerful presence as a memorial to the actual individual commemorated (who was the artist's uncle, William Reid), but there is also something of Phlebas the Phoenician in *The Waste Land*, or Puvis de Chavannes's *Poor Fisherman*, or perhaps, faceless and grand, his yellow oilskin like a suit of armour and carrying as his regalia the tools of his trade, he is the Fisher King himself, the king who died.

Like Eliot and Puvis, Maclean, in a single image, can reach from the immediate topicality of the present and personal to the permanence of myth, or indeed beyond, for the sea itself underlies all our consciousness, like the ultimate, Jungian symbol:

> An image o' the sea lies underneath
> A' men's imaginations — the sea in which
> A' life was born and that cradled us until
> We cam' to birth's maturity. Its waves bewitch
> Us still or wi' their lure o' peacefu' gleamin
> Or hungrily in storm and darkness streamin'.[24]

Like memories of childhood, fishing is another kind of living archaeology, an opening to a magic kingdom of memory and myth. As fisherman, man can be seen as a creature of nature, in touch with and dependent upon the natural world. The power of these fishing metaphors is that in this way they present man as once having had a place within nature's apparent harmony. Primitive religion and the ritual preserved in the romance of the Grail, according to this view, were a way of reinforcing that harmony, though the religion of the fishing people of Scotland, too, reflected their environment in a primeval way. Just as primitive man translated his understanding of nature into religious form, the unforgiving god of Calvinist predestination evoked in works by Maclean such as *Sea Lectern* (1989, *Pl. 40*) personifies the fierce indifference of the sea.

* * *

Within the western tradition, since the eighteenth century, time, perceived through history and even more through history's imaginative corollorary, folk-memory, has been seen by artists as a way into the deeper levels of the imagination and back to this imagined, natural state buried beneath our modern consciousness. It reflects the belief that at some remote point in time, as it were before our minds were made up according to the patterns of civilised convention, our beliefs and values assumed a simpler, more natural configuration. It is a version of the myth of the Golden Age; a myth as old as mankind, in one form it is in the book of Genesis and it was first called the Golden Age by Hesiod. It assumed a new importance in the eighteenth century in theories of the evolution of human society and its moral structure and the political interpretation given to them by Rousseau, but it was with Wilkie and John Galt that the specific contrast between past and present, though on a much shorter time scale, was for the first time used as a vehicle for direct, social criticism. After them, it was taken up by Thomas Carlyle who with some help from the Germans gave the idea a definitive form for the nineteenth century in his appropriately named book, *Past and Present.*

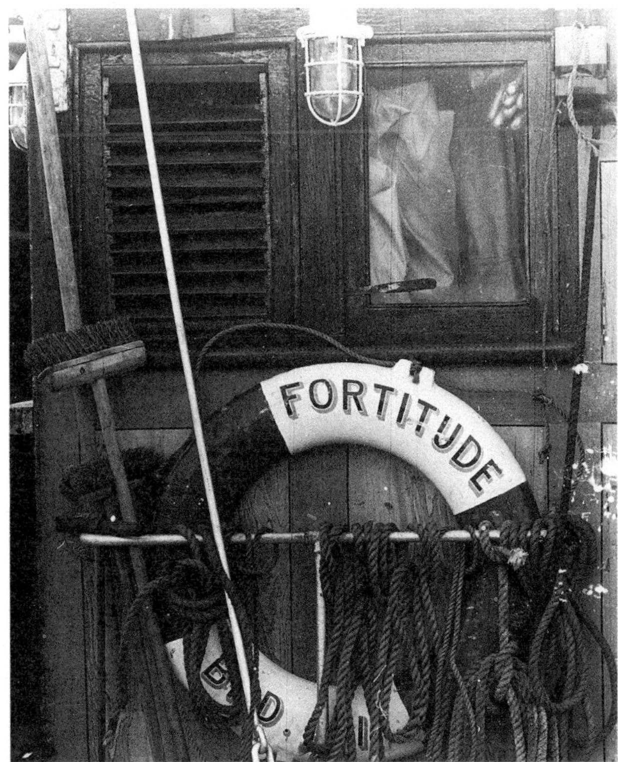

48. The wheelhouse of the *Fortitude*, photograph for the *Ring-Net* taken by the artist (1973)

The surrealists endorsed this tradition and substituted the psychologists' idea of the unconscious as the representative of the state of nature for the older, philosophical idea of the imagination and its corollorary, the relationship between freedom of imagination and purity of moral sense, but the motive remained the same; the moral ideal that man could not have been created as selfish and as wantonly destructive as recorded history suggests that he always has been. The Old Testament myth of the Fall — itself a version of the myth of the Golden Age — presented an alternative which, secularised, has served as one of the principal, underlying motives of modern art, but it is seen as a fall, not from the grace of God, but from nature. The sense of loss for the innocence of childhood — which could be equally the childhood of the individual or of the race — is seen as originating in loss of this natural communion.

If post-modernism stands for anything, it is really the recognition by critics of what has been understood by the most far-seeing artists for a long time, that the simplicity of this optimistic idea, the idea on which modernism was based, is attractive, but that its origins in the Utopian philosophy of the eighteenth century are so entangled with the origins of the idea of progress that in the end it is morally suspect. Modern history

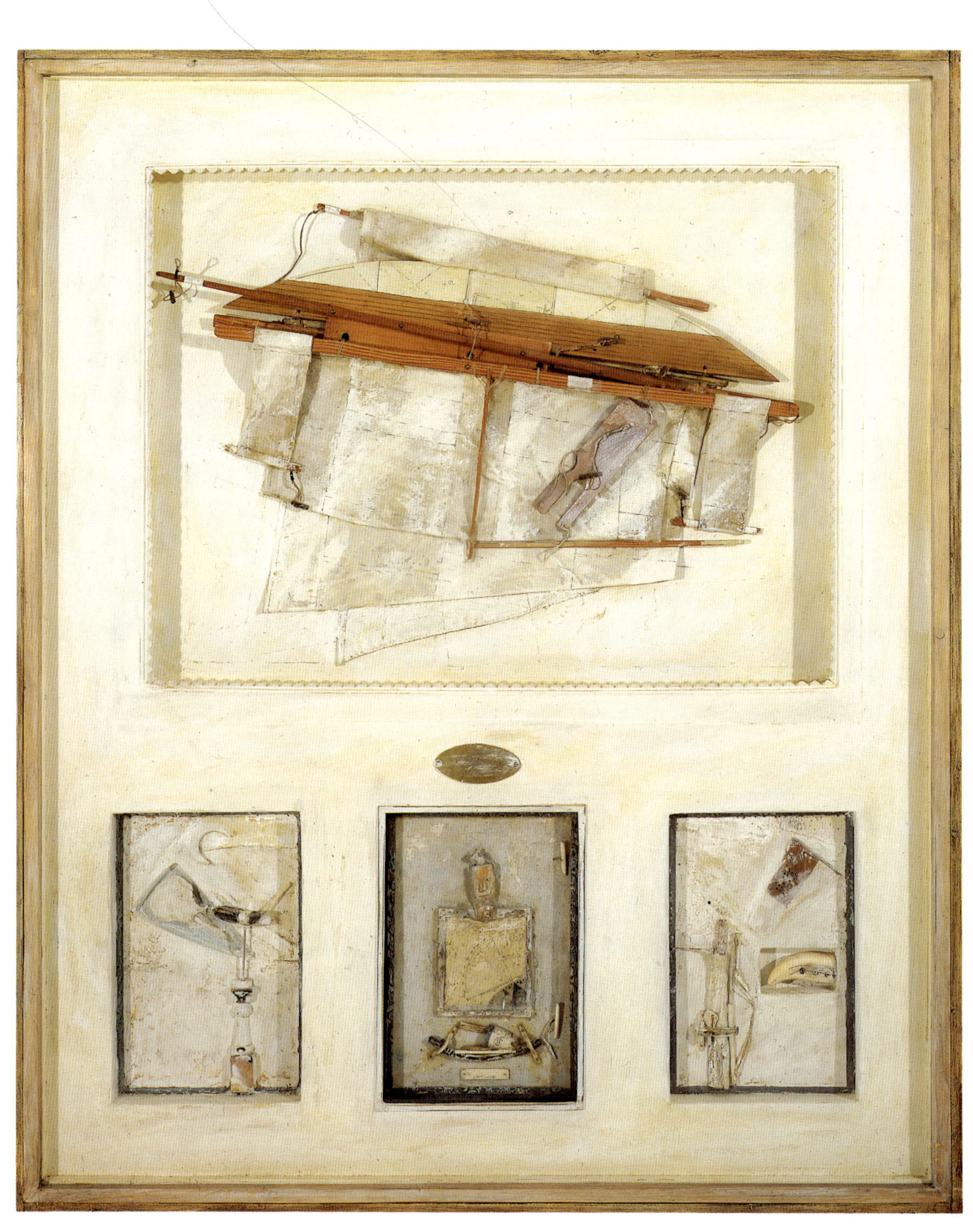

49. *Log Book I — Polar Voyage* (1986) (Cat. 108)

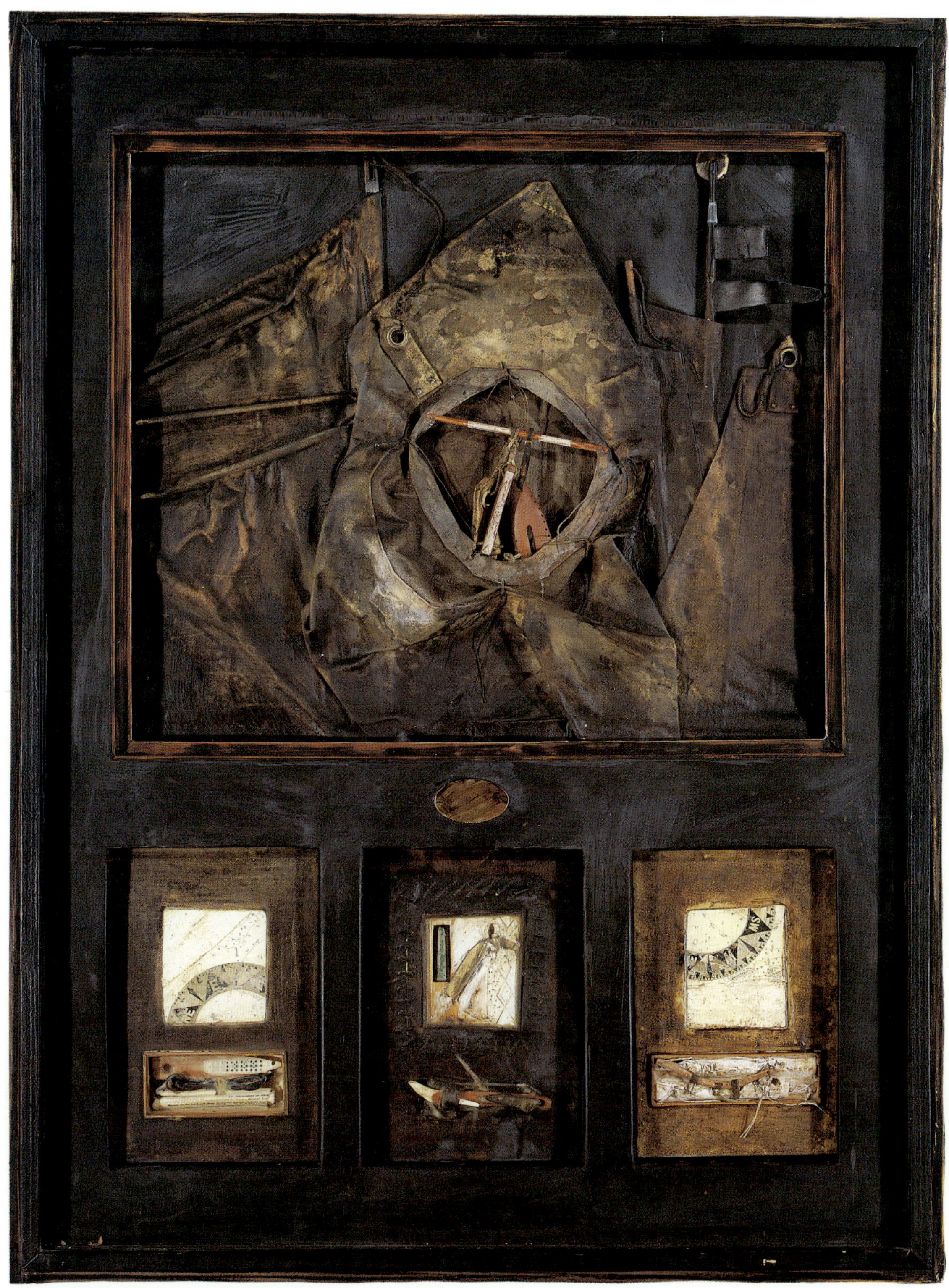

50. *Log Book II —Winter Voyage* (1986) (Cat. 109)

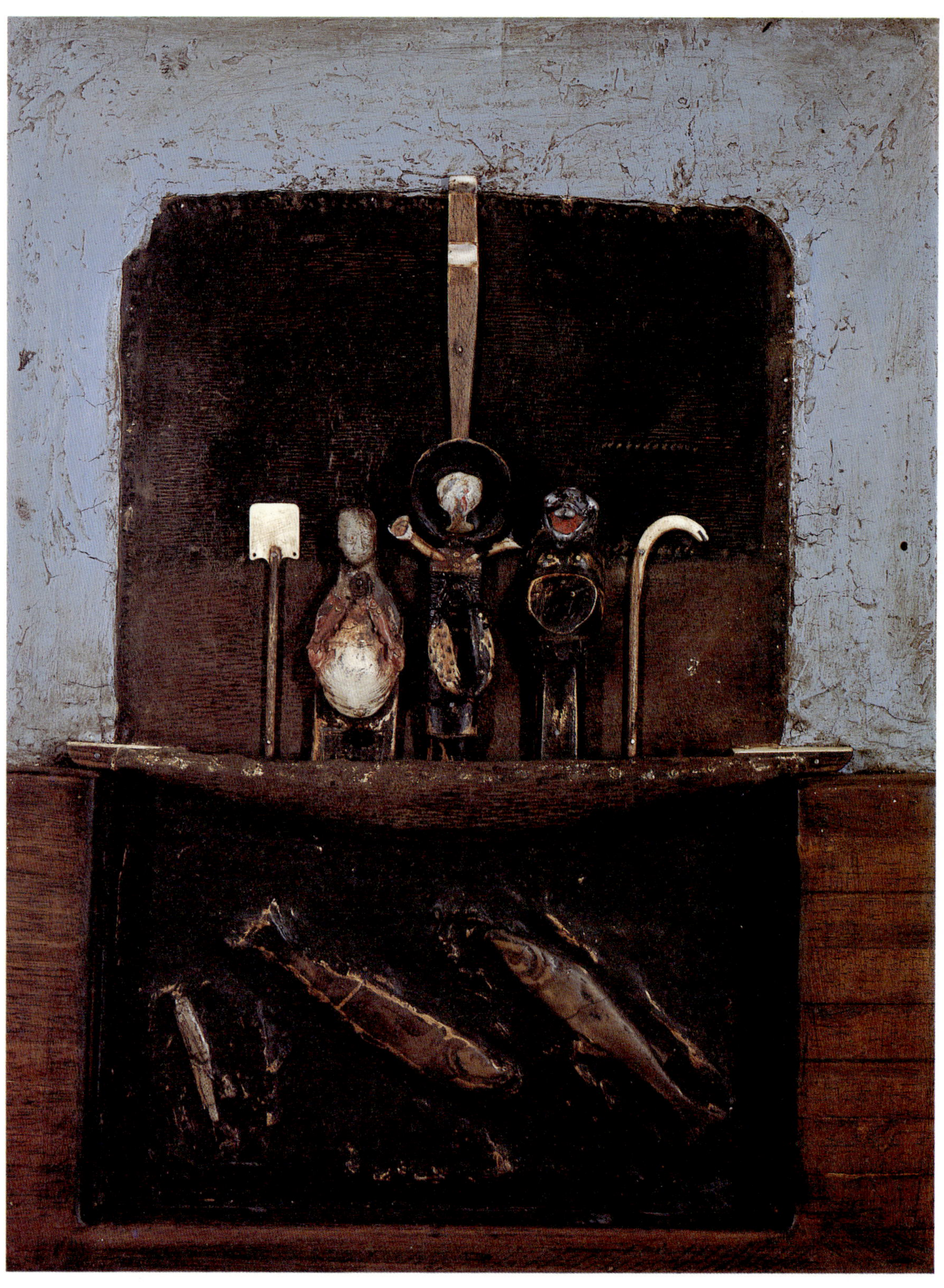

51. *Bard MacIntyre's Box* (1984) (Cat. 92)

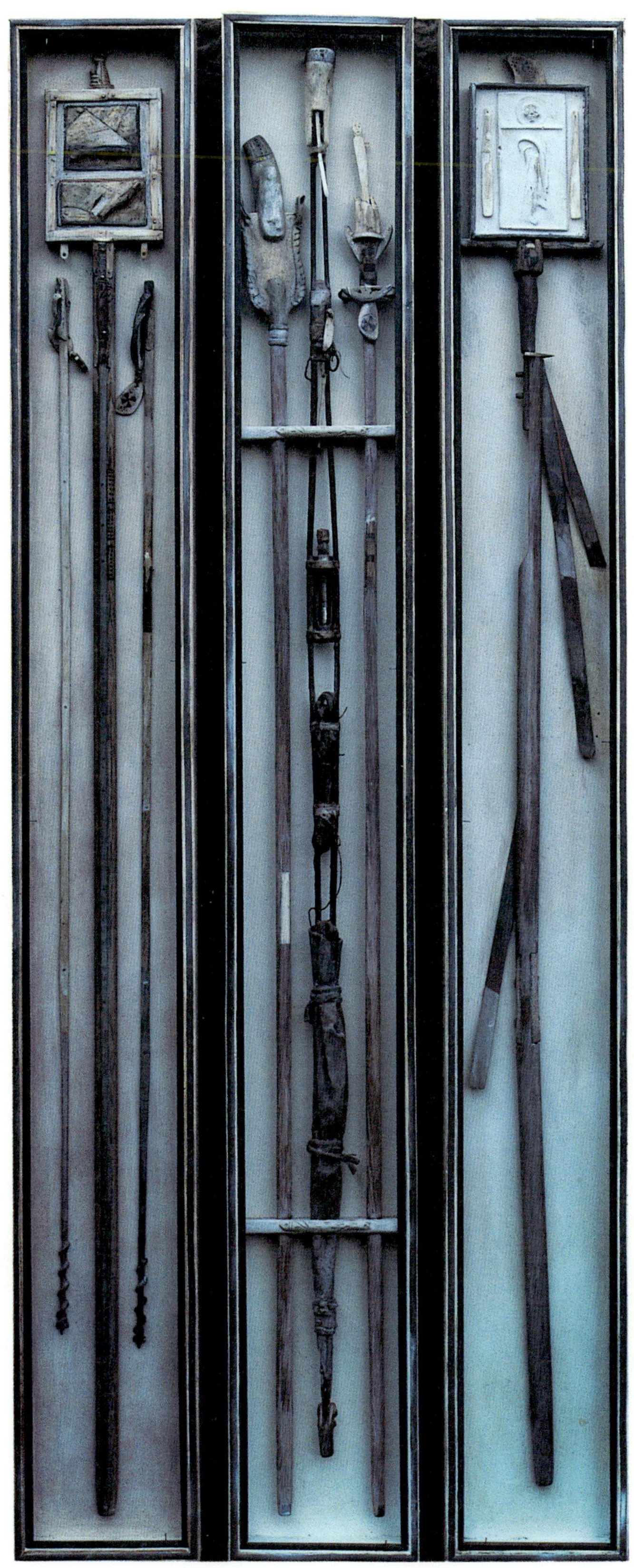

52. *Pole Marker Triptych* (1987) (Cat. 118)

has shown that the concept of progress is profoundly at odds with the real truth about the ambiguous part that nature plays in the compound, human nature. His insistence on this point has caused Ian Hamilton Finlay a deal of trouble and like Finlay, Paolozzi too recognised this long ago. Their art is imbued with a note of far less sentimental realism.

Finlay, too, uses fishing as Puvis de Chavannes did, as an image of the austerity of the true pastoral tradition, which he sees as a state of nature characterised, not by absence of rigour, but by the opposite: the supreme, intellectual and moral discipline needed to maintain it. It is a similar perception which gives moral complexity to Maclean's fishing imagery too. Fishing in its ancient form epitomises the ideal relationship of man and nature; in its modern form, like the Clearances, its breakdown. Like Finlay, Maclean's subject is not the ideal balance, but the destructive tension between man and nature — betweenCaptain Ahab and Moby Dick. In this, his implied belief in the role of the artist, if not his actual vision, is true not just to his post-modern contemporaries, but like them too, to the much older tradition of the bards. Blake saw himself as a bard in this sense and in the Highlands where the tradition of the bards survived for so long, this view does genuinely reflect something of their social role, recording, exhorting, celebrating and in the end standing for the transmission and evolution of values. MacDiarmid and Sorley MacLean stand for the revival, or perhaps the perpetuation of this tradition and Will Maclean joins them, for in his art he presents the ultimately insoluble, moral complexity of our situation, where innocence and experience must constantly coexist and are sometimes indistinguishable.

* * *

Outside the formality of religion, superstition and belief in the supernatural have always been instinctive ways of seeking to reconcile this paradox. Exploration of these areas and of experience at the edges of conventional consciousness has also for long been part of the literary tradition in Scotland, from the 'Bodach Glas' in *Waverley* to the importance of second sight in Neil Gunn's novels. It is a natural part of Maclean's art too therefore, and in pursuit of such ideas he turned in the late 1970s to explore these traditions in the Highlands, recorded in such books as John Gregorson Campbell's *Superstitions of the Highlands and Islands of Scotland.*[25] As well as following the literary tradition though, in doing this he was acting very much along lines pioneered in visual art in Britain by Paolozzi and Davie. When Davie compares the artist's role to that of a shaman, he is suggesting that he can be an intermediary between this world and a metaphysical one, in primitive terms a world of spirits. William Johnstone was a pioneer of this Jungian view of art in Britain and through Johnstone, Davie and Paolozzi are also linked to the Scottish poets and the novelists. All three though are ultimately indebted to the surrealists, and Maclean too is equally dependent on their inspiration.

In his work, it is possible to see the direct influence of Magritte, for instance in the painted landscape within the bookcase in *Interior Wester Ross*, but also beyond the surrealists, the influence of De Chirico who was such an important inspiration to them

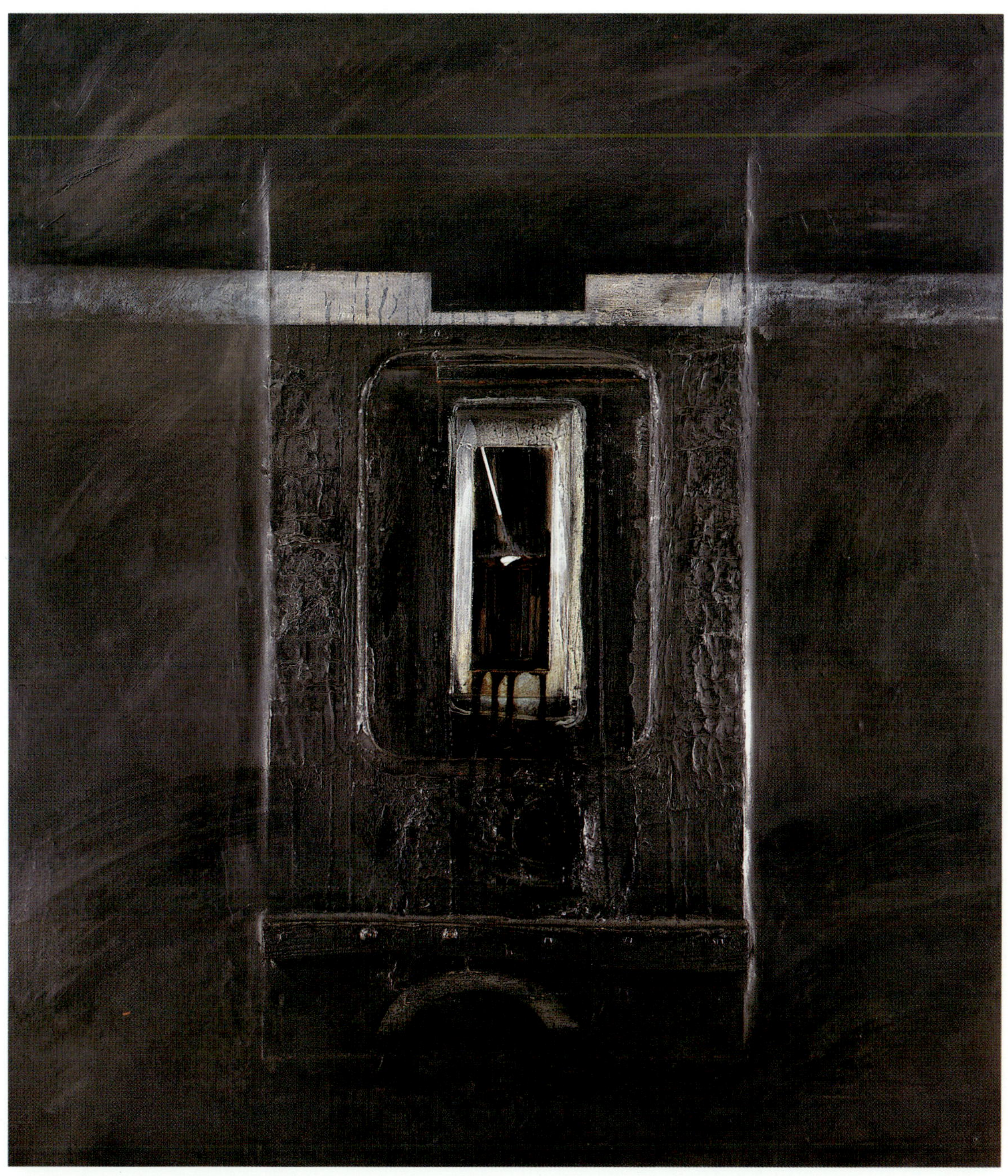

53. *Winter, North Atlantic* (1988) (Cat. 127)

is also apparent. In *Navigator's Locker* (1982, *Pl. 41*), for example, two white spheres sit on a shelf in a white-painted, but empty space. This luminous, structured emptiness recalls De Chirico and so do the shapes themselves, though they are also reminiscent of James Cowie. They are made up from cut and reassembled navigation instruments whose geometric shapes suggest the kind of enigmatic, pseudo-mathematical forms often seen in De Chirico's painting. Perhaps too, they suggest some kind of anarchic or metaphysical system of navigation.

Museum for a Seer (1983, *Pl. 42*) makes a direct connection between surrealist iconography and Highland prophecy. The seer in the title is the Bran Seer. He had a divining stone and it appears as an enigmatic object in the foreground, carved from wood. The rest of the work is equally enigmatic, for it is shrouded in a cloth, also carved and painted. To us the future is concealed. Only the seer can lift the cloth. The simplicity of this work and the way it is executed recall Magritte's subversive realism, but perhaps once again the work of De Chirico. *Window Visitation, North Uist* (1980, *Pl. 43*) shows a similar inspiration and in this case the artist is explicitly exploring the transitional territory beyond the margins of conventional consciousness.

In technique, this work is close to *Abigail's Apron.* It is beautifully made of wood and is basically a simple representation of something seen. The face of an old man, pale and obviously ill, glimpsed at a cottage window inspired it. The artist has reproduced the window, framing the man's face, and the stone weights holding the roof in place, but at the man's mouth and eyes are black butterflies. According to one Highland superstition, it is in this form that the soul leaves the body[26] and so here the butterflies are a premonition of death, or of the soul's transference.

Few places, at least in the west, present such vivid and tenacious folk memory as the Highlands. Premonition and second sight are, of course, central among Highland superstitions and the idea of the possibility of a shift between actual and spiritual vision is a constant theme with Maclean. One important drawing of this period, for example, is *Two Sights of the Sea* (1982, *Pl. 44*). It is an actual view of the corner of a room with a view through a window and it includes in the foreground an image of the related, contemporary construction, *The Drowning,* with an image of an upturned boat in the waves. In the drawing, there is a view of the outside world and the sea beyond, both through the door and through the window — a visual pun on the Gaelic for second sight which is literally 'two sights'.

An old man can be seen sitting outside the window against the open view, but he has been given a bird's head, like a primitive, ceremonial mask. As a bird, he is a creature of nature and can move freely in the world beyond. Miró uses birds as images of spiritual or imaginative freedom, freedom in this case to move in the imaginary landscape reached through the window. Bellany, too, uses them as Maclean does as metamorphic figures, in much the same way as animal and bird masks are used by primitive people, not as a pretence or disguise, but to claim identity with the creature represented.

Windows are one of the most frequent motifs in these constructions. Sometimes they are used to enclose the work, but at other times they are more directly part of the iconography. This is especially true when they are the windows of the wheelhouses of fishing-boats which are in effect the subject of several works, for instance, *China Nights* (1983, *Pl. 45*), *Wheelhouse Triptych* (1981, *Pl. 46*) and *Wheelhouse Study II* (1981, *Pl. 47 & 48*). The first has echoes of Conrad, memories of the east, invoked by a broken bamboo screen and a junk mysteriously, but only indirectly visible in a mirror in the dark interior of the work. In *Wheelhouse Study II*, a dog-fish and other fishes are visible in a wheelhouse window. The sailors have undergone a metamorphosis and there is salt trapped between two panes of glass. Like Actaeon, the hunters have joined the hunted. It is a ghost ship, under water.

Wheelhouse Triptych is more ambitious. It is a large work made up of the three sides of a wheelhouse, opened out and laid flat to create a triptych. Within the windows, the fishermen are seen in metamorphic form as seals and birds, creatures that can move freely in their natural element. The ship itself invoked by the wheelhouse is part of the metaphor too. With its freedom to move over the sea, it is a metaphor for the movement of the work of art within the imagination, or, in Sorley MacLean's poem, 'The Ship', the ship is Gaelic culture itself. Like Bellany's mask figures, the figures reflect the idea of metamorphosis, codified by Ovid in his *Metamorphoses* on the basis of primeval folk-memory, as a way of describing the spiritual continuity which underlies the apparent difference between man and the other creatures of nature. It is a belief that of course appears in Highland superstition in many forms, of which the best known is the silkie, the man-seal, visible here in the window of the wheelhouse. The ship in *Wheelhouse Triptych* is a fairy ship therefore, one that can sail beyond the world of men and such magical vessels of course also play a part in folk-tradition and in fact just such a ship inspired one of Maclean's best known works of the early 1980s, *Bard MacIntyre's Box* (1984, *Pl. 51*).

Maclean's interest in Gaelic culture naturally led him to the bardic poetry which is such an important part of it. Later he produced an important series of prints illustrating this body of verse and including this poem, but *Bard MacIntyre's Box* was one of his first works in this field. This kind of exploration of the territory of the imagination was of course the business of the bard and the poem called 'The Ship of Women' in the *Book of the Dean of Lismore* from which the image is taken is an example of its richness:

> What ship is this on Loch Inch, or can it be
> reported? What has brought the ship on the
> loch? . . .
>
> An old ship without anchors, without oak
> timber;
> we have not known its like; she is all one ship of
> leather:
> she is not a ship complete for sea-going.
>
> What is yon crew in the black ship, pulling her
> among the waves? — A crew without fellow-
> ship, without sense, a woman band of mind
> disordered.
>
> A band loud-voiced and talkative, loquacious,
> chanting, negligent; flighty, quarrelsome,
> greedy, ravenous, evil, of ill desires.
>
> A party thick-rumped and lascivious is that
> around the twosides of Loch Inch; they have all
> been cast into the ship on the chill ridge of the
> sea.
>
> A good woman would not venture into the
> Ship . . . [27]

Worthy of Dürer or Breughel, this ship with its crew of crazy women is a kind of

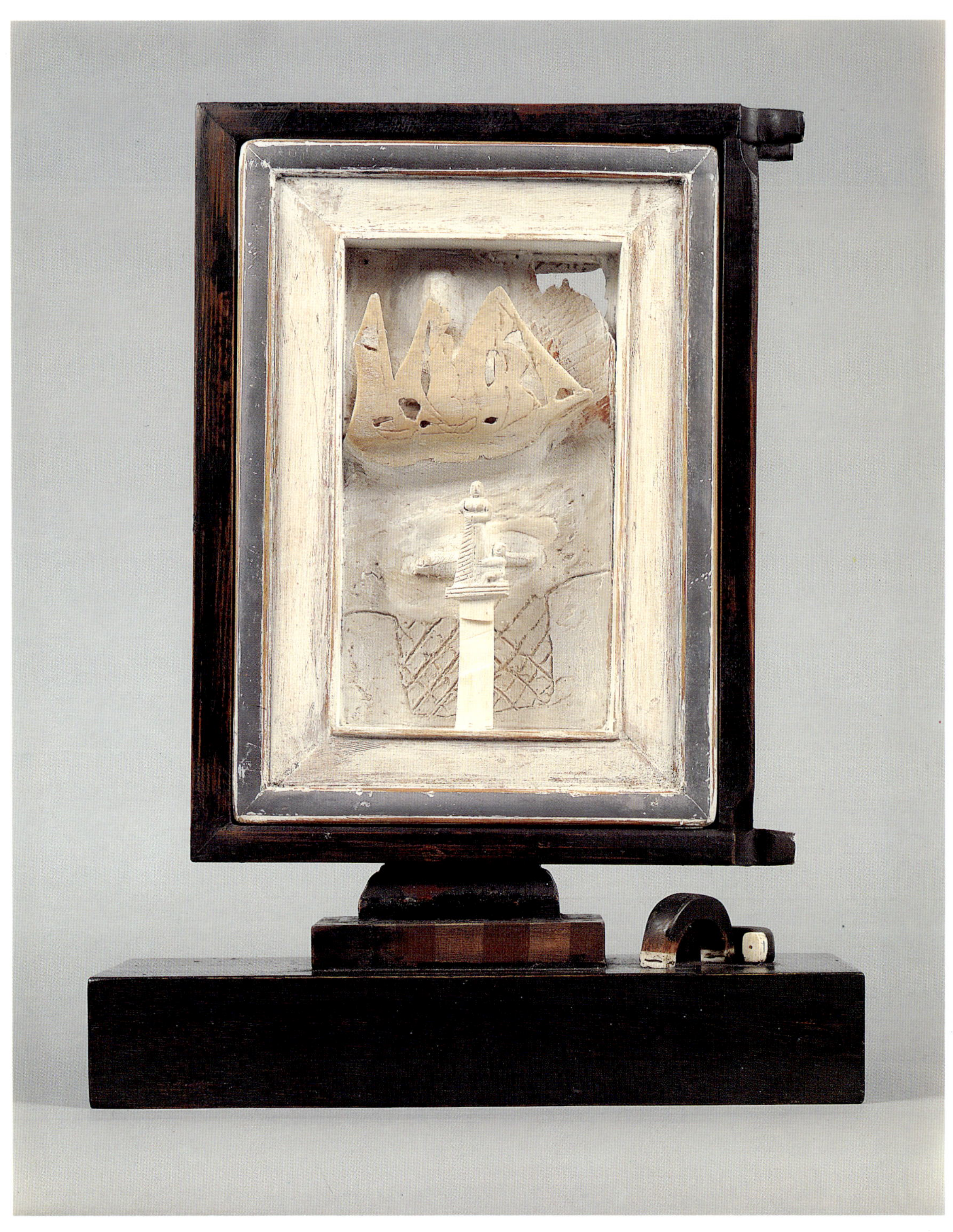

54. *Arctic Sea Marker* (1987) (Cat. 115)

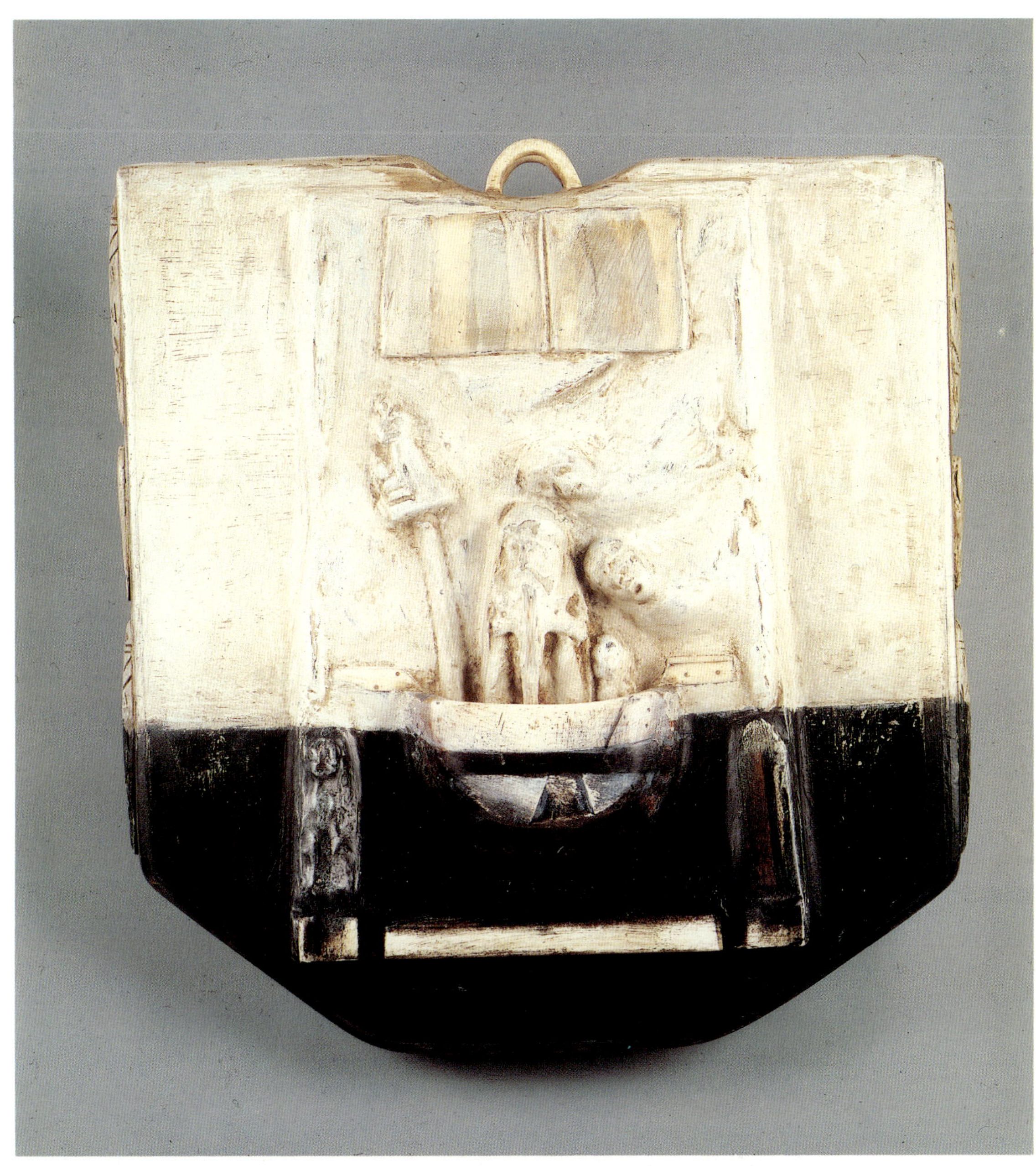

55. *Stern-Sheet Icon* (1987) (Cat. 116)

ship of fools, but also, perhaps, of temptation. The bard's high moral tone implicitly acknowledges the seductive power of such anarchic femininity. In Maclean's construction, three grotesque women present themselves to us like figures in a black mass. The central one has a grotesquely oversized vagina formed from two seal's teeth, truly the *vagina dentata* that weds fear with desire. In the dark water below the boat, threatening fish swim like the mind's unacknowledged motives swimming in the darkness of the unconscious.

A variation of *Bard MacIntyre's Box* is also the subject of one of the etchings in the set *Night of Islands* with the title, *The Author of this is . . .* (The published poem is headed with the words 'The Author of this is the Bard MacIntyre'.)

Such imagery is a reminder that neither the true Highland culture, nor Maclean's metaphoric use of it, is any more morally simple than human culture anywhere. We do not have in his work, therefore, merely the opposition of idealised past innocence to present corruption, but a moral universe in microcosm in which this polarity is perpetual and under constant tension. This polarity is frequently presented as a temporal opposition though, and as such it is an important element, not just in Maclean's art alone, but in the whole tradition to which he belongs.

* * *

The image of the ship in *Bard MacIntyre's Box* is part of Maclean's iconography of the sea. The strange sailors in *Wheelhouse Triptych*, for example, could be compared to Bard MacIntyre's bizarre crew, but, as we have seen, fishing itself is an integral part of Maclean's imagery. Like the history of the Highlands of which it is part, as he uses it though, it is the tap-root of a wider metaphor. It is a metaphor though which also starts in his own personal experience. In *Memories of a Northern Childhood*, for instance, as he did in *Symbols of Survival*, he took the imaginative intensity of his own remembered childhood as the starting point.

This work shows how much fishing had encompassed his ambition as a child, but there was also boyhood fascination with tales of adventure in the Arctic. A good many works of the 1980s, like *Log Book I—Polar Voyage* (1986, *Pl. 49*), *Log Book II, Winter Voyage* (1986, *Pl. 50*), *Pole Marker Triptych* (1987, *Pl. 52*), *Arctic Signs 1, 2, 3 &4* (1984-6), *Winter, North Atlantic* (1988, *Pl. 53*), or *Arctic Sea Marker* (1987, *Pl. 54*) or *Stern Sheet Icon (*1987, *Pl. 55*) reflect the artist's fascination with such stories. *Polar Voyage*, for instance, takes its subject from one of Franklin's voyages and a prominent detail is a representation (upside-down) of a folding boat that he took with him. *Pole Marker Triptych* was inspired by an account of Peary, in effect being taken to the North Pole by three Eskimos. They were not seen as heroes, so this is their memorial.

At one level such works invoke the simple atmosphere of sailors' yarns, even if touched with irony. Such tales of men living in the face of nature can work at two levels, though. As Melville showed, they can be both a good story and a metaphor of the original, human condition, and something of the complexity of vision which Melville and Conrad, too, built out of such material is there; the dark side revealed when men follow their instincts. For instance, Maclean has made various works on the theme of the *Raft of*

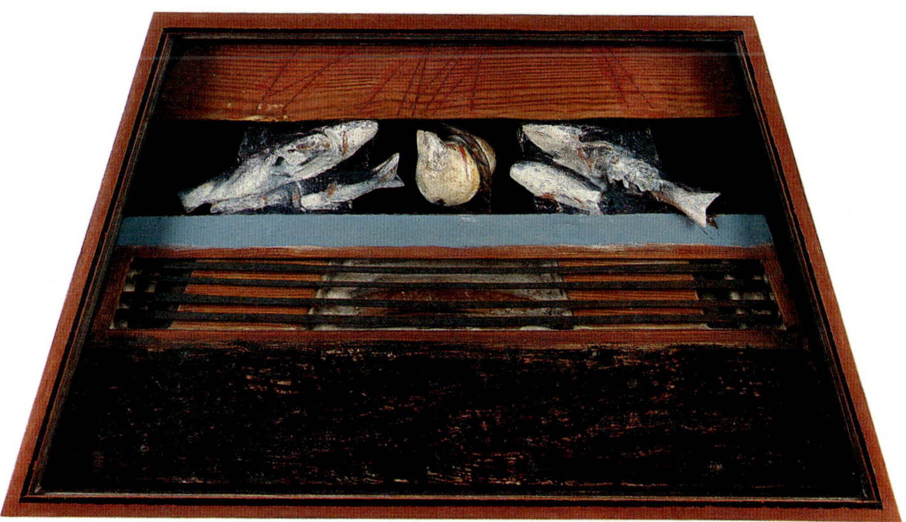

56. *Raft of the Medusa II* (1985) (Cat. 106)

the Medusa. These contain an obvious reference to Géricault in their subject, but he has gone back to the original testimony of the survivors to provide his own commentary on the horror of the tragedy. *Raft of the Medusa II* (1985, *Pl. 56*), originally part of a three-part work, is a schematic model of the raft, scored by cutlasses and bloodstained from the fighting over a lemon, one of the last scraps of food left to the survivors, while fish wait ominously below. In *Fisherman's Log* (1987), a fish, in the shadowy form of a shark, threatens a sailor directly as he clings to the raft. *Raft* (*Pl. 57*), a work on this theme made in 1990, superimposes a modern, inflatable life-raft over a photo-etching of the engraved plan of the Medusa's ill-fated, timber construction.

This recognition of the dark side of man's relation to the natural world and of its brutality informs Maclean's whaling imagery too. In *Leviathan Elegy* (1982, *Pl. 58*), for instance, there are three rows of relics of a whale. The first shows the detached arrangement of a museum display. The second is like a group of Eskimo artifacts and tools. The third presents the brutality of modern whaling. *Arctic Signs No. 3 Line Box* (1984, *Pl. 59 & 60*) shows rows of whales' tails, stamped with the poundage of oil extracted from each creature, and presented as the whaling captains recorded them in their log-books. Below are the instruments of torture, the harpoons, the boats and the log-books themselves.

Arctic Signs No. 4 — Mayday (*Pl. 61*) presents a more complex idea. At the centre of it is a wreath. This is a reference to the sailors' practice of hanging a wreath on the mast on Mayday. When the ship docked, the town boys raced up the mast, competing for the wreath as innocently as girls to be May Queen. Above this wreath is a ship carved from whalebone, a sailor's memento of a whaling voyage and an image that

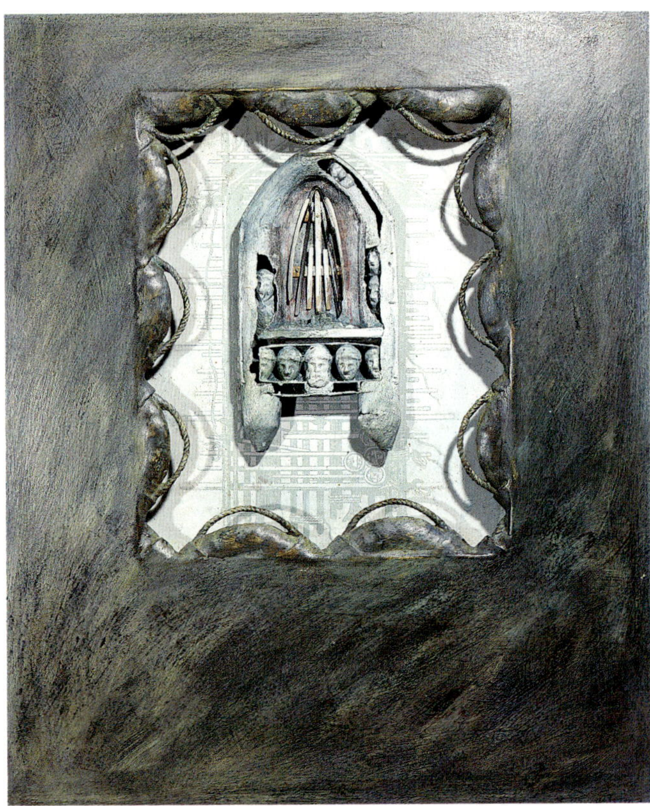

57. *Raft* (1990) (Cat.158)

reappears in several related works, but below is a harpooned and dying whale. The pun on Mayday makes a cruel contrast as the whale cries for help. It is an image in which innocence and experience are indivisible.

The irony is reinforced by the beauty of this work, which is also an outstanding example of the artist's use of the techniques of painting in his constructions. It is a rich blue, rubbed to white so cleverly that the recessed boxes work both as containers and as pictorial space, but the iconography makes it clear that there is no simple purity even in such beauty. *Arctic Signs No. 3* shows the same rich textures, using paint, metal and inlay, but again this beauty underlines the cruelty of the image. With these and related works, the construction itself is set into a wide, painted, flat surround which now functions very much as a picture field, rather than as a simple framing device.

* * *

The histories of deep-sea fishing and whaling encapsulate the duality of the relationship of man and nature which religion has sought to resolve in the idea of the Fall. On the one hand, nature represents the ideal of the innocence of Eden, on the other hand, also in Eden, it is on the natural side of humanity that the darkness lies. Had Adam refused the apple, he would not have been true to his nature. As fishing has evolved from a kind of living archaeology, the same is true. It only needed technology to show where

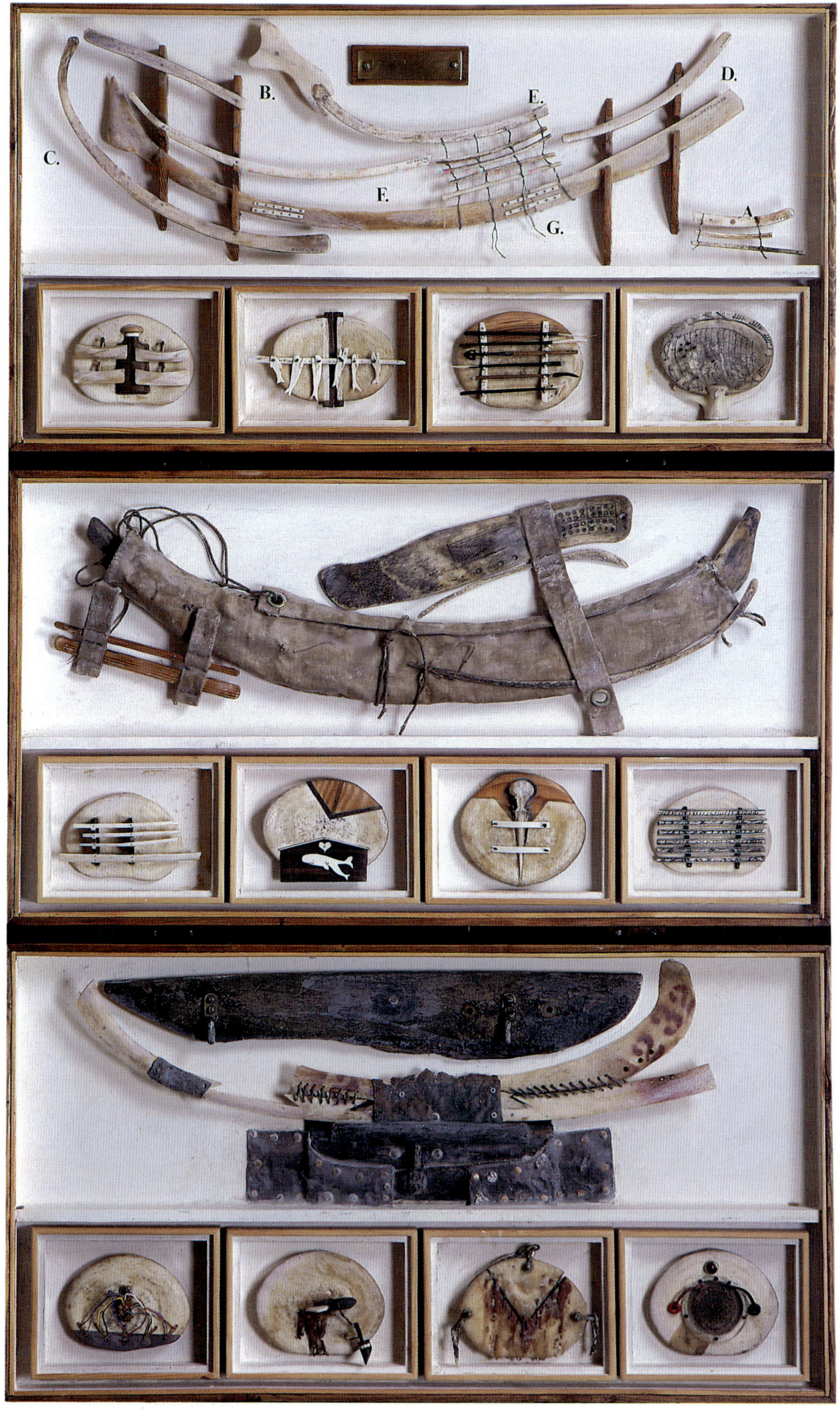

58. *Leviathan Elegy* (1982) (Cat. 66)

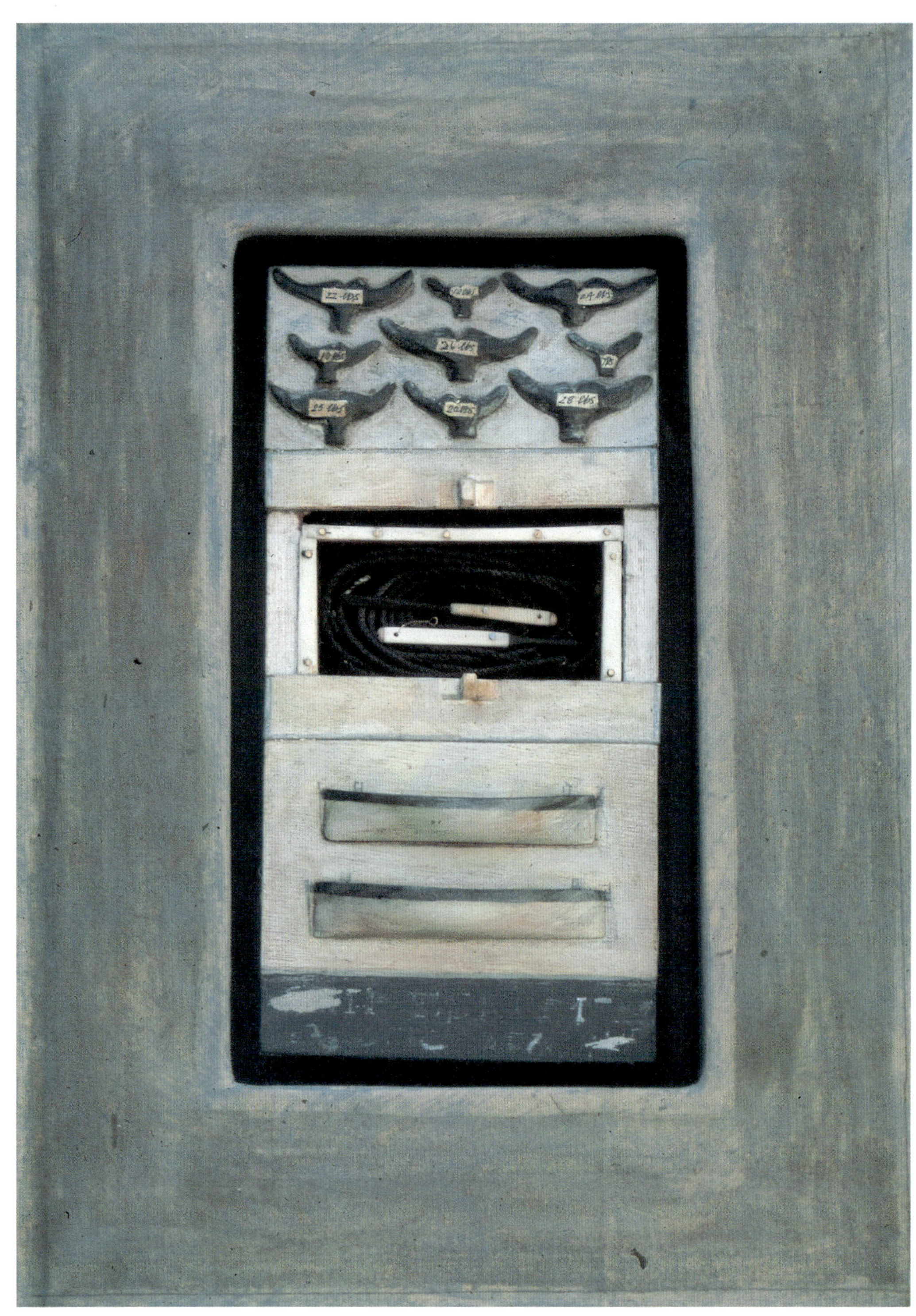

59. *Arctic Signs No. 3 Line Box* (1984) (Cat. 96)

men are concerned, how quickly the innocence of the state of nature can become the cruelty of experience. Thus illustrations of the metaphor of the Fall are easily found in modern life.

The Clearances themselves, Maclean's own starting point, are a perfect illustration of the destruction of a way of life by science in the service of economics, of the conjunction of knowledge and greed, just as when Adam plucked the apple — in this case these were represented by new agricultural methods employed in the interest of economic improvement. Indeed in 1983, Maclean made a beautiful work, *I didn't go willingly, I went sadly* (*Pl. 62*) which presents the consequences of the dislocation of Highland life in terms of the Expulsion from the Garden. This is the title of a poem by Murdo MacFarlane of Lewis and the subject is the sadness of all the girls sent out to exile in domestic service, far from their Highland homes. At the centre of the work is a photo-etching of such a group of girls. The rest, infused with melancholy, suggests the bareness of an attic in a stranger's house with a sprig of bog-cotton in a jam-jar, a pathetic reminder of home.

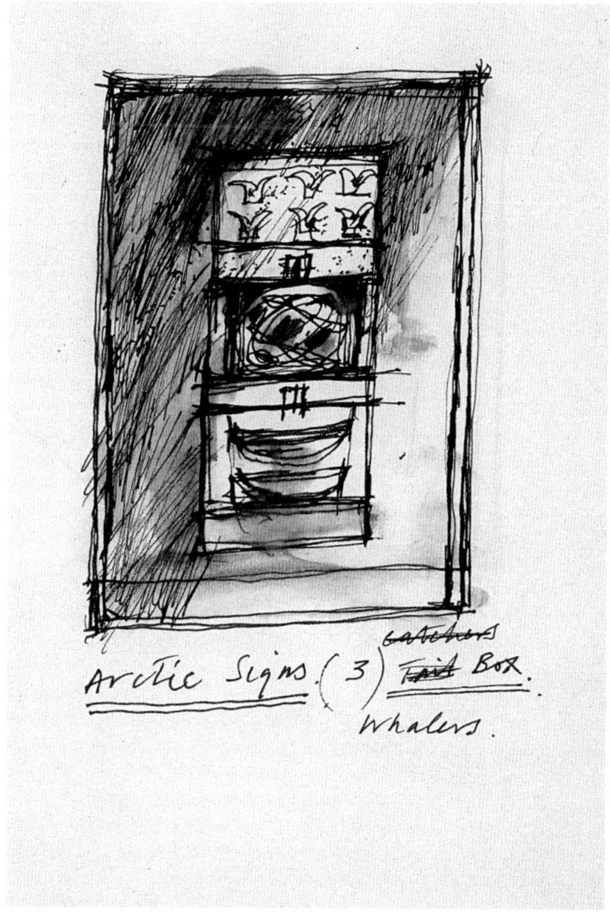

60. Study for *Arctic Signs No. 3 Line Box*, page from a sketchbook, pen and blue wash, 14.4 x 20.8 cms (1984)

In the 1970s in Scotland, one of the most effective presentations of the linkage between past and present in the disastrous march of progress in the history of the Highlands was *The Cheviot, the Stag and the Black, Black Oil*, written by John McGrath and performed by the 7:84 Theatre Company. Since then, the signs of impending ecological disaster have been added to this black picture. The Clearances were not themselves ecological, but they prefigured the present situation, reflecting the same ruthless, shortsighted exploitation of resources in the interest of gain which in the end was to leave only an empty land. Now, it seems, it will leave us an empty sea as well, for the same situation has evolved in the fishing industry. There technological change and the departure from historical methods are clearly leading to ecological disaster and have already seen the beginning of social changes which will eventually bring about a transformation as calamitous as the Clearances themselves.

In the early 1980s, Maclean extended this theme to include the new image of the nuclear submarines which are a constant threatening presence on the west coast, the epitome of destruction and a fearsome, vengeful metamorphosis of the

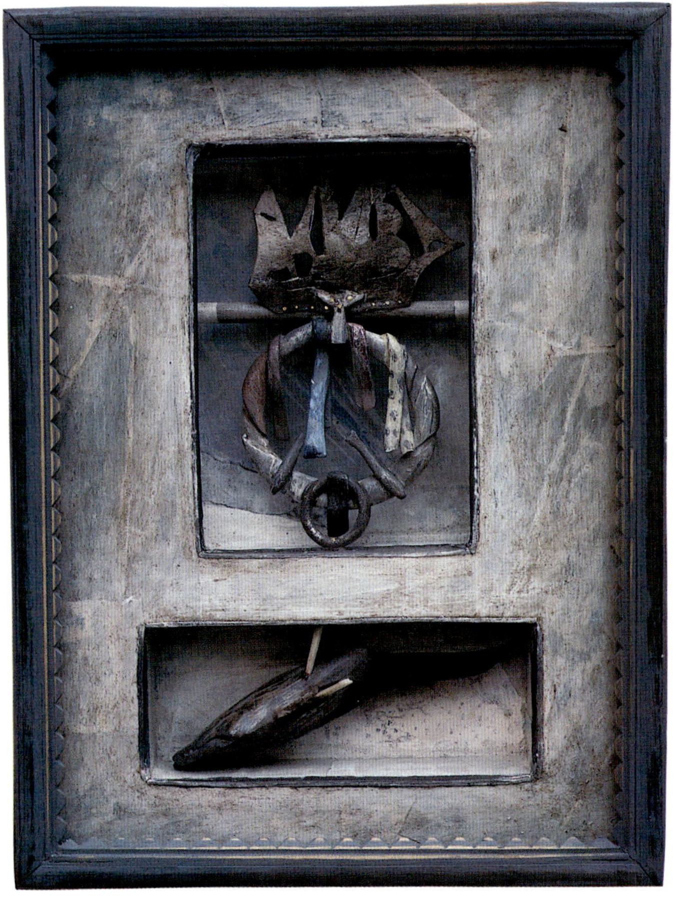

61. *Arctic Signs No. 4 – Mayday* (1986) (Cat. 97)

whale. This also reflects his close association with Sorley MacLean and *Sabbath of the Dead* was followed by a series of drawings on this theme. In his poem, 'Screapadal', the poet associates the destruction of the Clearances directly with this new image of violent destruction (in these verses, Rainy was the individual responsible for the clearance of Screapadal):

> Dh'fhàg Rèanaidh Screapadal gun daoine
> Gun taighean, gun chrod ach caoraich,
> Ach dh'fhàg e Screapadal bòidheach;
> R'a linn cha b'urrainn dha a chaochladh
>
> Thogadh ròn à cheann
> Agus cearban a sheòl,
> Ach an diugh anns an linnidh
> Togaidh long-fo-thuinn a turraid
> Agus a druim dhubh shlìom
> A'maoidheadh an ní a dheanadh
> Smùr de choille, de lianagan's de chreagan,
> A dh'fhàgadh Screapadal gun bhòidhche
> Mar a dh'fhàgadh e gun daoine . . .
>
> Tha tùir eile air an linnidh
> A'fanaid air an tùr a thuit
> Dhe mullach Creag a'Chaisteil,
> Tùir as miosa na gach tùr
> A thog ainneart air an t-saoghal:
> Peireascopan's sliosan slioma
> Dubha luingeas a'bhàis . . .
>
> *Rainy left Screapadal without people,*
> *with no houses or cattle, only sheep,*
> *but he left Screapadal beautiful;*
> *in his time he could do nothing else.*
>
> *A seal would lift its head*
> *and a basking shark its sail,*
> *but today in the sea-sound*
> *a submarine lifts its turret*
> *and its black sleek back*
> *threatening the thing that would make*
> *dross of wood, of meadows and of rocks*
> *that would leave Screapadal without beauty*
> *just as it was left without people . . .*
>
> *There are other towers on the Sound*
> *mocking the towers that fell*
> *from the top of the Castle rock,*
> *towers worse than every tower*
> *that violence raised in the world;*
> *the periscopes and sleek black sides*
> *of the ships of death . . .*[28]

In a series of drawings, the nuclear submarine appears as the death-fish, a sinister, man-made Leviathan, identifying, not only the Clearances, but also the persecution of the whale with the destructiveness epitomised by the nuclear submarine. In 1983, *Death Fish* (*Pl. 64)* and *Death Fish Study II* (P. 63) show the metamorphosis of the submarine's sinister shape into that of a shark. In *Inner Sound* (1984, *Pl. 65*), the malign, dark shape of the submarine's conning tower is seen through a broken, boarded-up window in an abandoned cottage. It is a sinister gloss on two lines from 'Hallaig' and a new and even more destructive incarnation of the forces which drove away the people who once lived there:

> Tha bùird is tàirnean air an uinneig
> troimh'm faca mi an Aird an Iar
>
> *The window is nailed and boarded*
> *through which I saw the West . . .*[29]

Hebridean Cruise (1985, *Pl. 66*) has an ironic title and in it, a piece of military hardware found on the beach echoes the shape of the conning tower of a submarine. In a more recent drawing, *Hunter's Vision* (1989, *Pl. 67*), three submarines move past as though underwater, but the scene is in a forest. Bird skulls hang like macabre creepers and in the ground, the sleeping shape of the Celtic god of hunting, Herne the Hunter, antlered like Actaeon, can just be made out. He is a mysterious figure from Celtic art and mythology who reappears in a number of Maclean's works, for instance in *Winter Kyle Elegy* (1989, *Pl. 68*). The submarines themselves seem partly entangled in the fluttering rags of funerary banners, like the rags on the *Cloutie Well* on the Black Isle.

These suggest the nets of fishing boats as the entangling of nets by submarines in this way has been the cause of too many tragedies on the west coast. One of the worst was the sinking of the *Antares* in 1990. In an extraordinary and disturbing coincidence,

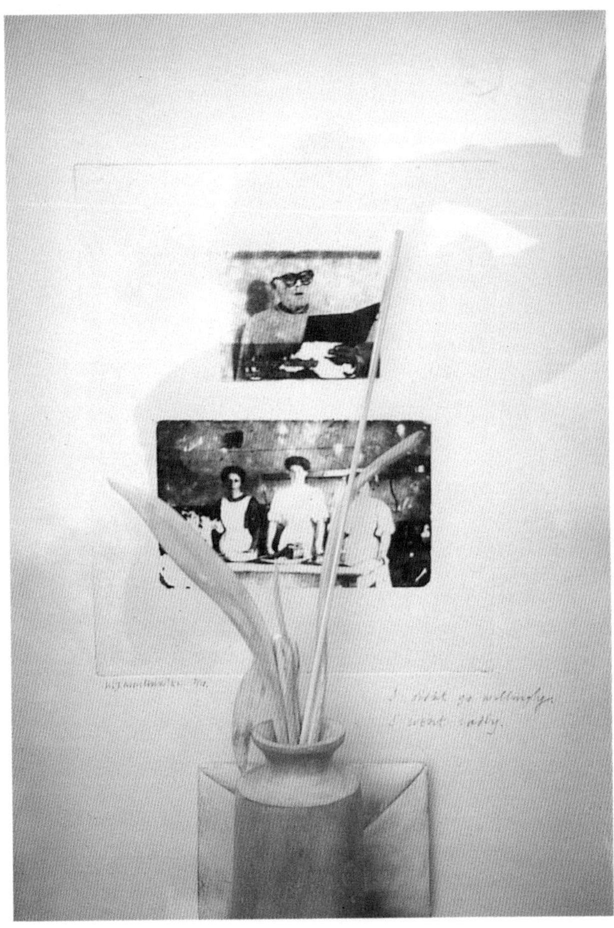

62. *I didn't go willingly, I went sadly* (Detail)(1983) (Cat. 84)

even experience of second sight, Maclean had incorporated the name of the *Antares* from a fish-box into his work *Skye Fisherman: In Memoriam* a year before. Thus the memorial predated the tragedy.

These reflections on the dark side of progress are a constant theme in the work of the writers of the Scots Renascence. For instance, specifically invoking the fall from a forgotten Golden Age, Gunn wrote in *Highland River* (in the novel the hero had been gassed in the first war):

> Voices of foreign secretaries as solemn today
> as the voice of Memphis. More money.

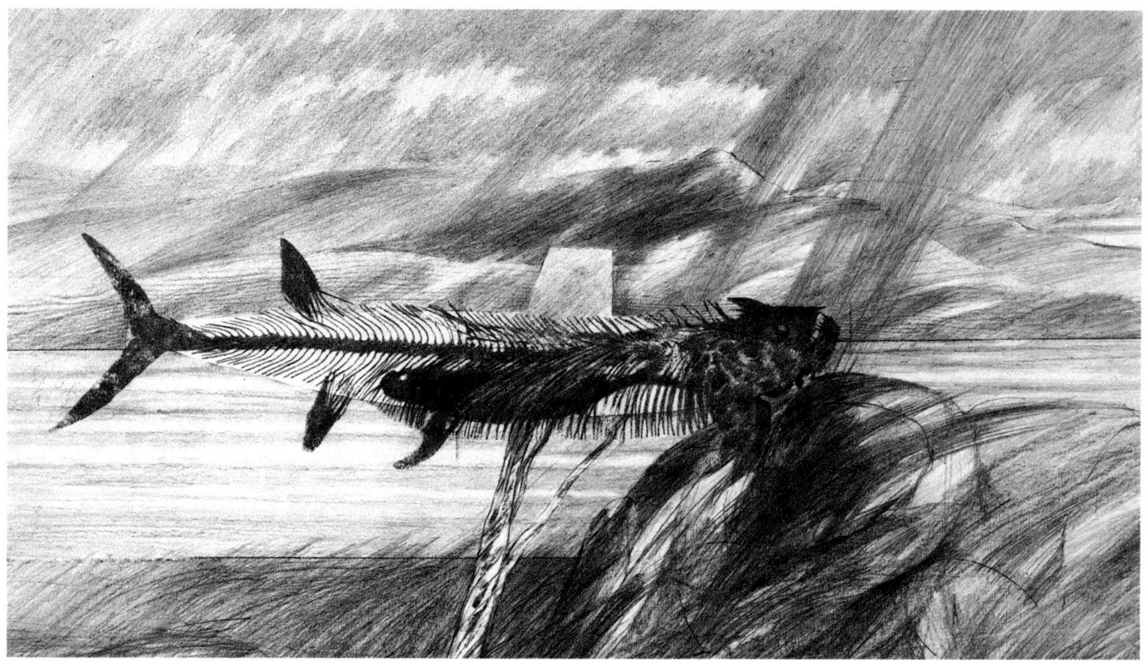

63. *Death Fish Study II*, pencil, 34 x 56 cms, British Museum (1983)

> More high explosive. More gas. In the name of Civilisation, we demand this sacrifice . . . It's a far cry to the golden age, to the blue smoke of the heath fire and the scent of the primrose! Our river took a wrong turning somewhere![30]

Maclean's own art continued to develop these themes of social concern, but in a new direction, following a visit to America in 1989 and his exposure there to the dark side of modern capitalism. The purpose of the trip was to visit the whaling museums of New England which are repositories of wonderful collections of the kind of things that had been central to his inspiration for so long. Ironically though, he found a different inspiration, its underlying concern the same, but now more urgent in his response to the experience of America and the diminution of humanity that results from the stark facts of urban alienation which he witnessed there. He recognised in it the same dissociation of sensibility as created the moral blindness that, in the name of wealth and profit, had destroyed the communities of the Highlands. This was the more ironic as it was America that had been the destination and the promised land of so many of those who were driven out. *The Emigrants, America* is, for instance, the wildest and most tragic of McTaggart's paintings on this theme painted a hundred years earlier.

Continuing the saga, in response to what he saw, Maclean created a series of images of modern America as telling and, because of the development of his technique, even more immediate than his own earlier works. *Central Park* (1989, *Pl. 69*), for example, is a graphic account of homelessness. At its centre, a man is sleeping with a cardboard box on his head and another on his feet, just as the artist saw him in Central Park. In *Manhattan* (1988, *Pl. 70*), Maclean contrasts the soaring beauty of the Empire State

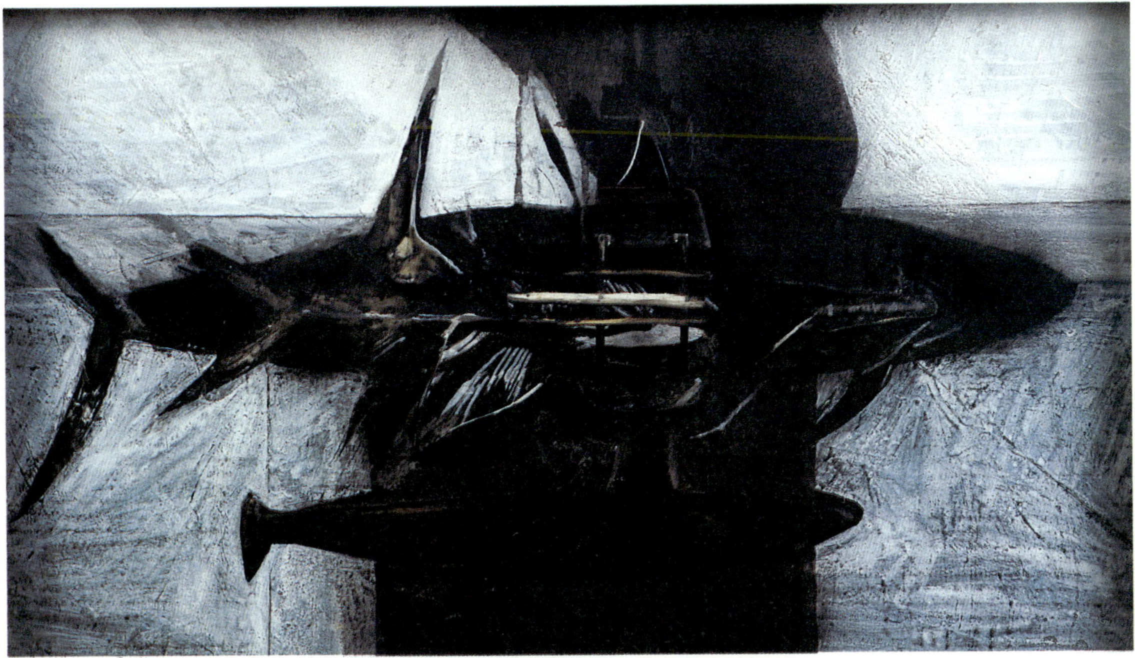

64. *Death Fish* (1983) (Cat. 80)

Building with the human darkness at its feet. *Nantucket Front and Back* (1989, *Pl. 71*) is a dark totem which dramatically opposes the front, the now tidy world of the whalers in the New England museums, all death and danger safely distant, all passion spent, to the insane tidiness of a poor woman seen in a bus waiting-room, crazily packing newspapers into a left-luggage locker, her fractured sense of order as remote from reality as the whaling museums.

In these and other recent works, although he continued to develop the underlying themes that had been his preoccupation for so long, Maclean uses a much freer, more open manner. Previously, using drawings, he had generally planned his work carefully. Collage or assemblage, too, had been his main medium since 1975, but increasingly he combined it with painted surfaces which serve a properly pictorial purpose in a way that reflects his original training and its preoccupations. *Manhattan*, for instance, includes a directly pictorial image of a skyscraper. *Fisherman with Coalfish* (1990, *Pl. 72*), *Island Ferry — Cape Cod* (1990, *Pl. 73*) and *Bone Circle* (1990, *Pl. 74*) are paintings as much as constructions. In all of these, intelligibility of the image depends on the use of paint and colour.

The discovery of the new medium of assemblage had been a liberation from the constraints of painting and it had allowed the artist to develop a rich and complex subject matter, but he had never become a narrative artist for whom formal considerations were secondary to its demands. They went together and had it not been for the skill and economy with which he unifies his image so that we are always struck first by its apparent simplicity, his art would not be so effective.

The Dada artists and the surrealists used these techniques to promote startling conjunctions in which the objective was to

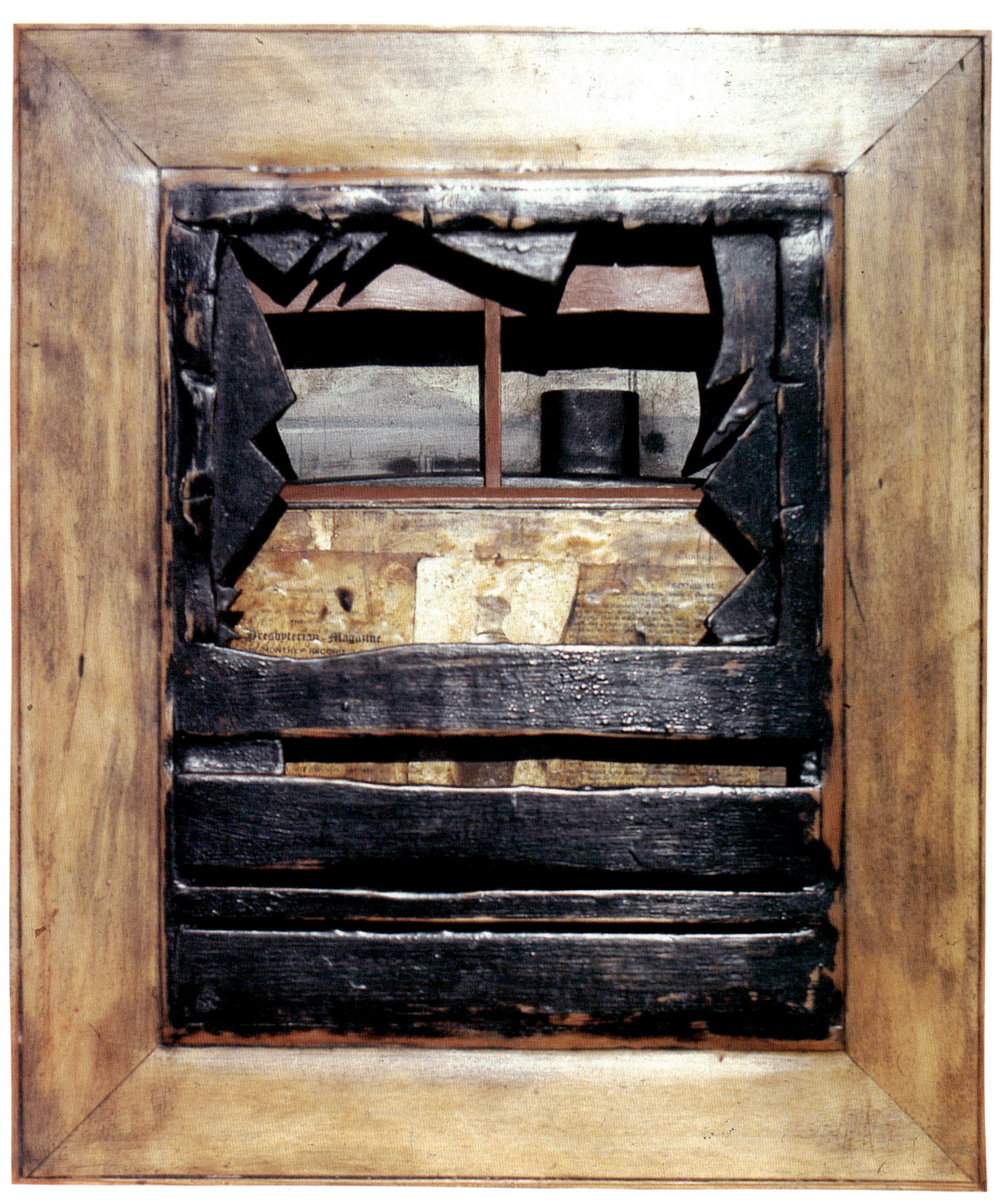

65. *Inner Sound* (1984) (Cat. 88)

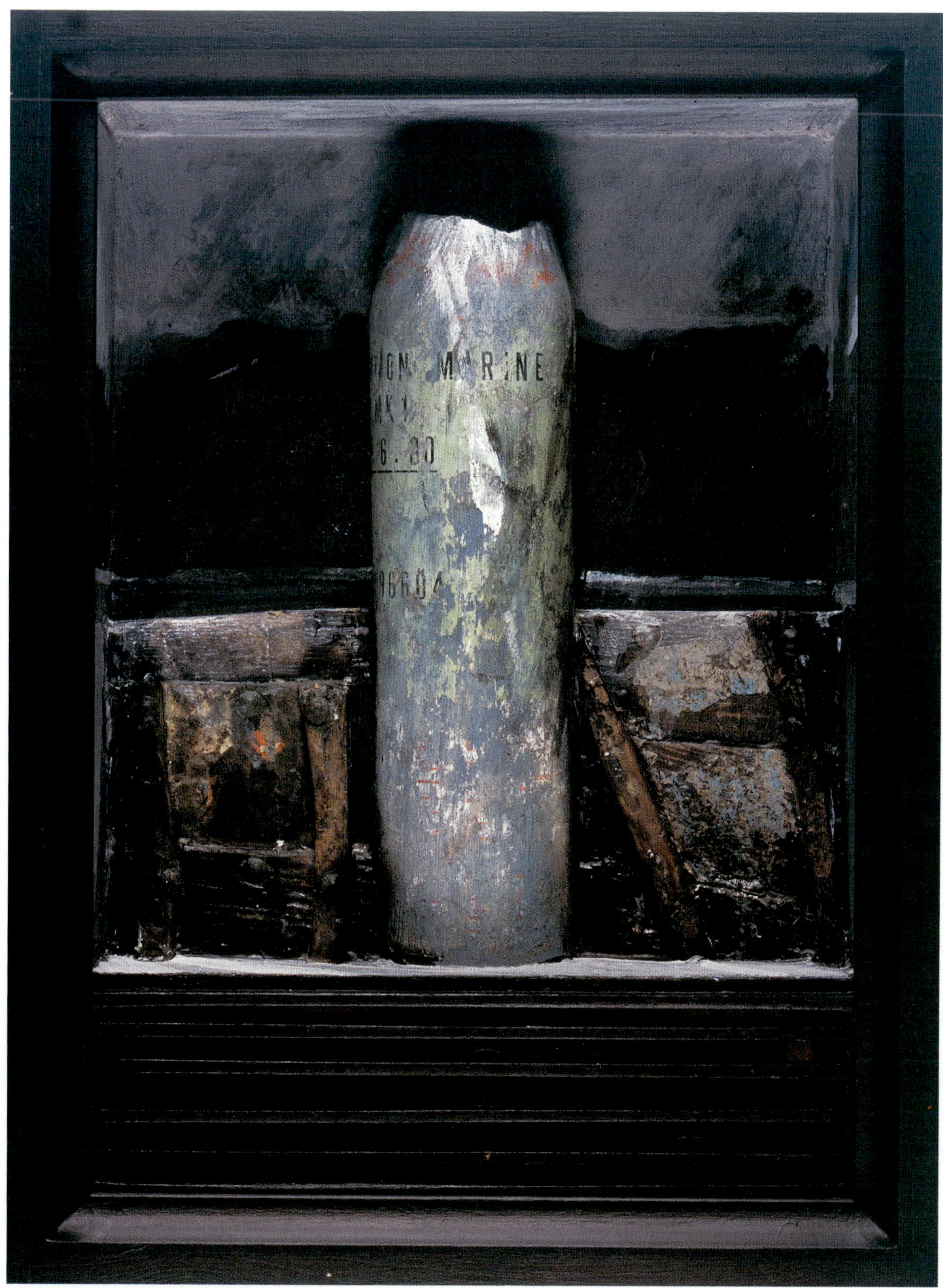

66. *Hebridean Cruise* (1985) (Cat. 107)

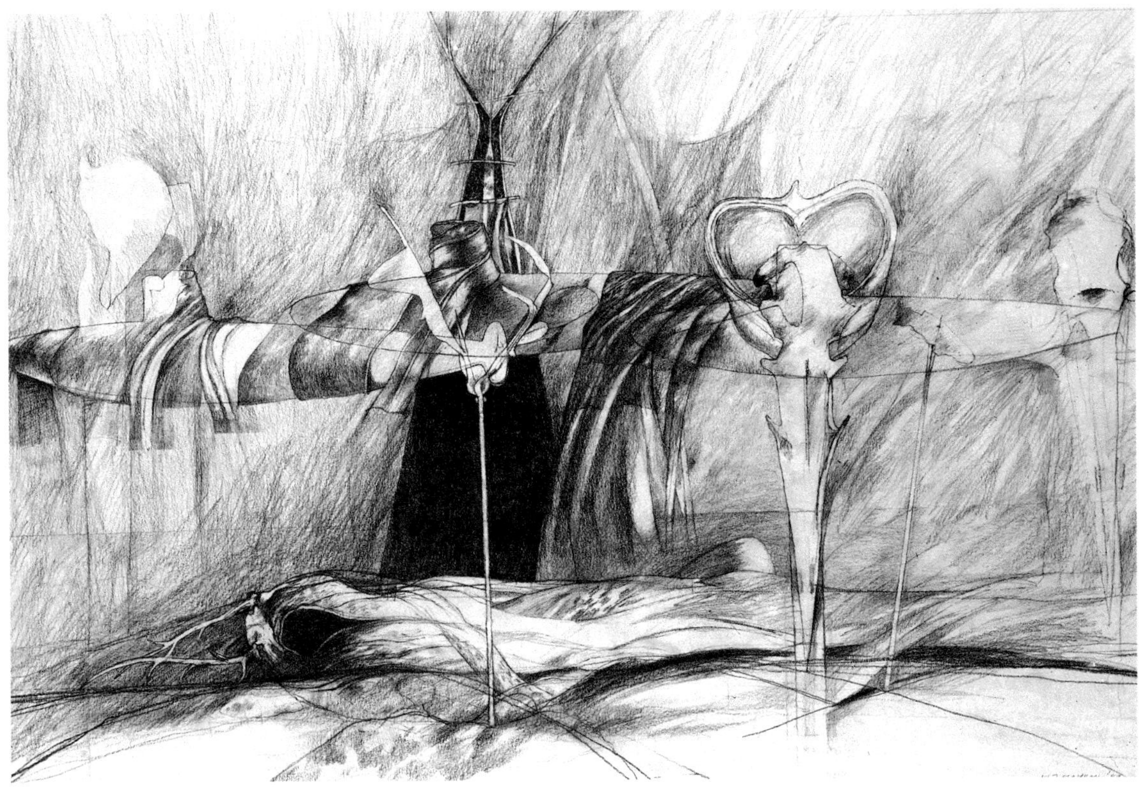

67. *Hunter's Vision*, pencil, 76 x 98 cms, Private Collection, London (1989)

break down the expected, or conventional associations of familiar objects and to replace them with new ones. The theories of Freud and Jung led artists to see that such processes might reflect deeper, unconscious connections in the mind. Just as Paolozzi saw non-western societies adapting western products to more imaginative uses, such images can then have an autonomous power like that with which a totem is endowed; autonomous because it is not dependent on any explicit intention or interpretation, but is an intrinsic quality of the image. To create something truly totemic in this sense has been one of the driving ambitions of western artists since the surrealists. Maclean's art, too, reflects this ambition.

The shrine-like quality which is such a common characteristic of so many of his works is a reflection of this. Even when there is also a particular set of references invoked, it gives his art a hieratic quality and he frequently stresses the central, vertical axis so that the image becomes formal, suggesting some kind of primitive ritual image. Other works like *Sea-Creed Banner* (1984, *Pl. 75*), *Enigmatic Figure* (1984, *Pl. 76*), *Tide Column* (1986) and *Ancestor Figure* (1986, *Pl. 77 & 78*), all free-standing, are intended to be mysterious and to work at a level of imaginative suggestion without precise context, though in the latter, suggestively the figure in the work is carved from the butt of a shotgun. Sometimes these works invoke a particular kind of mythological image, though without suggesting a precise interpretation. *King Fisherman* (1989, *Pl. 79*), for instance, uses a cast of an

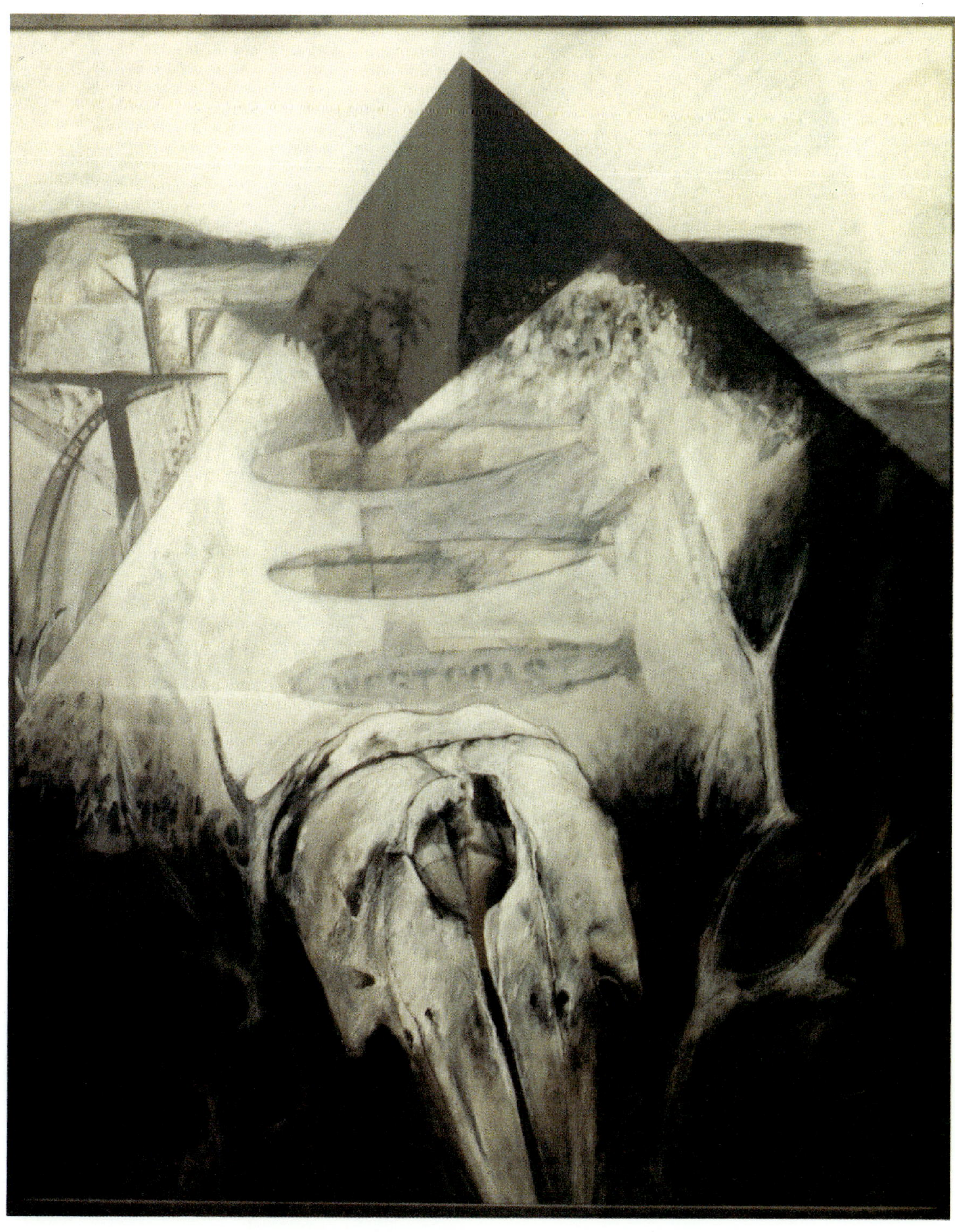

68. *Winter Kyle Elegy*, pencil, 220 x 98 cms, BBC Scotland (1989)

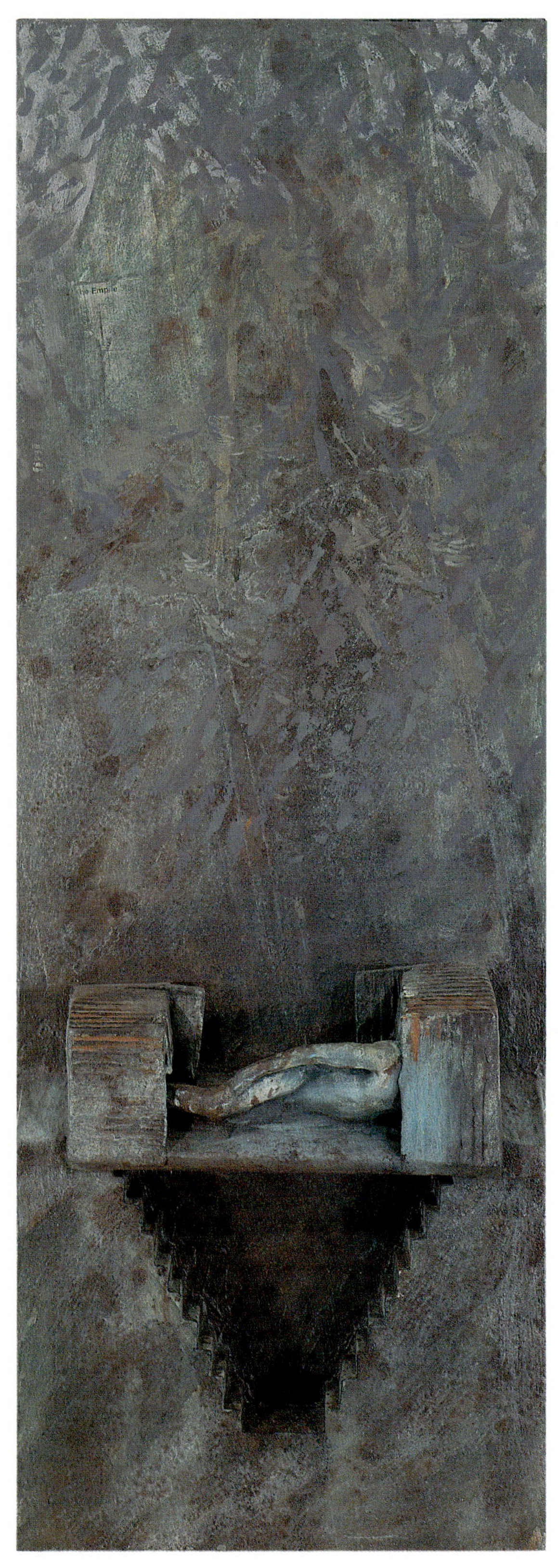

69. *Central Park* (1989) (Cat.139)

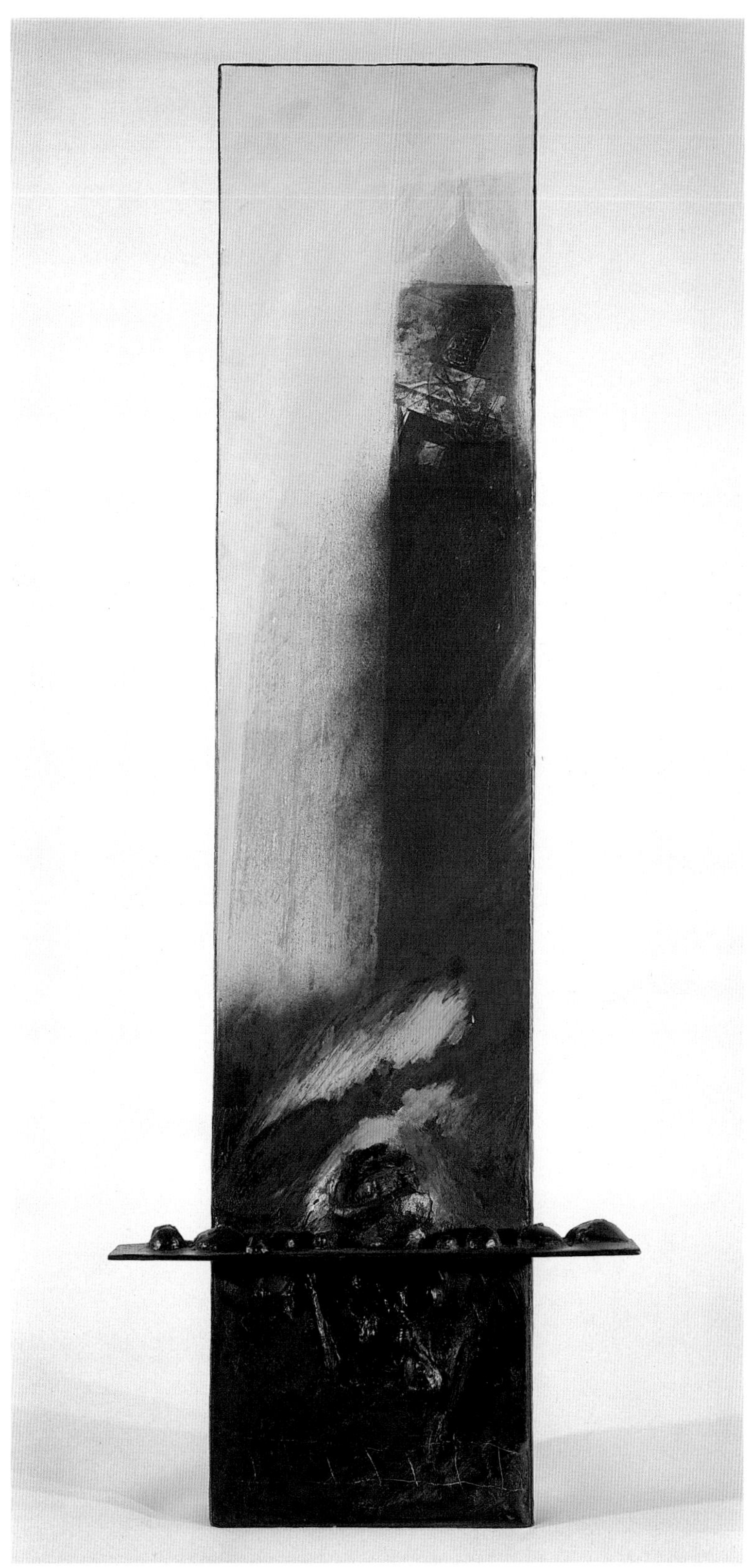

70. *Manhattan* (1988) (Cat. 137)

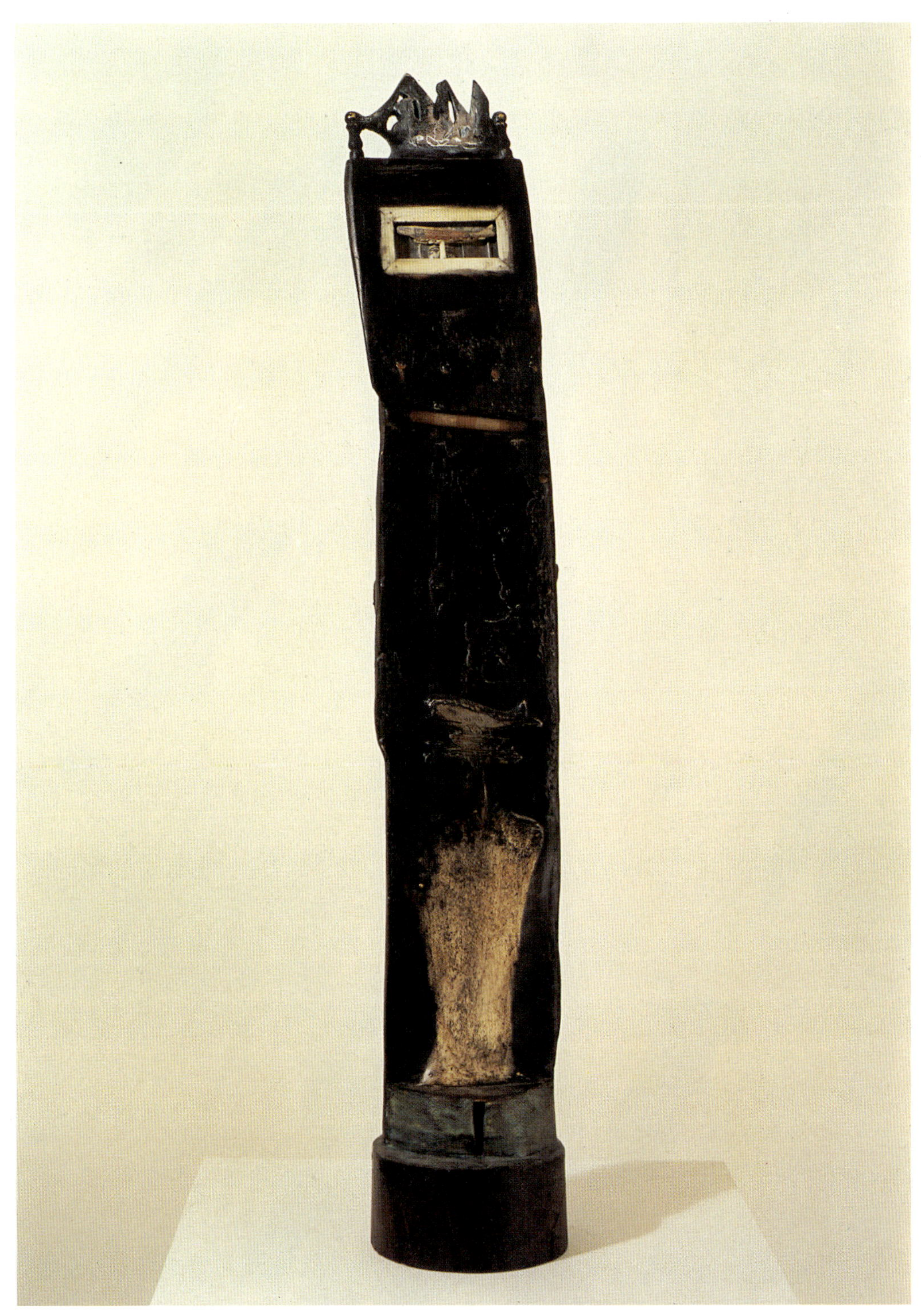

71. *Nantucket Front and Back* (1989) (Cat. 152)

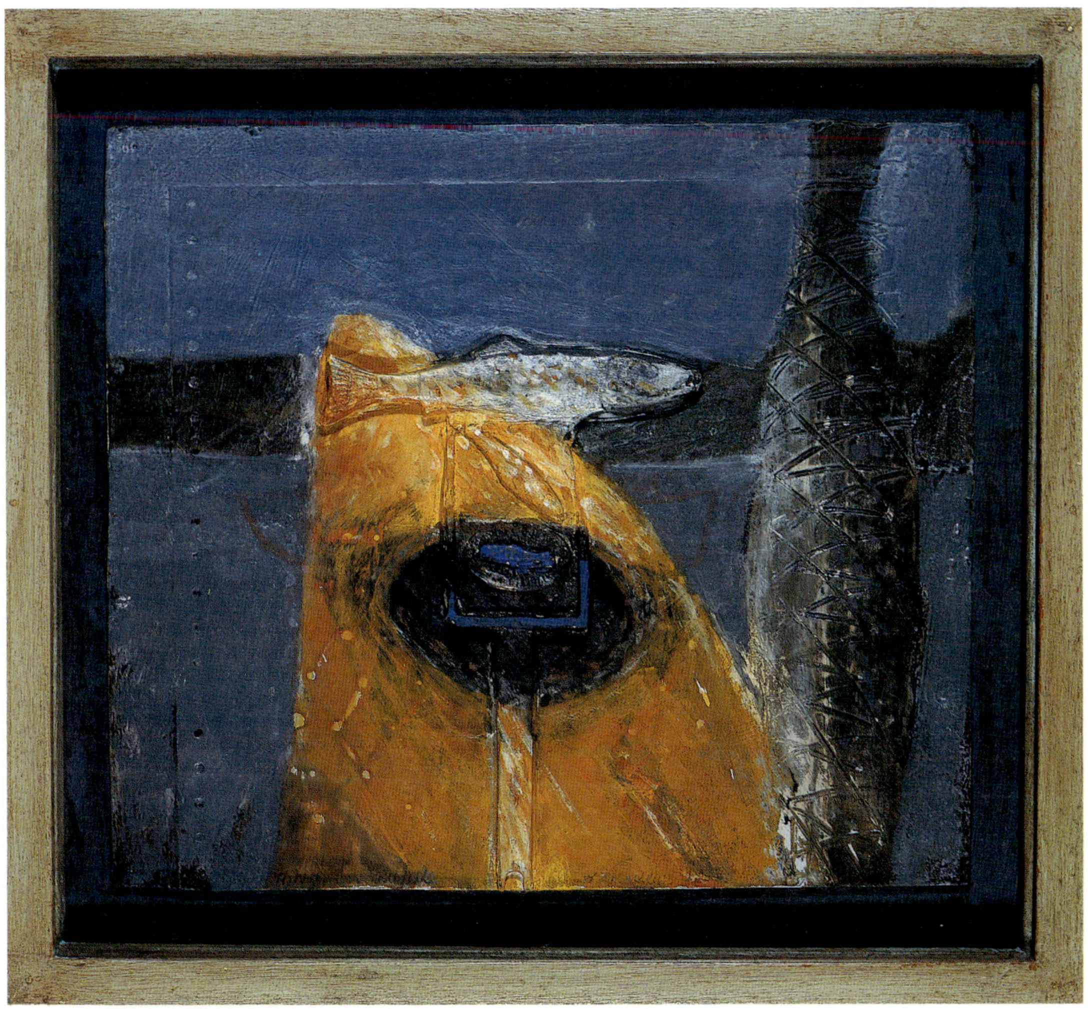

72. *Fisherman with Coalfish* (1990) (Cat. 163)

Egyptian figurine to suggest an ancient king standing on a boat, like a kingfisher on a branch. The Skye fishermen used to call a successful fisherman, a 'king fisherman', so he became a kingfisher, but once again, and this time explicitly, he is the Fisher King.

Apart from the symbolism that it invokes, this little figure is also an example of the artist's use of casting, something he has done frequently over the last few years. It has freed him from the obvious constraint that he was under when, as he generally did earlier, he incorporated a unique object into an assemblage. He could only use it once, but casting allows him to combine and recombine objects in different ways and so much more freely. A beautiful example of this way of working and one which also invokes some of the central themes of his art is *The Archaeology of Childhood* (1989, *Pl. 80*).

In this work, he uses toys and tiny, china pudding-dolls (porcelain charms to be hidden like sixpences in a pudding). Some are on sticks like primitive standards, others are ranged hieratically like figures in a shrine or

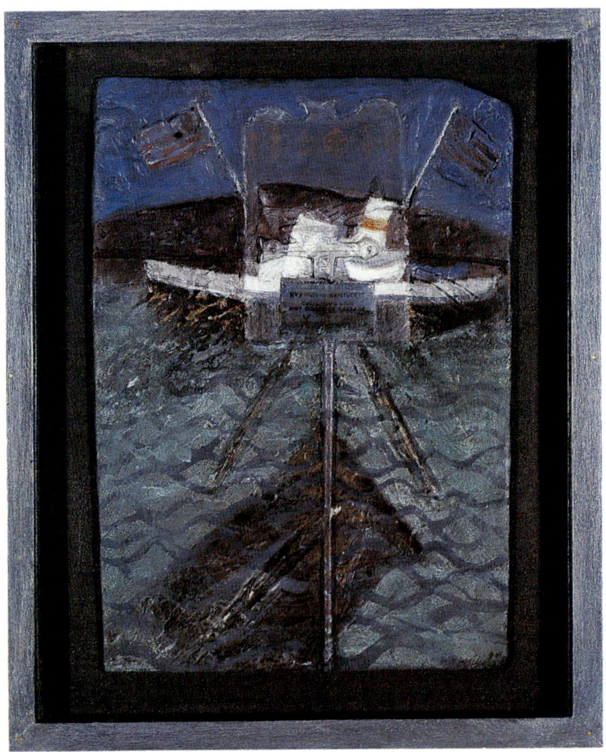

73. *Island Ferry — Cape Cod* (1990) (Cat. 157)

an altar frontal. Using paint and resin, he combines them in a unity whose scumbled, bluish-white surface seems insubstantial. Some of the forms are shrouded too, as though glimpsed in a dream. Whereas in his earlier work, memory was invoked additively. This is now done by suggestion. The image is incomplete, inchoate. Because of the freedom of execution, the spectator's imagination is also free. The links between the world of modern children and that of the religious imagery and ritual objects of primitive or preclassical art are suggested, not stated, and so are given greater imaginative force.

In his new way of working therefore, the structure of associations that he sets up is much more intuitive, musical even. *Red Ley Marker* (1989, *Pl. 81*), for instance, is a work that uses an image familiar to the artist, a red-triangle, warning beacon at the entrance to the harbour at Kyleakin. In a sense therefore, this is a landscape, but the work is not tied to that reference. Instead, it takes a familiar sign and reinvests it with mystery, but it does this pictorially. The central placing of the red triangle and the definiteness of its form within a roughly painted context are what give the image force. In such works, he was confidently incorporating into his own pictorial language the formal lessons of abstract expressionism and its successors in the early 1960s, Rauschenberg and Johns — a pictorial language that had given him such difficulty twenty years before. This kind of freedom is even more vividly apparent in the series of collages made in Italy in 1992 on the theme of the *Stations of the Cross* and these follow on from the freedom of the etchings in the suite *A Night of Islands* (see below).

He did not abandon his use of symbolism though, even as he constructed his images more freely. *Bird Altar* (1988, *Pl. 82*), for example, is one of the first works of this kind and it combines both found objects and casts or mouldings taken from them with a freely painted surface. As an image, it looks right back to his first constructions, like *Memorial for a Clearance Village* (1974, *Pl. 83*) and the paintings contemporary with them, works like *Beach Allegory* and *Three Fires, Achnahaird.* Its freedom leaves interpretation open, but is powerfully suggestive.

The idea echoes the discovery of the remains of a bird cult on Orkney. There are half-formed bird skulls in the upper corners, suspended in the lightness of the sky. Between them hangs a kind of shrine with an ominous skull. It is looking down on a little figure, crouched like Atlas holding up the heavens. He is on a narrow and

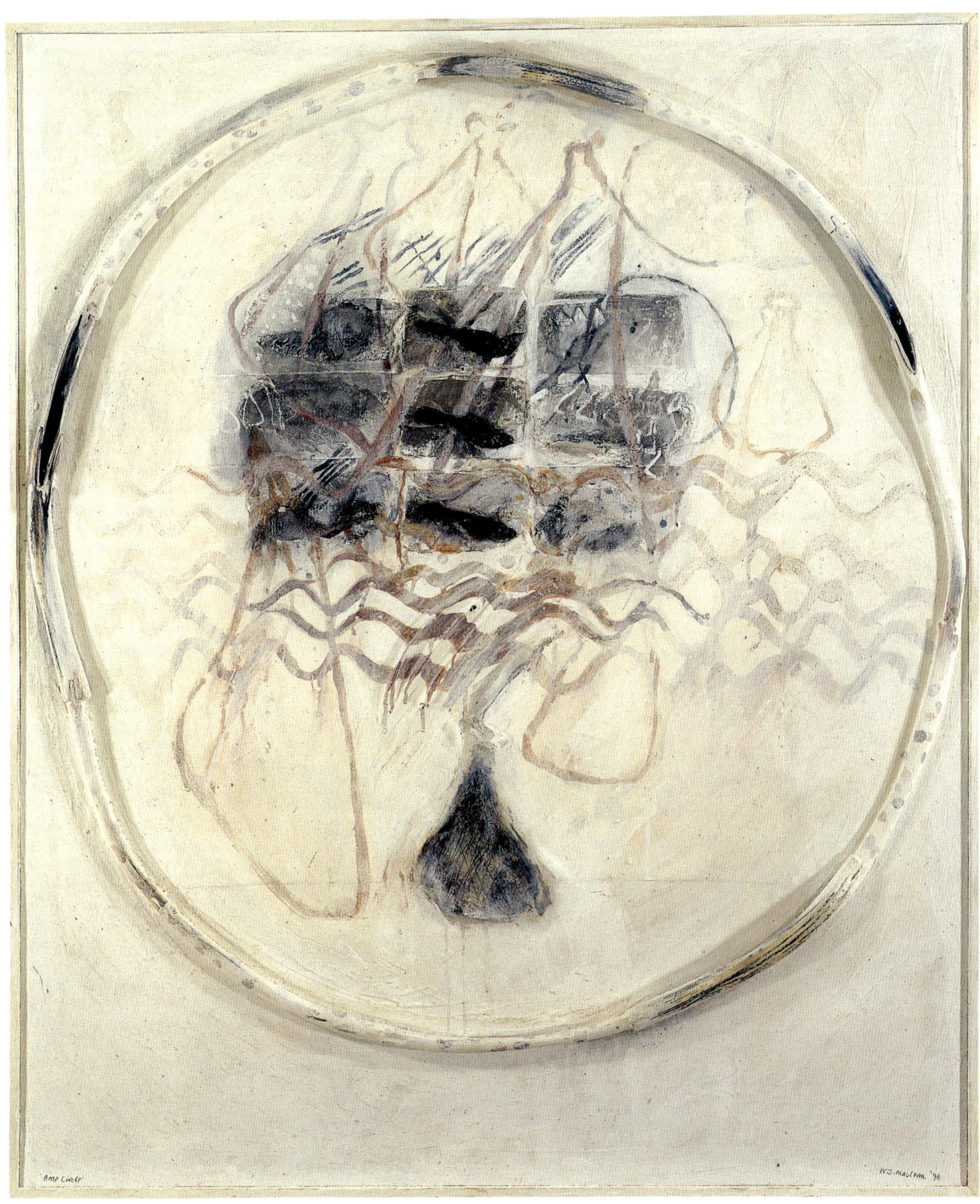

74. *Bone Circle* (1990) (Cat. 160)

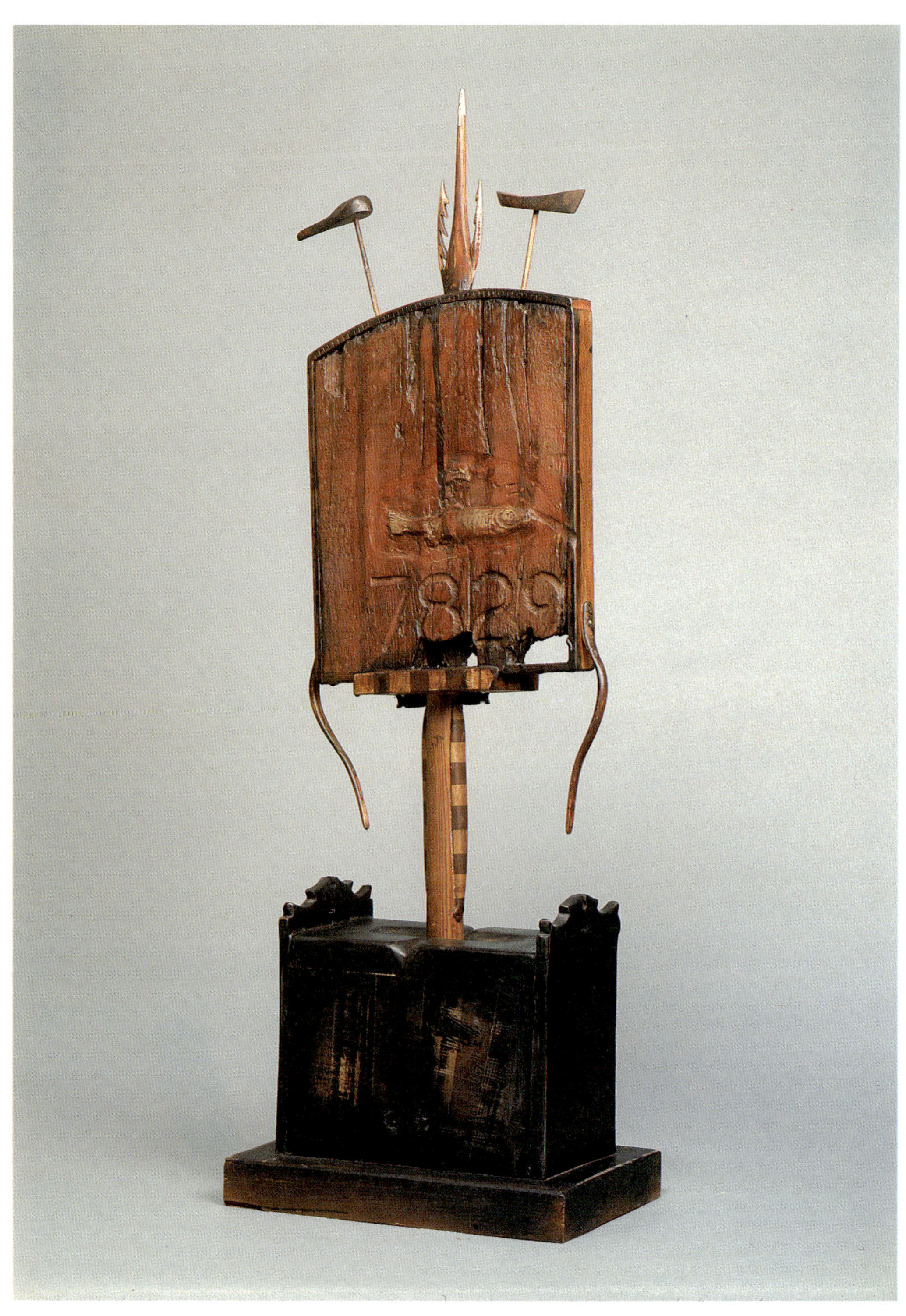

75. *Sea-Creed Banner* (1984) (Cat. 90)

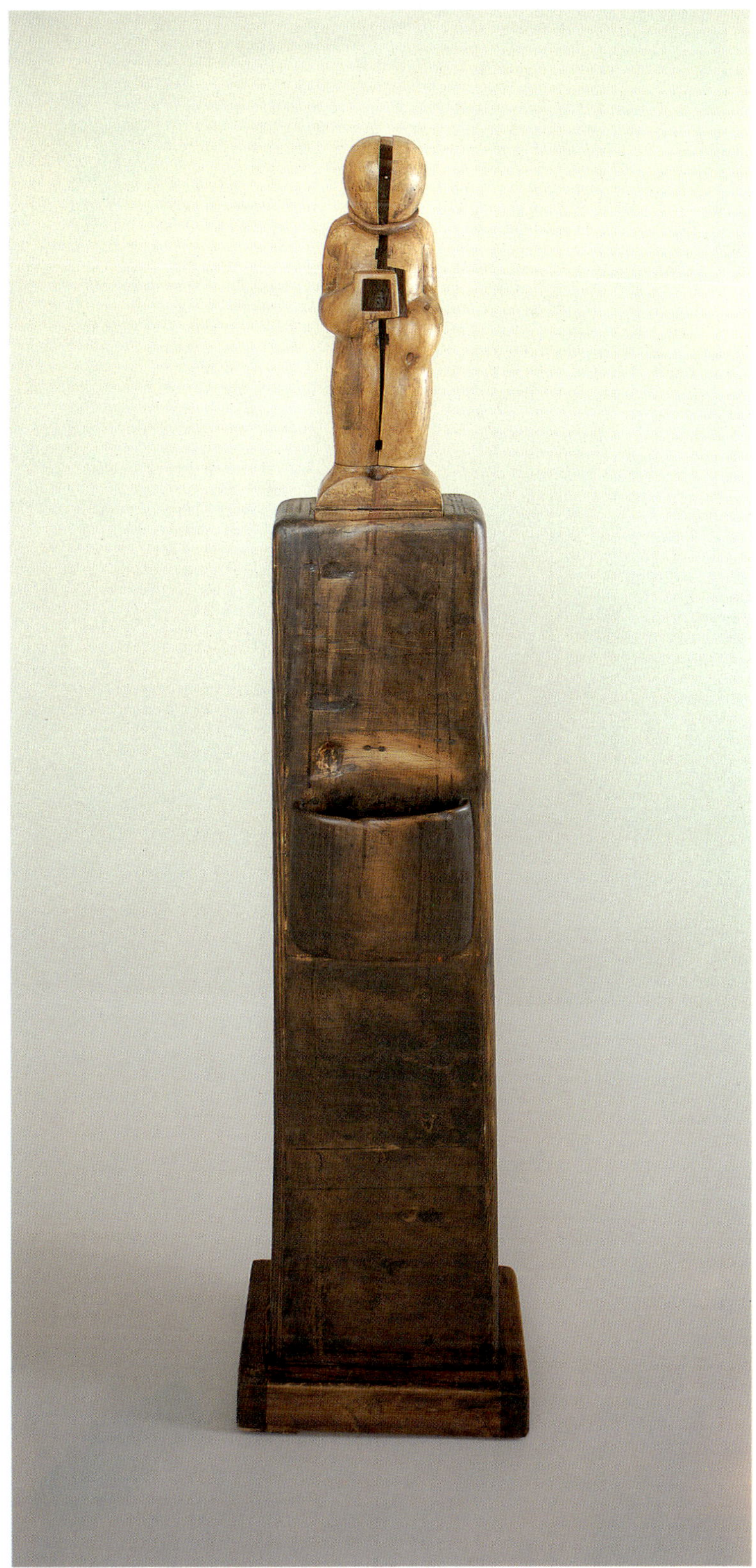

76. *Enigmatic Figure* (1984) (Cat. 89)

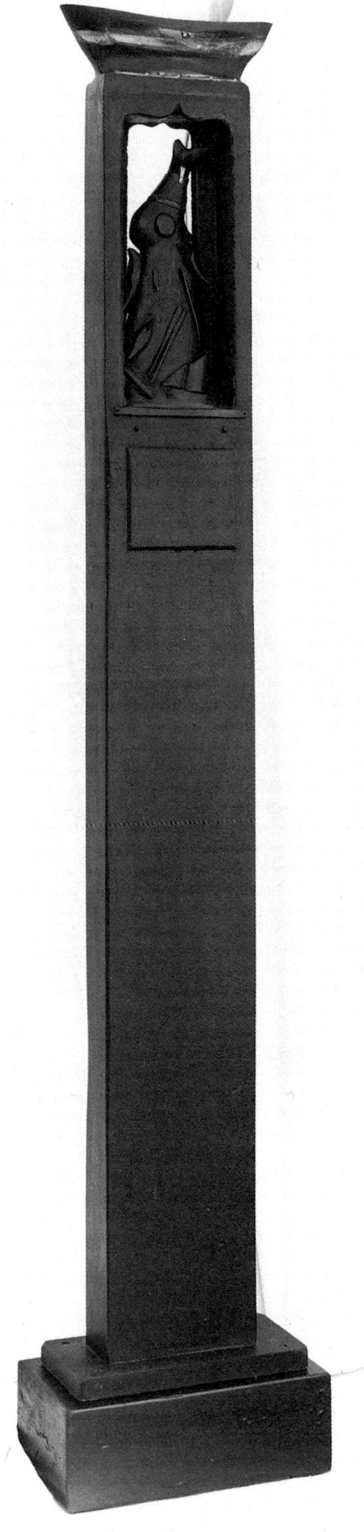

77. *Ancestor Figure* (1986) (Cat. 110)

insubstantial platform while beneath him surge the creatures of the sea. Among them a tiny ship is overwhelmed. Between death by air and death by water, it is an apocalyptic vision, but it is surely a topical one. It is an image of man in nature and Maclean's whole art explores the relationship between this and its corollorary or obverse, nature in man. It is their imbalance which has led to our present, environmental crisis.

There is another dimension to this work, too. According to the myth, not Atlas himself, but his brother Prometheus was the sacrificial victim on just such a bird altar. His crime was to steal fire from Olympus and give it to men. Like the apple in Eden, it was a dangerous gift which, although it has borne untold benefits, has also ultimately evolved into the ominous shape of the nuclear submarine as the poets and artists describe it. Patrick Geddes foresaw the consequences if human nature got out of balance with itself, or with the natural world. He described it in terms of Stevenson's metaphor for the twentieth century, Dr Jekyll and Mr Hyde, the divergence between the raw fact of human inquisitiveness and ingenuity and the humanity which should temper them.

In some memorable lines in his long poem *The Cuillin*, Sorley MacLean also invokes the legend of Prometheus:

'S ioma car a chuir an saoghal
on chunnaic Aeschylus aogas
suinn-dé-duine crochte màbte
air Caucasus nan sgurra gàbhaidh:
an dia fhuair dealbh air cruth daonda,
Iupiter borb, le iadach claoine
ag cur nam biatach acrach mùinte
a shrachad's a dh'ithe ghrùdhain:
an cinne daonna air na creagan
ag ceusadh anama fhéin ri sgreadan
nan eun is nam brùidean fiadhaich

a fhuair an toirt fhéin on bhiathadh.
Dh'aom Iupiter, an gealtair brùideil,
agus Iahweh an t-Iùdach
ach cha dànaig ám riamh
's nach d'fhuair uachdarain dia
a chrochadh air na þeanntan cràbhach
colann ìobairt nan sàr fhear.
Chrochadh Crìosda air crois-ceusaidh
agus Spartacus le cheudan;
bha ioma biatach dé am Breatainn
a rinn an obair oillteil sgreataidh,
agus cheusadh ioma Criosda
an uiridh agus am bliadhna.

Many a turn the world has taken
since Aeschylus saw the likeness
of hero-man-god hanged, lacerated
on Caucasus of the dangerous peaks
the god fashioned after man's image
barbarous Jupiter, with oblique jealousy
sending the hungry, obedient vultures
to tear and eat his liver:
mankind on the rocks
crucifying his own soul to the screeches
of the birds and savage animals
that got their own good from the feeding
Jupiter, the brutal coward has failed
and so has Jahweh the Jew
But a time has never come
when rulers have not found a god
who hangs on pious mountains
the sacrificed bodies of surpassing men
Christ was hanged on the cross
and Spartacus with his hundreds;
there were many god-vultures in Britain
who did the loathsome hateful work
and many a Christ has been crucified
last year and this year

(*The Cuillin*, VII)[31]

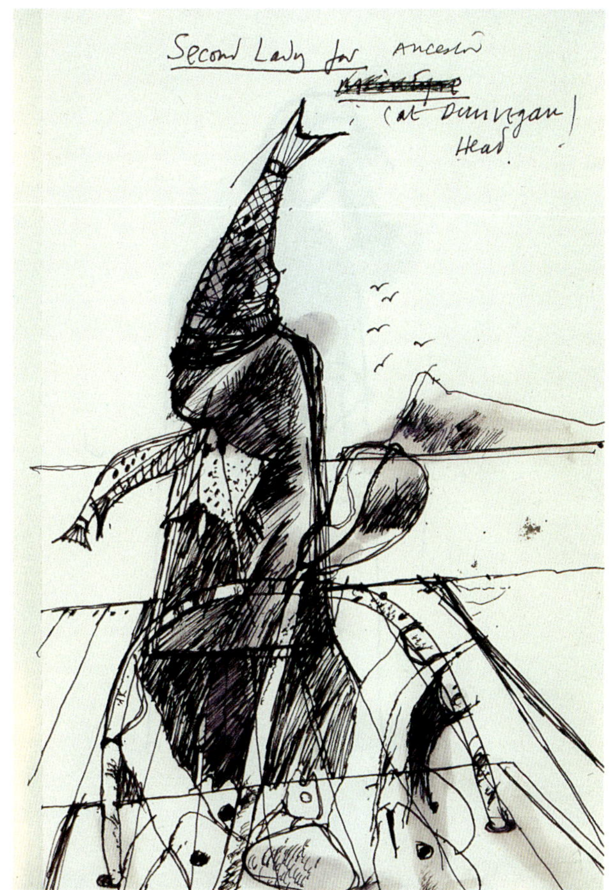

78. Study for *Ancestor Figure*, page from a sketchbook, pen and wash, 14.4 x 20.8 cms (1986)

The poet seems to gloss the legend to suggest that Prometheus was a sacrificial victim on just such a bird altar as the artist has created. In the poem too, he uses the image to condemn man's inhumanity to man and, like Blake in his *Illustrations to the Book of Job*, he unmasks the way that we elevate the structures of law that we create for ourselves in the forms of religion and then justify our inhumanity by our obedience to them. Blake's view was the same as Geddes's. He saw that this kind of religion was the consequence of a split between reason and imagination; between the factor's perception of the economic advantage to be gained from the cleared land and the failure of imagination in his inability to perceive and sympathise with the human suffering entailed in its clearance. For Adam Smith, sympathy, as the agent of the imagination, was the cement that binds society and was the vehicle of morality, so for Blake, as for Geddes and the artists of the Scots Renascence who have followed him,

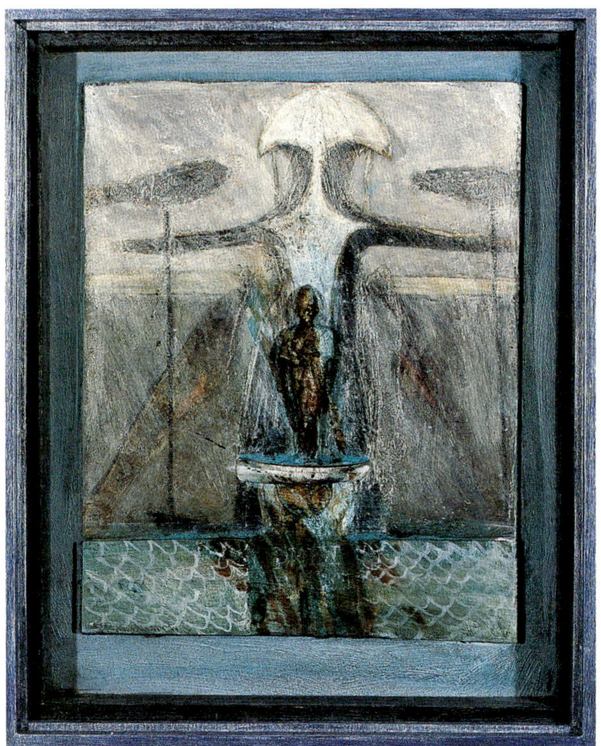

79. *King Fisherman* (1989) (Cat. 146)

to avoid this kind of consequence, reason and imagination had to be unified and art was a principal agent in the realisation of that unity.

In the context set by the whole of Sorley MacLean's poem, there is a shift from the local history of the Highlands to a universal symbolism. It is this same shift which Will Maclean achieves in his mature work. His most important recent work, the set of ten prints to Gaelic poetry, *A Night of Islands*, which was commissioned by Charles Booth-Clibborn, is a summary of these concerns. These are large and complex, coloured etchings involving as many as four plates in each. Unlike his earlier etchings which follow his drawings, these take their form from his constructions. Each has a framing border which relates to the central image which is in a reserved area like the window, or the box in his constructions. One of the most moving images illustrates Derick Thomson's poem, 'Strathnaver' (*Pl. 86*), which commemorates one of the most notorious of all the Clearances, undertaken on behalf of the Duke of Sutherland by his factor, Patrick Sellar. The etching is dark. The border suggests smoke and in the centre is an image made up of the horns of sheep piled in a creel. Above this are raised two smoking roof-timbers from a destroyed cottage. The roof-timbers were essential for shelter. Their destruction left the people without protection beneath the stars, and in the print the sky above is dark and starry.

At the time of going to press, Maclean has under way a major work, *The Emigration Ship*, which also draws on the story of Strathnaver and so focuses his central concerns thematically, but also the way in which they open towards a universal symbolism. Its title is a homage to McTaggart's *The Emigrant Ship*, painted almost exactly a hundred years ago, but it is also a major statement of one of Maclean's own central themes. It looks back to *Emigrant's Voyage* (1987, *Pl. 87*) for instance, to the etching, *The Melancholy of Departure* (1986, *Pl. 84 & 85*; commissioned by An Lanntair in Stornoway on the occasion of the exhibition on the theme of the Clearances, *As an Fhearann*, organised by that gallery in 1986), or to the major work, *Composite Memory (Vessel)* (1987, *Pl. 88*). The latter is a construction shaped like a cross-section of a boat. Within it is visible a dark, confused jumble of figures whose unnatural disorder suggests their suffering and is iconographically reminiscent of Rodin's *Gate of Hell*. It was inspired by the tragic story of the *Exmouth*, in effect a slave ship carrying emigrants to America in 1747,

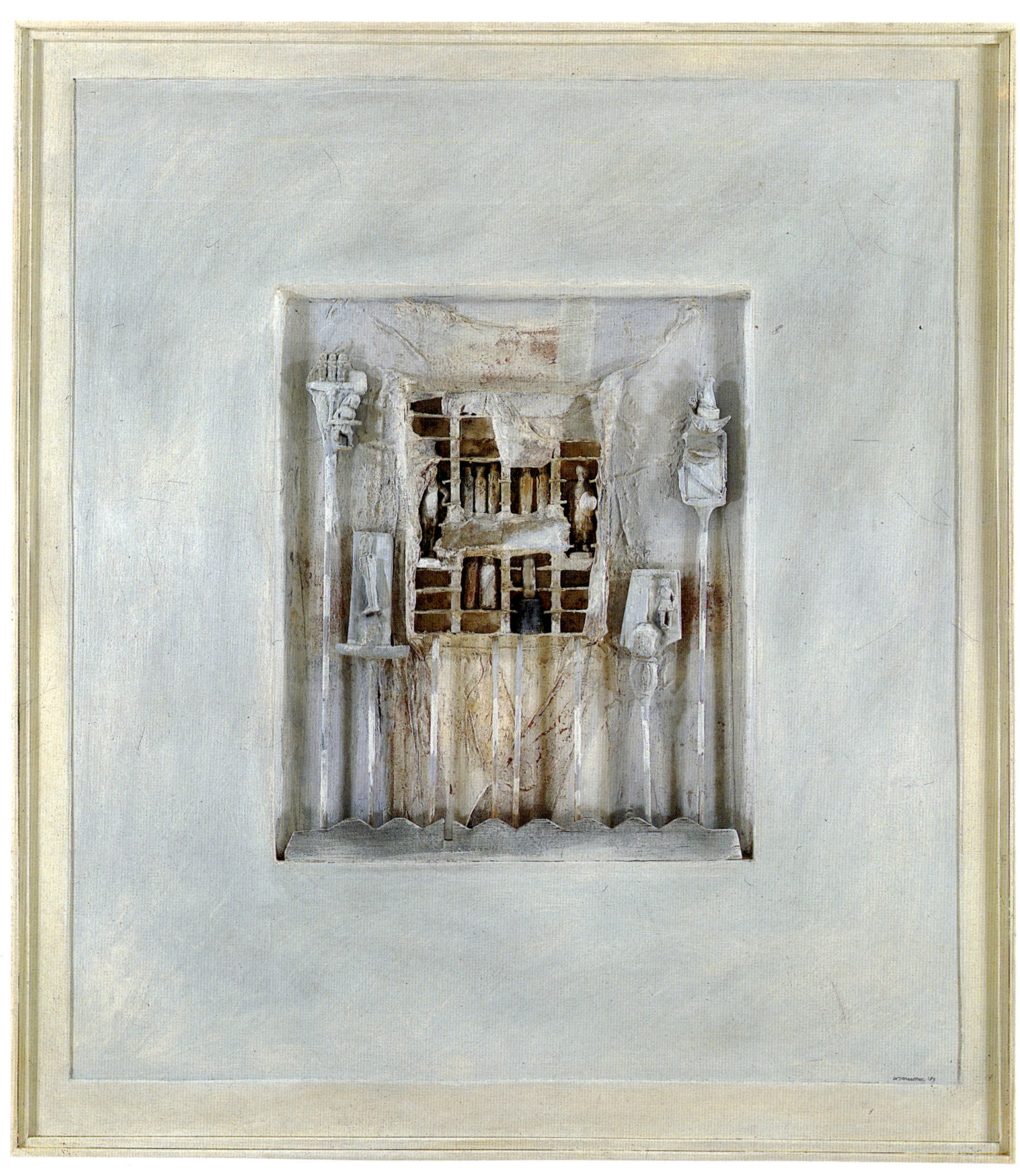

80. *The Archaeology of Childhood* (1989) (Cat. 148)

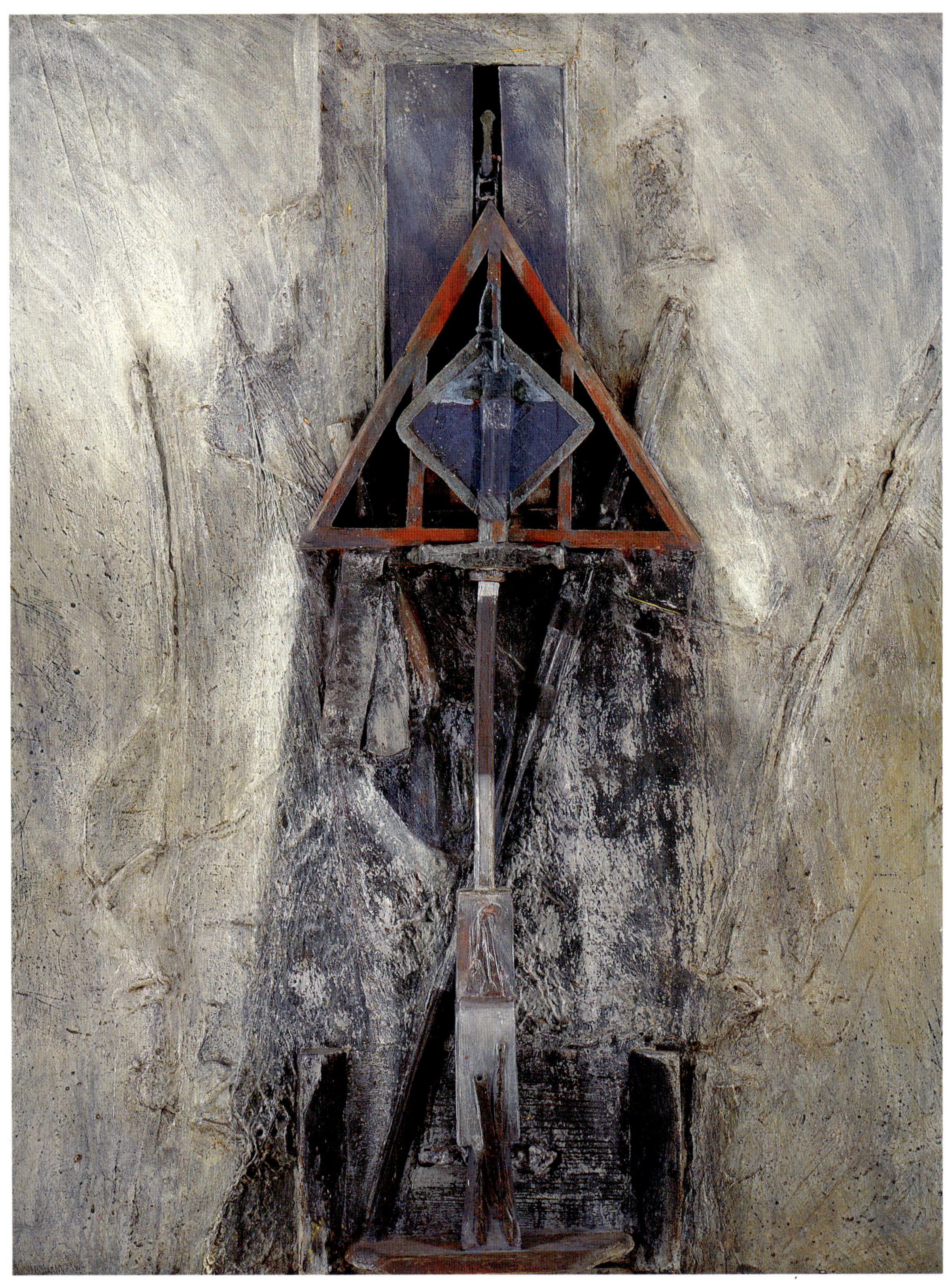

81. *Red Ley Marker* (1989) (Cat. 154)

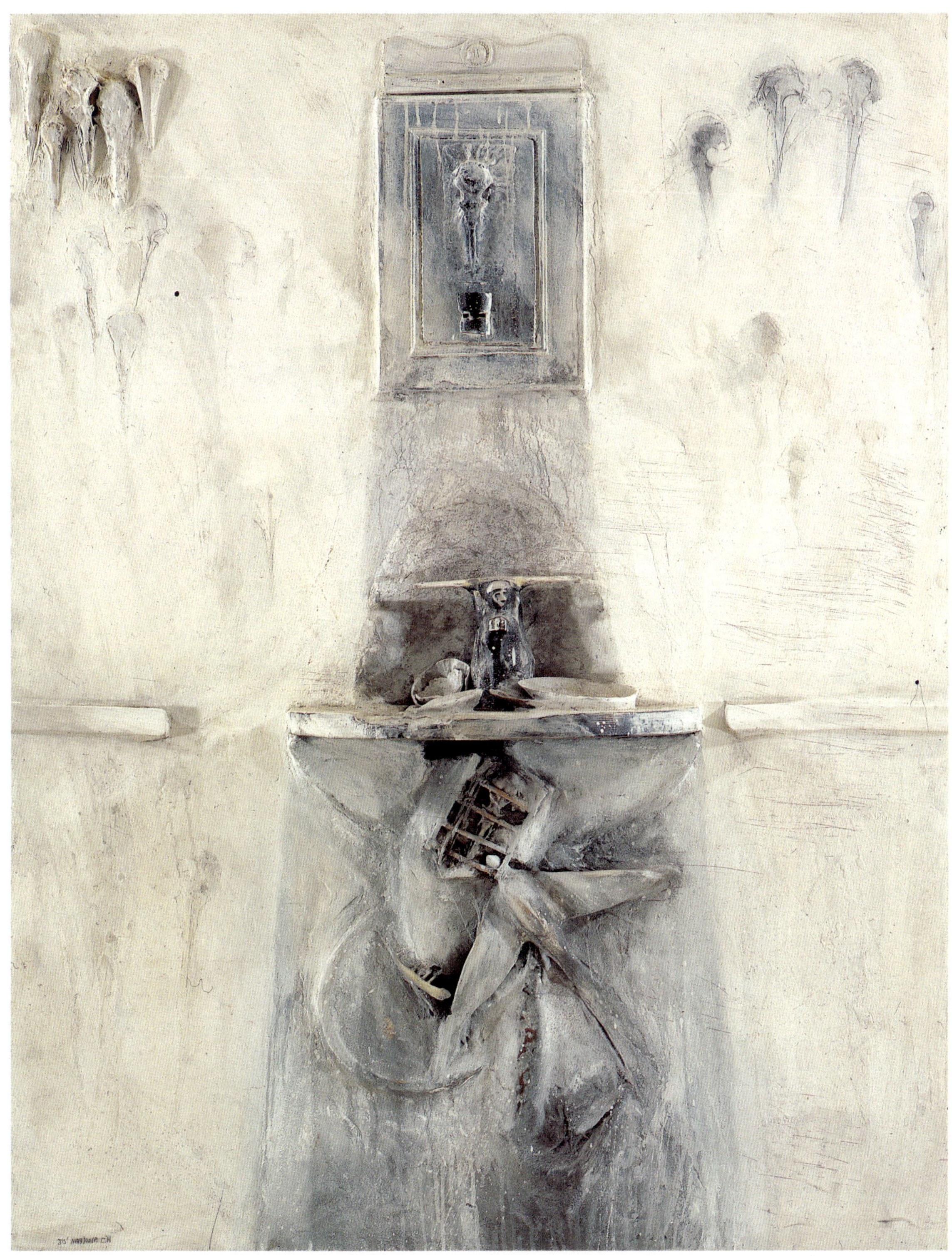

82. *Bird Altar* (1988) (Cat. 136)

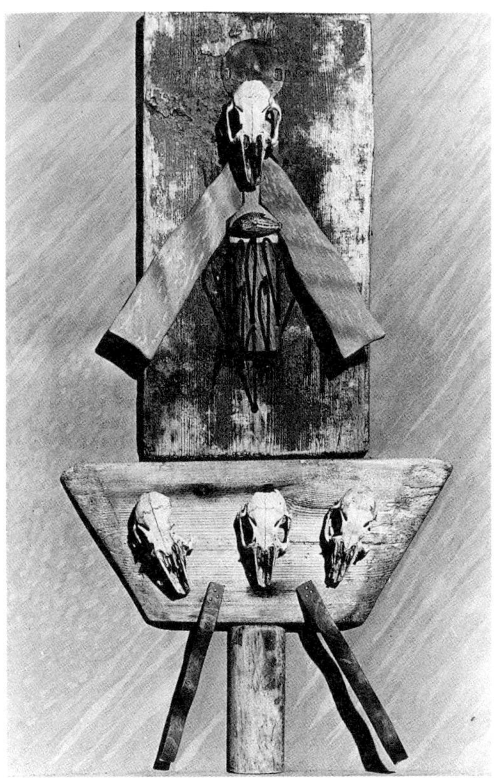

83. *Memorial for a Clearance Village* (1974) (Cat. 12)

but wrecked off the coast of Islay with terrible loss of life.

The Emigration Ship includes an image of a sailing ship, found scratched in the plaster of a ruined school on Mull. It also has as its centrepiece a slate, scratched with the diamond pattern of the glass of the window of the church at Glencalvie in Sutherland. Within the diamonds of the panes are written various inscriptions relating to the story of the people of Strathnaver. One of these is a quotation of something actually written on the window of the church. When they were driven out of their homes by Patrick Sellar, exposed to the elements, they sought shelter by the church at Glencalvie, but they were refused admission. In the confusion of their innocence, they scratched on the window that it was they who were 'the wicked generation'. Inexplicably, in their despair the crucified people took upon themselves the guilt of those who persecuted them. They could not believe that they were the victims of such inhumanity without being somehow guilty themselves. They present us with a tragic paradigm of the perpetual struggle between innocence and experience which is the nature of morality and the human condition. This is not just a nostalgic lament for Highland culture, therefore. Maclean's art draws on the past, but it does so to speak urgently to the present.

In the last of the ten prints in the set *A Night of Islands*, Maclean takes for his text the poem, 'Clann Adhaimh' or 'Adam's Clan' by George Campbell Hay:

Sud bàrca beag le antrom gaoìthe sìorruidh
'na siùil chaithte, a'dìreadh cuain gun chòrsa,
s i leatha fhéin an cearcal cian na fàire,
is gul is gaireachdaich troimh chéil' air bòrd
dhith.

Tha Bròn, Aoibh, Aois is Oige, Sàr is Suarach
a'tarruing nam ball buan a ha ri'brèidibh;
tha Amaideas is Gliocas, Naomh is Peacach
air a stiùir mu seach is càch 'gan éisteachd.
Fo speur tha uair grianach, uair sgreunach,
— clais is cìrein — fèath is doinionn — théid i,
gu fàire nach do leum siadh riamh no sùilean,
s a lorg s a h-ùpraid ghuth 'dol bàs 'na déidhse.

Ceangal

Sud i is brù air a siùil s i 'deuchainn gach sgòid,
long àrsaidh le sunnd is sùrd is léireadh air
bòrd,
fàire làn rùn nach do rùisgeadh fo cheann a
croinn-spreiòd,
is cop uisge a stiùrach a'dúnadh s'ga chall
sa'mhuir mhóir.

Yonder sails a little bark, with the grievous burden of an eternal wind on her worn sails, climbing an ocean that has no coast, alone within the distant circle of the horizon, with a confusion of weeping and laughter aboard her.

Grief, Joy, Age and Youth, Eminent and Of-No-Account are heaving at the everlasting gear that trims her canvas; Folly and Wisdom, Saint and Sinner take her helm in turn, and all obey them. Under a sky now sunny, now lowering — trough and crest — calm and tempest — she goes on to a horizon that neither stem nor stern nor eye yet overlept, and her track and her tumult of voices die astern of her.

Envoi

There she goes with a curve on her sails, putting each sheet to the test, an ancient ship with bustle and cheer and suffering aboard her; a horizon full of secrets unrevealed under her bowsprit head, and the foam of her wake closing and losing itself in the great sea astern.[32]

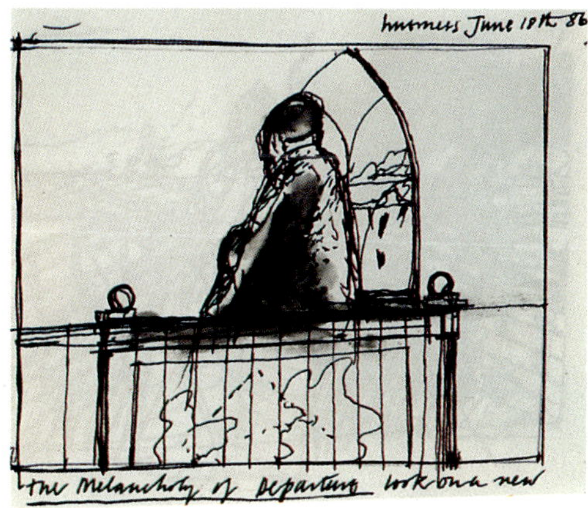

84. Study for etching, *The Melancholy of Departure*, page from a sketchbook, pen and wash, 14.4 x 20.8 cms (1986)

Maclean illustrates this beautiful poem with a view through the rigging of a nineteenth-century sailing ship, careering through the sea like the Flying Dutchman (*Pl. 89*). Both poem and print recall Bard MacIntyre's ship and Sorley MacLean's ship of Gaelic poetry in his poem, 'The Ship', but now instead of the ship of Gaelic culture alone, it is the ship of all the world.

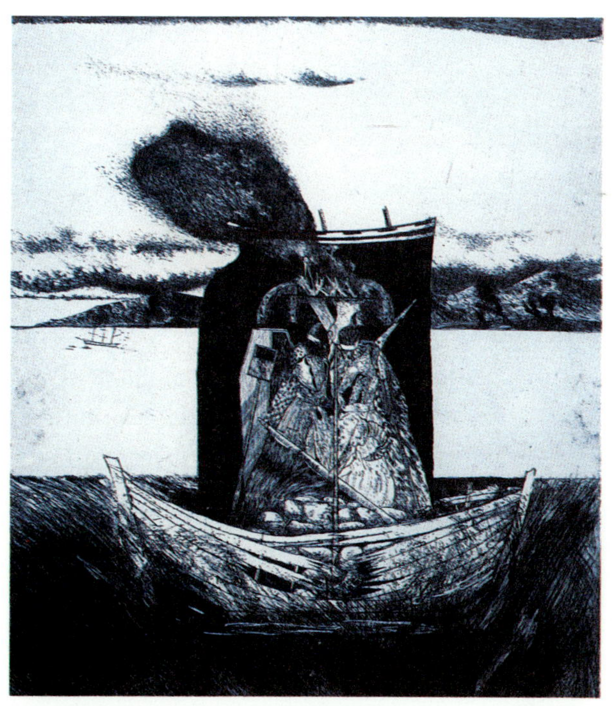

85. *The Melancholy of Departure*, etching, edition of 45, 46 x 35 cms (1986)

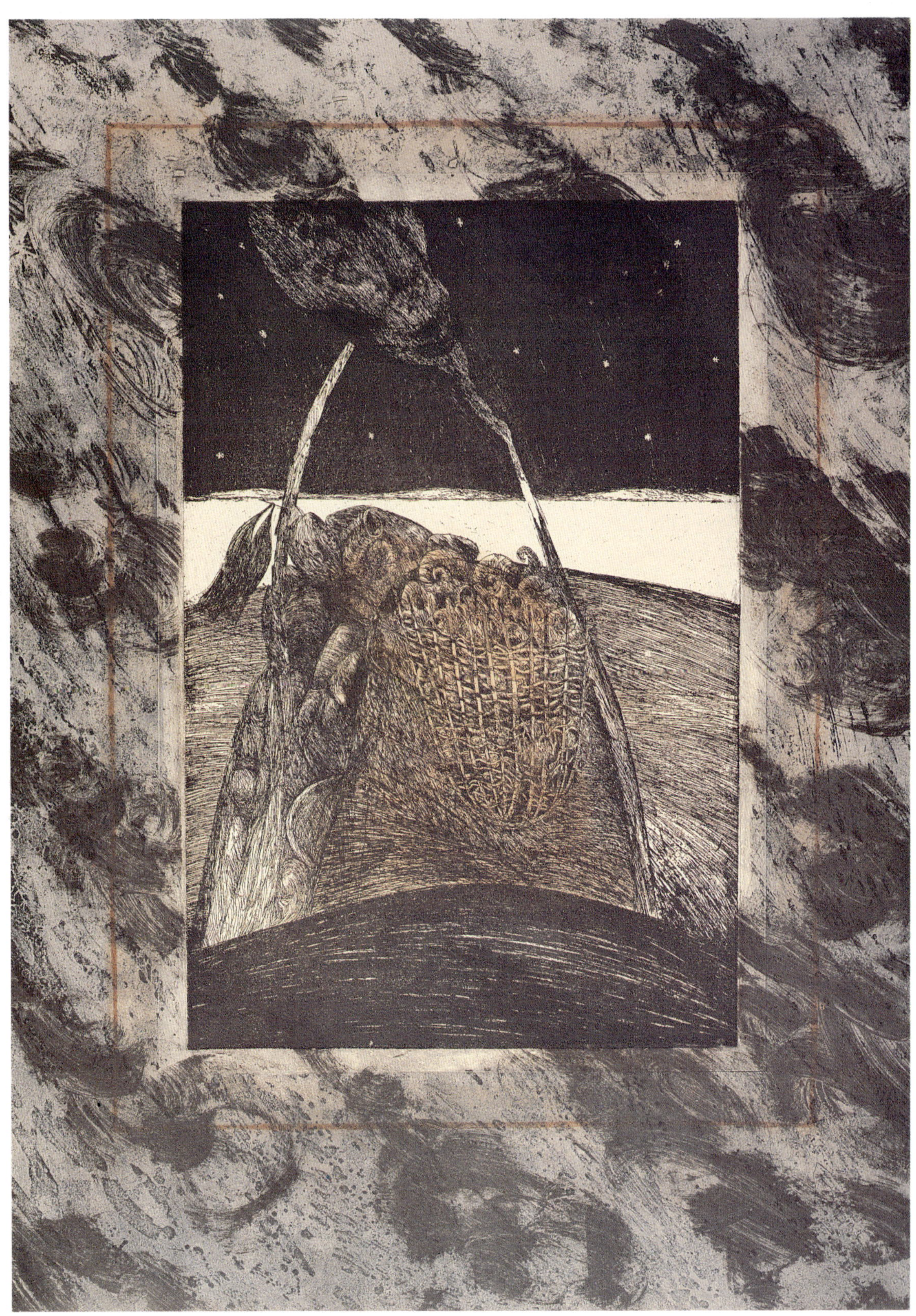

86. *Strathnaver*, coloured etching from *A Night of Islands* suite of twelve, 80 x 55 cms (1991)

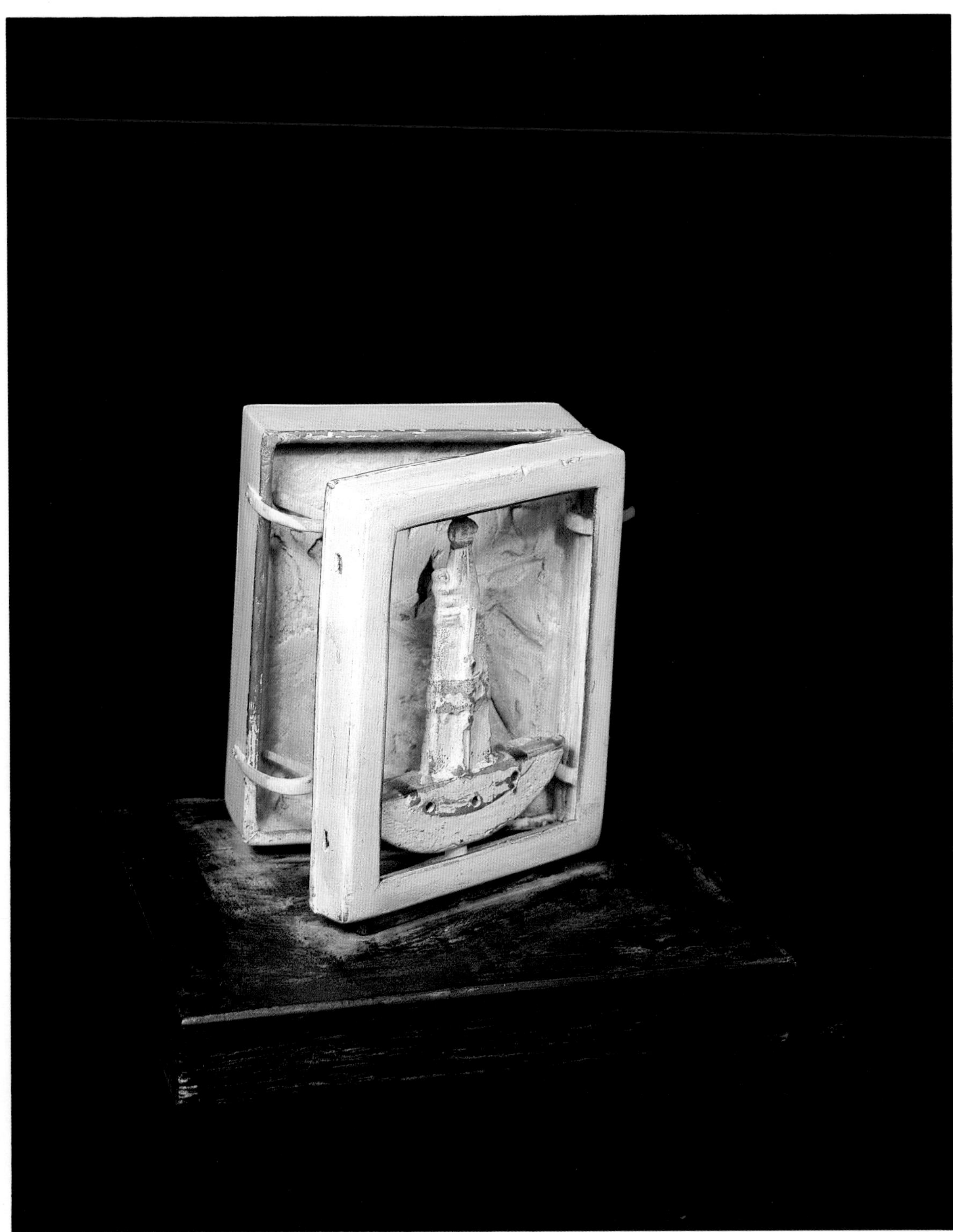

87. *Emigrant's Voyage* (1987) (Cat. 124)

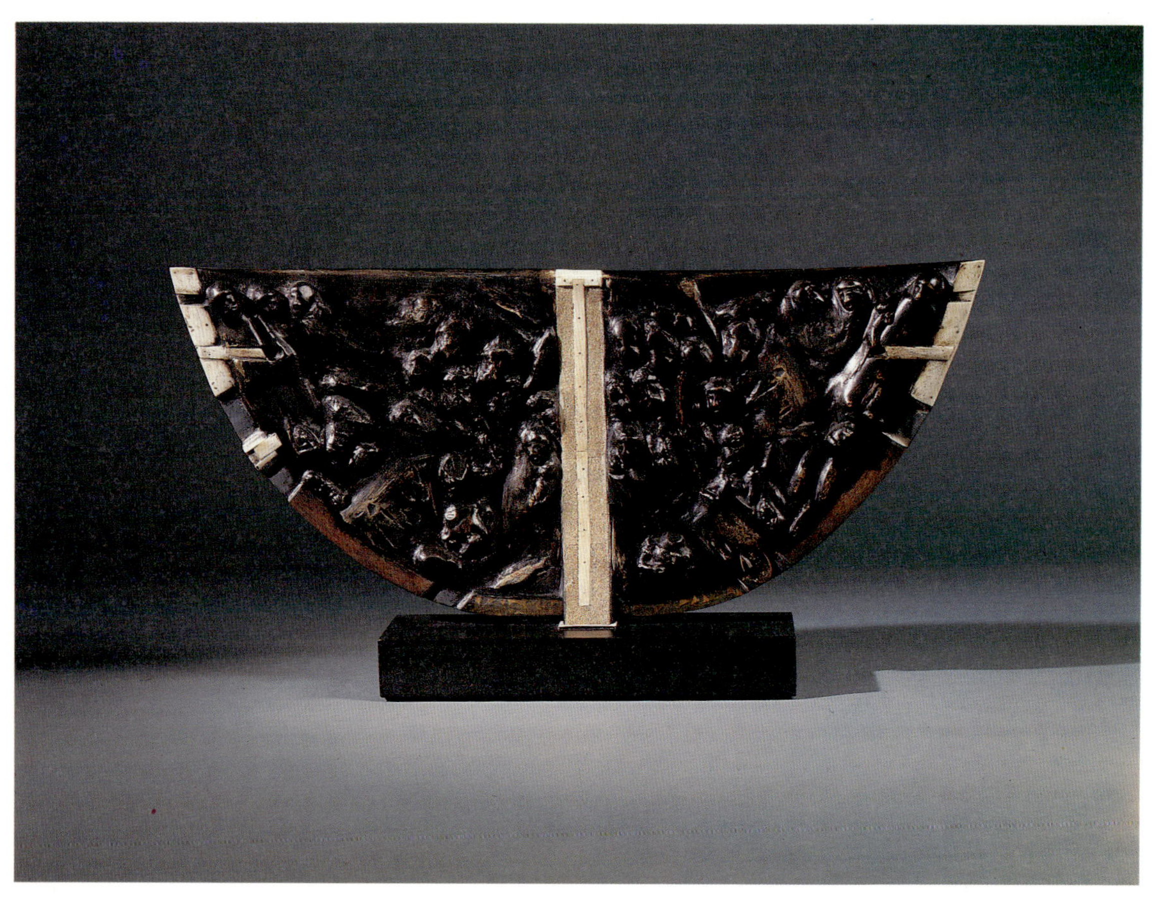

88. *Composite Memory (Vessel)* (1987) (Cat. 119)

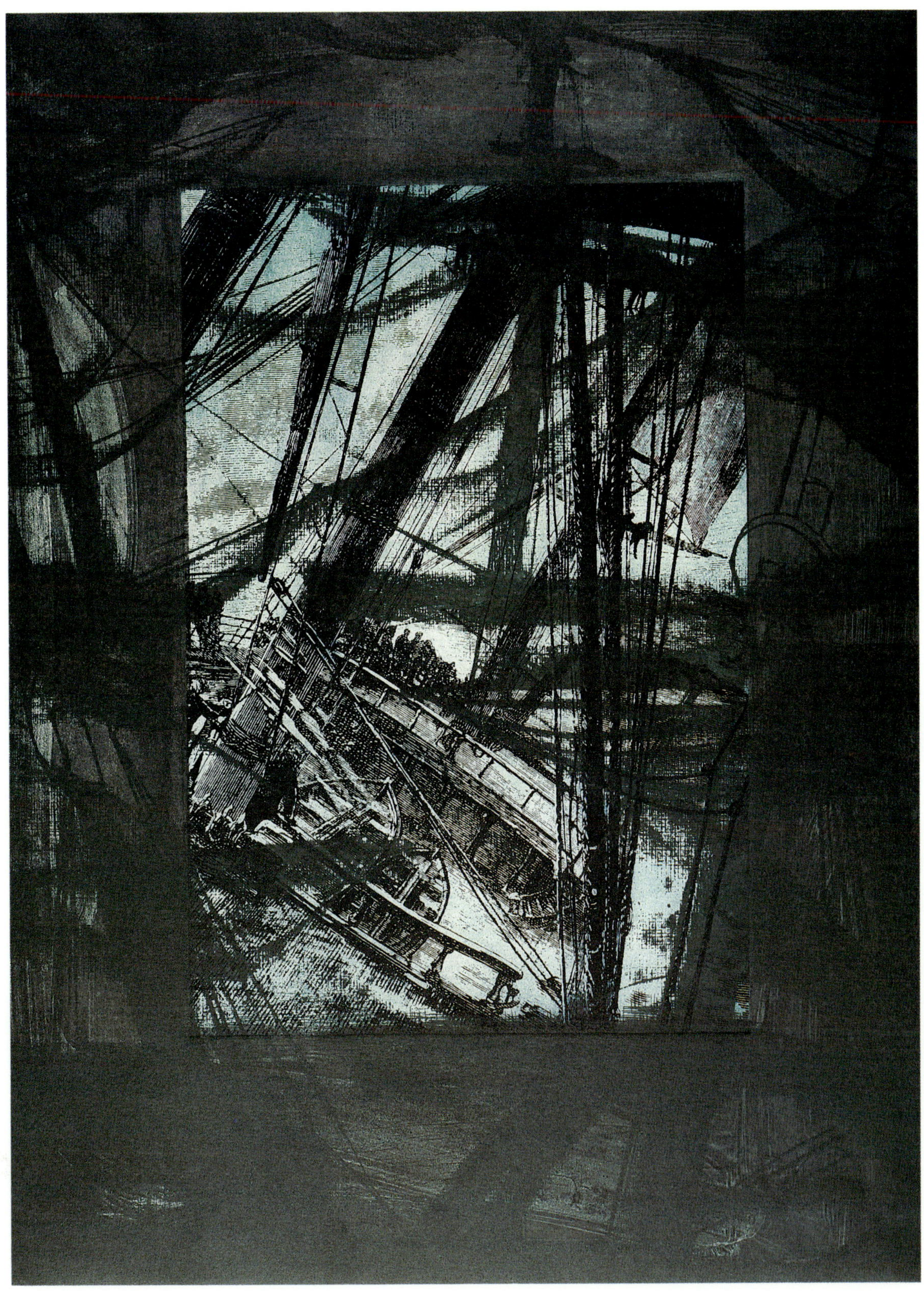

89. *Adam's Clan*, coloured etching from *A Night of Islands* suite of twelve, 80 x 55 cms (1991)

CATALOGUE RAISONNÉ

CONSTRUCTIONS AND ASSEMBLAGES BY WILL MACLEAN, 1974-1992

This catalogue incorporates the *Catalogue Raisonné* published in 1987 by Claus Runkel.That list has been brought up to date and the suite of numbers extended to include work done since then. Where no collection is named, works belong to the artist.

1. *Requiem Construction (John Maclean)*; painted wood and found and painted objects, 30 x 25 x 8 cm. The McManus Gallery, Dundee (1974) Plate 19

2. *Fore-Father's Tale*; painted found objects on board, 46 x 26 x l0 cm. The Scottish Arts Council Collection (1974)

3. *Mackerel Passage*; found objects, painted wood and enamel on copper, 46 x 30 x 7 cm. Private Collection (1974)

4. *Memorial to the Sperm Whale*; wood, bone, lead and acrylic, 44 x 18 x 12 cm. (approx.) Fife County Collection (1974)

5. *Nightmare for a Herring*; mixed media, wood and perspex, 50 x 38 x 10 cm. (1974; reworked 1987)

6. *Canna Memorandum*; painted wood and metal, 61 x 35 x 8 cm. Private Collection (1974; reworked 1987)

7. *North Minch Allegory*; painted wood and metal, 51 x 38 x 8 cm. The Scottish Arts Council Collection (1974)

8. *Trap Image No. 3*; painted metal and pencil on board, 38 x 51 x 6 cm. The Scottish Arts Council Collection (1974)

9. *Northern Totem*; wood, metal, slate and dogfish skin, 51 x 33 x 13 cm. Ferens Art Gallery, Hull (1975)

10. *Predatory Voyage*; painted wood and bone, 56 x 28 x 10 cm. The McManus Gallery, Dundee (1975)

11. *Hebridean Catafalque*; carved and painted wood, bone and horn, 50 x 35 x 12 cm. Private Collection (1975)

12. *Memorial for a Clearance Village*; found and painted objects, wood and bone, 58 x 41 x 8 cm. Private Collection, Edinburgh (1975) Plate 83

13. *Symbols of Survival*; yellow pine, bone and acrylic, 84 x 104 x 10 cm. Private Collection, Scotland (1976) Plate 20

14. *Ray Fish Shrine*; painted wood, metal and bone, 61 x 41 x 15 cm. Arts Council of Great Britain, London (1976) Plate 37

15. *Legendary Predator*; carved and painted wood, 52 x 150 x 14 cm. (approx.) Private Collection, London (1976)

16. *Nostalgic Locker*; carved and painted wood and found objects, 56 x 30 x 15 cm. Private Collection, Scotland (1976) Plate 36

17. *Spirit Boat*; carved and painted wood, 69 x 71 x 8 cm. Private Collection, Edinburgh (1976)

18. *Spectre of Famine*; found objects, wood, metal and fur, 84 x 56 x 13 cm. Collection David Gilbert, Germany (1976)

19. *West Highland Memorabilia*; carved and painted wood and found objects, 94 x 48 x 6 cm. Private Collection (1977)

20. *Memories of a Northern Childhood*; wood, slate and found objects, 48 x 35 x 15 cm. Private Collection, Cambridge (1977) Plate 28

21. *Secrets*; carved wood and slate, 63 x 36 x 8 cm. Collection John Maclean, Tayport (1977)

22. *Song for the Solan*; mixed media, wood, metal and bone, 56 x 28 x 12 cm. Private Collection (1977)

23. *Homage to Hirta*; acrylic on board with mixed media and found objects, 150 x 118 x 25cm. The National Trust for Scotland, Edinburgh (1977)

24. *Primeval Image*; wood, metal and penguin skin, 40 x 30 x 8 cm. (approx.) Formerly the Scottish Arts Council Collection (1977)

(25.) *Skate Offering*; carved and painted wood and found objects, 44 x 56 x 8 cm. Dismantled (1977)

26. *Sabbath of the Dead*; oil and acrylic on wood with metal and bone, 38 x 69 x 15 cm. Private Collection, Glasgow (1978) Plate 25

27. *Letter to an Exile*; carved wood and watercolour, 69 x 46 x 22 cm. Inverness Art Gallery (1978)

28. *Dark Shore Box*; carved and painted wood, canvas and found objects, 46 x 52 x 15 cm. The Scottish Arts Council Collection (1978)

29. *Fladday Reliquary*; found objects, bird and bone, 55 x 43 x 10 cm. Inverness Art Gallery, (1978) Plate 29

30. *Icon for a Fisherman*; painted wood, metal and ceramic, 61 x 60 x 10 cm. Private Collection, New York (1978) Plate 30

31. *Metamorphic Bird*; collage, carved and painted wood, 58 x 68 x 10 cm. Private Collection, Cambridge (1978)

32. *Mysterious Voyage*; carved and painted wood, 25 x 66 x 10 cm. Private Collection, London (1978)

33. *Inshore Presage*; collage, carved and painted wood, 66 x 46 x l2 cm. Private Collection, Cambridge (1978)

34. *Marine Harvest*; mixed media and drawing on board, 36 x 36 x 8 cm. Private Collection, Glasgow (1978)

35. *I.N.S. 232*; carved and painted wood, 43 x 43 x 8 cm. Collection David Gilbert, Germany (1978)

36. *Mystical Box with Lure* (I); found object and acrylic, 8 x 10 x 8 cm. Formerly the Scottish Arts Council Collection (1978)

37. *Mystical Box with Lure* (II); found object and acrylic, 8 x 10 x 8 cm. Formerly the Scottish Arts Council Collection (1978)

38. *Ex-Voto Box (for Mary-Isabella Reid)*; pencil drawing with carved and painted wood, 64 x 38 x 5 cm. Private Collection, Skye (1978)

39. *The Elders*; carved and painted wood, metal and bone, 64 x 38 x 5 cm. Claus Runkel, London (1978)

40. *Hunter's Dream No. 1*; pencil on board, with bone and wood, 30 x 46 x 8 cm. Private Collection, Scotland (1979)

41. *Hunter's Dream No. 2*; pencil on board, with wood and bone, 38 x 50 x 8 cm. Private Collection, Switzerland (1979)

42. *Scribe's Box*; ceramic and inlaid wood, 65 x 45 x 10 cm. Galerie Gilbert, Germany (1979)

43. *The Prisoner*; carved and painted wood, 60 x 45 x 10 cm. (approx.) Private Collection, Cambridge (1979)

44. *Traveller's Box*; acrylic on board with carved and painted wood, 60 x 40 x 10 cm. (approx.) Private Collection, Cambridge (1979)

45. *Anatomy of a Myth*; ceramic and painted wood, 102 x 81 x 20 cm. Private Collection, USA (1979)

46. *Time Passage No. 1*; painted wood, 28 x 68 x 8 cm. Private Collection, Scotland (1979)

47. *Time Passage No. 2*; painted wood, 28 x 68 x 8 cm. Private Collection (1981)

48. *Window Visitation North Uist*; carved and painted wood, 104 x 46 x 18 cm. Inverness Museum and Art Gallery, (1980) Plate 43

49. *Abigail's Apron*; painted wood, bone and metal, 214 x 50 x 15 cm. Private Collection, Cambridge (1980) Plate 21

50. *Pouch for an Exile*; carved and painted wood and bone, 94 x 43 x 10 cm. Private Collection, Switzerland (1980)

51. *Plate-Rack*; carved and painted wood, 85 x 104 x 12 cm. The Scottish Craft Collection, Edinburgh (1980)

52. *Healer's Cabinet*; steel, leather, lead and wood, 80 x 40 x 15 cm. (approx.). Private Collection, Scotland (1980)

53. *Interior Wester-Ross*; carved and painted wood, 137 x 56 x 23 cm. Private Collection, London (1980) Plate 24

54. *Dead Reckoning*; painted wood, mixed media and found objects, 76 x 96 x 10 cm. Private Collection, Inverness (1981)

55. *Wheelhouse Triptych*; carved and painted wood, bone and slate, three parts (a.) 122 x 91 x 16 cm. (b.) 122 x 61 x 10 cm. (c.) 122 x 61 x 10 cm. Private Collection (1981) Plate 46

56. *Wheelhouse Study No. 2*; carved, painted wood and collage with resin, 96 x 71 x 7 cm. Kirkcaldy Museum and Art Gallery (1981) Plate 47

57. *Night Voyage*; wood and bone, 50 x 40 x 7 cm. Collection David Gilbert, Germany (1981)

58. *Quiet Waters*; found objects and painted wood, 56 x 68 x 10 cm. Private Collection, Scotland (1981)

59. *Sailor's Home*; carved and painted wood, 43 x 43 x 8 cm. Private Collection, Switzerland (1981)

60. *Composite Image — East Neuk*; wood and found objects, 34 x 28 x 8 cm. Private Collection, Basel (1981)

61. *Easter at Polbain*; collage, carved and painted wood, 80 x 120 x 12 cm. Private Collection (1981)

(62.) *Tingle Box*; lead, wax, painted wood and bone, 51 x 97 x 10 cm. Dismantled (1981)

63. *Alignment Frame Paradox*; painted wood, bone and metal, 71 x 56 x 18 cm. Private Collection, London (1982)

64. *Black Priests' Box*; painted wood, bone and found objects, 46 x 36 x 20 cm. Private Collection, New York (1982) Plate 31

65. *Navigator's Locker*; carved and turned wood, bone and ivory, 64 x 56 x 25 cm. Private Collection, USA (1982) Plate 41

66. *Leviathan Elegy*; painted whalebone and found objects on three panels (joined) 203 x 137 x 10 cm., complete; 76 x 46 x 10 cm. each. Aberdeen Museum and Art Gallery, Aberdeen (1982) Plate 58

67. *Kelvin Red*; lead and painted metals on board, 25 x 41 x 10 cm. Private Collection, London (1982)

68. *Fisherman's Icon*; found objects, painted wood and bone, 43 x 40 x 28 cm. Private Collection, New York (1982)

69. *Summer at Roussillon*; found objects, collage and painted wood, 140 x 60 x 22 cm. Private Collection, London (1982)

70. *Portrait of Angus Mackenzie*; collage, slate, bone, canvas and wax, 46 x 56 x 7 cm. Private Collection, London (1982) Plate 23

71. *Fladday Memory*; wood, found objects and wax, 69 x 38 x 7 cm. Private Collection (1982)

72. *Talisker Tabernacle*; carved and painted wood, lead and found objects, 66 x 56 x 12 cm. Private Collection, Chicago (1982)

73. *The Drowning*; carved and painted wood, 15 x 20 x 71 cm. Private Collection, New York (1982)

74. *Days of the Fathers*; carved and painted wood, 89 x 61 x 8 cm. Private Collection, Venice (1982)

75. *Black Shrine*; painted wood and metal 58 x 38 x 8 cm. Private Collection (1982)

76. *The Observation of Christmas*; painted wood and photo-etching, 79 x 61 x 7 cm. Private Collection, London (1982) Plate 4

77. *Star of the Sea*; carved and painted wood, 30 x 25 x 5 cm. Fitzwilliam Museum, Cambridge (1983) Plate 26

78. *Raasay Window*; collage, carved and painted wood, 58 x 40 x 7 cm. Private Collection, Aberdeen (1983)

79. *Museum for a Seer*; carved and painted wood, 53 x 46 x 25 cm. (1983) Plate 42

80. *Death Fish*; collage and found objects, 42 x 69 x 5 cm. Collection David Gilbert, Germany (1983) Plate 64

81. *China Nights*; painted wood and mirrors, 85 x 61 x 10 cm. Glasgow Art Gallery and Museum (1983) Plate 45

82. *A Day at the Seaside*; mixed media construction, 84 x 61 x 5 cm. Private Collection (1983)

83. *Small Forecastle Reliquary*; carved and painted wood, wax and lead, 28 x 48 x l0 cm. Private Collection, Scotland (1983)

84. *I Didn't Go Willingly – I Went Sadly*; carved and painted wood and photo-etching, 61 x 40 x 10 cm. Private Collection (1983) Plate 62

85. *Sea-Pouch Offertory*; found objects, leather and lead, 66 x 61 x 8 cm. Private Collection, Scotland (1983)

86. *Death Fish Study*; painted wood, collage and bone, 30 x 45 x 5 cm. Private Collection, London (1983)

87. *Ritual Object/Didactic Showcase*; carved and painted wood and found objects, 117 x 41 x 8 cm. Private Collection, London (1983)

88. *Inner Sound*; painted wood, 70 x 50 x l0 cm. Private Collection (1984) Plate 65

89. *Enigmatic Figure*; carved and painted wood, 128 x 30 x 41 cm. Private Collection, London (1984) Plate 76

90. *Sea-Creed Banner*; found objects, painted wood and metal, 86 x 40 x 25 cm. (1984) Plate 75

91. *Gannet Shore Box*; carved and painted wood, bone and found objects, 43 x 23 x 7 cm. Private Collection (1984)

92. *Bard MacIntyre's Box*; mixed media (leather, shell, resin, wood, wax), 61 x 46 x 7 cm. Scottish National Gallery of Modern Art, Edinburgh (1984) Plate 51

93. *Ribhinn Bhan*; collage, painted wood and bone, 71 x 50 x 7 cm. Private Collection, New York (1984)

94. *Arctic Signs No. 1* – Green Tail Box; painted wood, cork and bone, 36 x 28 x 7 cm. Private Collection, London (1984)

95. *Arctic Signs No. 2* – Fleshing; lead, bone, acrylic and oil 36 x 28 x 7 cm. Mr and Mrs Michael Barrett, Washington, DC (1984)

96. *Arctic Signs No. 3* – Line Box; painted wood and bone, 48 x 33 x 7 cm. Collection Marian Maclean, Tayport (1984) Plate 59

97. *Arctic Signs No. 4* – Mayday; painted wood and bone, 38 x 28 x 7 cm. Private Collection (1984/86) Plate 61

98. *Egyptian Section*; mirror, wood, cast resin and metal, 43 x 33 x 10 cm. Private Collection (1984)

99. *Tourist Trips*; carved and painted wood and found objects, 86 x 61 x 12 cm. Private Collection, London (1984)

100. *La Palette*; carved and painted wood, 79 x 45 x 10 cm. Private Collection, London (1984)

101. *Rudder Requiem*; painted wood and metal, 50 x 43 x 12 cm. Private Collection, Cambridge (1985) Plate 38

102. *Shark Stones*; painted wood, slate, bone, leather and canvas, 76 x 122 x 10 cm. Private Collection, London (1985)

103. *Fire Figure*; laburnum wood and mixed media, 51 x 36 x l0 cm. (1985) Plate 32

104. *White Whale Box*; mixed media on board, with bone and collage, 46 x 31 x 8 cm. Claus Runkel Fine Art Ltd. London (1985)

105. *Raft of the Medusa I*; painted wood, plaster and bone, 43 x 72 x 10 cm. (1985)

106. *Raft of the Medusa II*; painted wood and plaster, 50 x 54 x l0 cm. (1985) Plate 56

107. *Hebridean Cruise*, painted wood and found objects, 54 x 40 x 8 cm. Private Collection, Chicago (1985) Plate 66

108. *Log Book I – Polar Voyage*, painted wood, canvas and mixed media, 112 x 82 x 7 cm. Private Collection, London (1986) Plate 49

109. *Log Book II – Winter Voyage*, painted wood, canvas and mixed media, 112 x 82 x 7 cm. Private Collection, London (1986) Plate 50

110. *Ancestor Figure*, painted wood, 152 x 18 x 6 cm. Uppsala Ekeby Ltd., Stockholm (1986) Plate 77

111. *Tide Column*, painted wood and ivory, 178 x 26 x 16 cm. Uppsala Ekeby Ltd, Stockholm (1986)

112. *Chart Box*, painted wood, found and carved objects, 79 x 51 x l0 cm. Private Collection (1986)

113. *Calotype for Schwitters*, collage and resin on wood, 41 x 28 x 4 cm. Private Collection, London (1986) Plate 27

114. *Arctic Signs — White Whale Box II*; carved and painted wood and bone, 40 x 33 x 7 cm. Private Collection, London (1986)

115. *Arctic Sea Marker*, painted wood, lead, resin, bone and whalebone, 40 x 30 x 5 cm. Private Collection (1987) Plate 54

116. *Stern-Sheet Icon*, painted wood, bone and resin, 36 x 33 x 4 cm. Private Collection (1987) Plate 35

117. *Excavator's Bureau*, mixed media, painted wood, bone and resin, 30 x 40 x 10 cm. Herbert Martin & Co., London (1987)

118. *Pole Marker Triptych*, mixed media, carved and found objects, 3 pieces, each 160 x 19 x 7 cm. Private Collection, London (1987) Plate 52

119. *Composite Memory (Vessel)*; painted wood, metal, resin and whalebone, 71 x 38 x 15 cm. Private Collection, London (1987) Plate 88

120. *Fisherman's Log*, mixed media and pencil on board, 122 x 122 x 10 cm. Private Collection, Germany (1987)

121. *Object of Unknown Use*, painted bone and acrylic on wooden base, 8 x 15.5 x 5.2 cm. (incl. base) (1987)

122. *Flenser's Fetish*, mixed media sculpture, 32 x 15 x 15 cm. Private Collection, London (1987)

123. *Black Tar's Post*, mixed media sculpture, 45 x 18 x 14 cm. (1987)

124. *Emigrants' Voyage*, sculpture, bone, carved and painted wood, 23 x 25 x 16 cm. Private Collection, Paris (1987) Plate 87

125. *Holy War*, construction, painted wood and resin, 48 x 37 x 8 cm. Private Collection, Germany (1988)

126. *Seagate*, bone, wood and painted resin, 41 x 34 x 7 cm. Private Collection, Rome (1988)

127. *Winter, North Atlantic*, painted wood & resin, 124 x 105 x 5 cm. (1988) Plate 53

128. *Landscape and Totems*, acrylic on board with mixed media, 125 x 125 x 5 cm. Private Collection, London (1988)

129. *Bottle Beach Part 1*; mixed media on board (1988), five pieces: *Salt*, 41 x 23 x 5 cm.; *Bone*, 41 x 23 x 5 cm.; *Ritual* 72 x 47 x 5 cm.; *Shell* 41 x 23 x 5 cm.; *Bottle Find 41 x 23 x 5 cm.*

130. *Bottle Beach Part 2*; mixed media on board (1988), five pieces: *Sand* 41 x 23 x 5 cm.; *Water* 41 x 23 x 5 cm.; *Measurement* 87 x 36 x 5 cm.;*Flint* 41 x 23 x 5 cm.; *Pigment* 41 x 23 x 5 cm. Plate 34

131. *Bottle Beach Part 3*; mixed media on board (1988), *Bronze* 41 x 23 x 5 cm.; *Skin* 41 x 23 x 5 cm.; *Warfare* 60 x 46 x 5 cm.; *Clay* 41 x 23 x 5 cm.; *Charcoal* 41 x 23 x 5 cm.

132. *West Coast*, mixed media, 56 x 71 cm. Private Collection (1989)

133. *Flounder and Cormorant*, tar, acrylic, and found wood, 26 x 25 x 4 cm. Private Collection, New York (1988)

134. *Sweeney Drinking from a Fountain*, acrylic casts and acrylic paint, 44 x 49 x 5 cm. Private Collection, London (1988)

135. *Death of Sweeney*, acrylic casts, acrylic and horn, 37 x 27 x 4 cm. Private Collection, Munich (1988)

136. *Bird Altar*, acrylic and wood on board, 38 x 103 x 28 cm. Private Collection, London (1988) Plate 82

137. *Manhattan*, mixed media, acrylic casts and collage on wood and board, 90 x 24 x 6.5 cm. Private Collection, San Francisco (1988) Plate 70

138. *Fisherman Listening for Herring*, found objects and acrylic on board, 34 x 39 x 2.5 cm. Private Collection, London (1988) Plate 35

139. *Central Park*, acrylic paste, plaster and wood on hardboard, 52 x 30 x 4.5 cm. (1988) Plate 69

140. *No Man's Land*, found objects and acrylic on wood, 26 x 48 x 7 cm. (1989)

141. *Ex-Voto/Kyleakin*, acrylic casts and oil on board, 27 x 35 x 5 cm. (1989)

142. *Kyles of Little Bernera*, acrylic paste and collage on board, 52 x 30 x 4.5 cm. Private Collection, Nurnberg (1989)

143. *Skye Fisherman: In Memoriam*, collage, found objects and acrylic on board, 135 x 125 x 6 cm. McManus Gallery, Dundee (1989) Plate 39

144. *Electro-Acoustic*, collage, acrylic and gouache on board, 45 x 45 x 3 cm. Private Collection, Germany (1989)

145. *Song of the Shellback*, found objects, acrylic and oil on paper and board, 91 x 76 x 6 cm. (1989)

146. *Kingfisherman*; acrylic and acrylic casts on board, 42 x 33 x 3 cm. Private Collection, London (1989) Plate 79

147. *Fishing Boat with Flag*; collage, wood and acrylic on board, 33 x 32 x 3 cm. Private Collection, London (1989)

148. *The Archaeology of Childhood*; found objects, and acrylic on paper and wood, 125 x 109 x 8 cm. (1989) Plate 80

149. *Sweeney Drinking at Evening*; acrylic and gouache on paper on board, 44 x 49 x 5 cm. Private Collection, Oxford (1989)

150. *Summer Fishing, Eriskay*; mixed media construction, 53 x 35 x 5 cm. Private Collection, Cambridge (1989)

151. *Sweeney Drinking*; acrylic on gesso, paper and board, 32 x 30 cm. Collection Turske Hue-Williams (1988)

152. *Nantucket Front and Back*; sculpture, painted wood, bone and resin, 82 x 14 x 14 cm. Private Collection, London (1989) Plate 71

153. *Sea Lectern*; sculpture, painted wood, bone and resin, 27 x 20 x 30 cm. Private Collection, London (1989) Plate 40

154. *Red Ley Marker*; mixed media on board, 136 x 105 x 7 cm. Robert Fleming Holdings Plc (1989) Plate 81

155. *Museum Casket*; mixed media sculpture, 44 x 28 x 14 cm. (1989) Plate 6

156. *Boston 'T'*; mixed media construction, 115 x 93 x 10 cm. RSA Diploma Collection (1989)

157. *Island Ferry, Cape Cod*; mixed media construction, 39 x 32 x 6 cm. Private Collection (1990) Plate 73

158. *Raft*; mixed media construction, 74 x 60 x 6 cm. (1990) Plate 57

159. *Wavy Navy*; mixed media construction, 42 x 36 x 4 cm. (1989)

160. *Bone Circle*; mixed media on board, 42 x 36 x 4 cm. (1990) Plate 74

161. *Landscape and Beacons*; acrylic on paper and board, 122 x 124 x 4 cm. (1990)

162. *Homeward Bound*; paper pulp, wood and baleen, 51 x 53 x 5 cm. (1990)

163. *Fisherman with Coal Fish*, painted resin and zinc, 33 x 36 x 4 cm. Private Collection (1990) Plate 72

164. *White Poet's Box*; mixed media construction, 56 x 61 x 8 cm. (1991)

165. *Poet's Blue Box*; mixed media construction, 63 x 61 x 10 ins. Private Collection, Edinburgh (1991)

166. *Kingfisherman and Storm Flag*; mixed media, acrylic on wood, 50 x 40 x 3 cm. Private Collection, London (1991)

167. *Whale Bethel*; mixed media construction, 126 x 126 x 3 cm. Private Collection, Toronto (1991)

168. *Postcard Series (1) Deep Sea*; mixed media construction, 56 x 30 x 12 cm. Collection David Maclean (1991)

169. *Postcard Series (2) Marché aux Pouces*; mixed media construction, 40 x 12 x 5 cm. (1991)

170. *Diviner's Wall*; mixed media construction, 162 x 162 x 8 cm. (1991) Frontispiece

171. *Memory Album*; painted and carved wood, 50 x 130 x 10 cm. Private Collection, Chicago (1991)

172. *The Battle of the Dog Fish*; collage and acrylic on card, 68 x 83 cm. Private Collection, Arizona (1991)

173. *The Emigrant Ship*; mixed media on board with slate and wood, 120 x 240.5 x 12 cm. (1992)

174. *Temple Vessel*; found objects and acrylic on board, 152 x 122 x 15 cm. (1992)

175. *Captain Ferguson's Vision* (1); acrylic and lead on board, 25 x 23 cm. (1992)

176. *Captain Ferguson's Vision* (2); acrylic and bone on board, 30 x 35 cm. (1992)

177. *Death of Sweeney*; sculpture, wood, metal and bone, 32 x 7 cm. (1992)

178. *Religio Scotica*; 12 parts, all mixed media and acrylic on wood, 35 x 26 x 8 cm. (1992)

BIOGRAPHY OF THE ARTIST

1941
Born Inverness 1941.
Education, Inverness Royal Academy.

1957-59
HMS *Conway*, N. Wales.
Midshipman. Blue Funnel Line, Liverpool.
Able Seaman Certificate.

1961-65
Diploma and Post Graduate Diploma, Gray's School of Art, Aberdeen.
Rowney Paint Prize, Hospitalfield Scholarship, Arbroath, George Davidson Memorial Scholarship.

1966
Scottish Education Department, Travelling Scholarship to Greece, Italy and France.
Studied at British School at Rome.

1968
Ring-net fisherman, Skye.
Married Marian Leven.

1969
Elected Professional Member, Society of Scottish Artists.
Dundee College of Education Teachers Training 1969, taught in various Fife primary schools.

1971
Appointed teacher at Bell Baxter High School, Cupar.

1973
Scottish Education Trust major bursary to study ring-net herring fishing.
Elected Associate of the Royal Scottish Academy.

1974
Worked on *Ring-Net* project.

1979
Scottish Arts Council Visual Arts Bursary.
Glasgow Group, Benno Schotz Prize.

1981
Appointed Lecturer, Fine Art, Duncan of Jordanstone,College of Art, Dundee.
Moved to Tayport, Fife.

1985
Scottish Arts Council Printmakers' Bursary, Dundee.

1987
Publication of *Catalogue Raisonné* by Claus Runkel.

1988
Visit to Maritime Museums in North America funded by Sir William Gillies Bequest, Royal Scottish Academy.

1991
Elected Royal Scottish Academician.
Publication of *A Night of Islands*, Paragon Press.

1992
Scottish Arts Council Award.

ONE MAN EXHIBITIONS

1967
British School, Rome.

1968
New 57 Gallery, Edinburgh.

1970
Richard Demarco Gallery, Edinburgh.

1971-73
Loomshop Gallery, Lower Largo.

1978
The Ring-Net, Third Eye Centre, Glasgow and Richard Demarco Gallery, Edinburgh, Leeds Art Gallery, Inverness Art Gallery, Campbeltown and Tarbert

1979
Compass Gallery, Glasgow.
Gilbert Parr Gallery, London.

1983
Richard Demarco Gallery, Edinburgh.
Landmark Centre, Carrbridge.

1984
Kirkcaldy Museum and Art Gallery, Retrospective Loan Exhibition.
Downing College, University of Cambridge.

1986
Ring-Net, Scottish National Gallery of Modern Art.

1987
Claus Runkel Fine Art, London.

1990
Runkel-Hue-Williams, Old Bond Street, London.

SELECTED GROUP EXHIBITIONS

1972
Four Figurative Painters, Demarco Gallery, Edinburgh.
MacLeod/Maclean, New 57 Gallery, Edinburgh.

1974
Dallas Brown/Maclean, Stirling Gallery.

1975
Six Coastal Artists, Saltire Society, Edinburgh.
A Choice Selection, Fruitmarket Gallery Opening Exhibition, Edinburgh.
200 Years of Scottish Painting, Marjorie Parr Gallery, London.

1976
The Need to Draw, Scottish Arts Council Touring Exhibition.

1977
Inscape, SAC Exhibition, selected by Paul Overy, Fruit Market Gallery, Warehouse, Covent Garden and Ulster Museum, Belfast.

1978
Scottish Arts Council Travelling Gallery Opening Exhibition.
Painters in Parallel, Scottish Arts Council, Edinburgh College of Art.

1980/81/82
International Art Fair, Basle; represented by David Gilbert Gallery, London and Germany.

1980
Compass Gallery, touring exhibition, Denmark.

1981
Art and the Sea, Third Eye Centre, touring exhibition, Glasgow, England and Wales.

1982
Inner Worlds, Arts Council of Great Britain, touring exhibition.
Artists Boxes, Xavier Berg Gallery, London.
Artender '82, Bilbao, Spain.
Mises en Boîte, touring exhibition, Belgium.

1983
Dusseldorf Arts Fair.
Six Scottish Artists, Cavallino Gallery, Venice.
Bath Arts Fair.
Leinster Fine Art, London.

1984
Barbican Art Fair, with Leinster Fine Art.
Scottish Contemporary Art in London and Washington. Will Maclean/Barbara Rae, Leinster Fine Art London and V.N. Gallery, Alexandria, Virginia.
A Festival of Scottish Drawing, Fine Art Society, Edinburgh.

1985
Hallaig, works for the film directed by T. Neat, touring exhibition.
Focus on Landscape , Fremantle, Australia.
Scottish Contemporary Drawings, Fair Maids Gallery, Perth.
10th Anniversary Exhibition, Third Eye Centre, Glasgow.
Represented Leinster Fine Art at the Chicago International Art Exposition.
Work for National Trust Collection exhibited at Scottish National Gallery of Modern Art.

1986
Wood Works, touring exhibition, Liverpool, Edinburgh and Inverness Art Galleries.
International Contemporary Art Fair, London.
Group exhibition with Leinster Fine Art.
Group exhibition Simon/Neuman Gallery, New York
Contemporary Art from Scotland, Leinster Fine Art.
As An Fhearann (From the Land), An Lanntair, Stornoway; and Royal Scottish Museum, Edinburgh — touring exhibiton, Canada.
Drawings from Sorley MacLean's 'Hallaig', STV.

1987
Will Maclean/Italio Scanga — Simon Neuman Gallery, New York.
Scottish Contemporary Art at Cambridge, Clare Hall.
Wood Works, Mixed Exhibition, Bluecoats Gallery, Liverpool, City Art Centre, Edinburgh.
Group Exhibition, Leinster Fine Art, International Contemporary Art Fair, London.
The Ring-Net, One-man exhibition, Scottish National Gallery of Modern Art.
Mixed Exhibition, C.D.R. Fine Art, London.
Contemporary Art from Scotland, Leinster Fine Art, London
Wrought Wood — Bolton Art Gallery.
The Scottish Show, touring exhibition, Wales.
Dundee Artists, Clare College, Cambridge.
The Chosen Few, Open Eye Gallery, Edinburgh.
Round the Scottish Coasts, Peacock Printmakers, travelling exhibition.

1988
Garden Exhibition, Fine Art Society, Glasgow.
Homage to MacDiarmid, Edinburgh Fesitival Exhibition, Richard Demarco Gallery,
Edinburgh Printmakers Workshop Festival Exhibition, invited artist
Modern Masters I, Claus Runkel Fine Art Ltd.
Modern Masters II, Claus Runkel Fine Art Ltd.
Clean Irish Sea, Greenpeace, Dublin, Cardiff and touring England and Germany.
Scottish Art, Middlesborough Art Society.
Opening Exhibition, Barbizon Gallery, Glasgow — Scottish Art.
State of the Art, Fine Art Society in Edinburgh and Glasgow.
Scottish Art Since 1900, Exhibition and Barbican Gallery, London.
Scottish National Gallery of Modern Art Festival.
Into the Highlands, Dundee City Art Gallery.
A Song of the Sea, Barrack Street Museum, Dundee.
The Stevenson Collection, Warwick Arts Trust, London.

1990
From the Directors Chair, Open Eye Gallery, Edinburgh.
Edinburgh Printmakers in London, Vanessa Devereux Gallery, London.
Boxes and Totems, England & Co., London.
Contemporary Arts Fair, Olympia, London, Runkel-Hue-Williams.
Jordanstone Folio. A collaboration with Writer-in-Residence included in the Kindred Spirits exhibition, Ancrum Gallery and Dundee College of Art.
Boites et Reliefs (4 person show), Gallerie de la Gare, Bonnieux, France.
Scotlands Pictures, the National Collection, RSA, Edinburgh.
Gallery Artists, Runkel-Hue Williams, London.
Glasgow's Glasgow, Art in the North, The Arches, Glasgow.
Scotland Creates—5000 Years of Scottish Art and Design, McLellan Galleries, Glasgow.

1991
The Artist and the Whale, Dundee Art Gallery.
Gallery Artists, Runkel-Hue-Williams, London.
RSW/Peacock Printmakers, RSA, Edinburgh, invited artist.
Wood Works, Covent Garden, London.
Towards a New Decade, 20th Century Scottish Art, The Fine Art Society, Glasgow and Edinburgh.
Scottish Art in Budapest, Hungary.
Will Maclean, *A Night of Islands*, Runkle-Hue-Williams, London.
New Prints, Cyril Gerber Fine Art, Glasgow.
Myth and Symbol, Highland Regional Council, touring exhibition.
20th Century Scottish Art, Bristol, North-

West Academy of the Arts.
Virtue and Vision, Sculpture and Scotland, National Gallery of Scotland in the Royal Scottish Academy.
Art in Boxes, England & Co, London.
The Artist as Voyager, Will Maclean and Richard Demarco, Aberdeen and Edinburgh.
The First 100 Years, invited artist, Society of Scottish Artists Exhibition.
The Scottish Artists and Artist Craftsmen Exhibition, invited artist.

WORKS IN PUBLIC AND CORPORATE COLLECTIONS

Aberdeen Art Gallery.
Argyllshire Education Trust.
Arts Council of Great Britain.
BBC Scotland.
British Transport.
British Museum.
Broadford Hospital, Skye.
Contemporary Art Society.
Clare College, Cambridge.
Comhairie Nan Eilean.
Department of the Environment.
Dumbarton Education Trust.
Dundee District Council.
Edinburgh City Art Gallery.
Fanim Hall Collection, Vancouver, Canada.
Ferens Art Gallery, Hull.
Fife Education Authority.
Fitzwilliam Museum, Cambridge.
Glasgow Art Gallery, Kelvingrove.
Inverness Museum and Art Gallery.
Inverness Education Authority.
Kirkcaldy Museum and Art Gallery.
Kings College, Cambridge.
McManus Art Gallery, Dundee
Motherwell District Council.
Mitchell Library, Glasgow.
National Library of Scotland.
National Trust for Scotland.
Perth Museum and Art Gallery.
Peterhead Museum and Art Gallery.
Readers Digest Collection, USA.
Robert Fleming Collection, London.
Royal Scottish Academy Collection.
Rhode Island School of Design, USA.
Scottish Arts Council.
Scottish Craft Collection.
Scottish National Gallery of Modern Art.
Scottish Television.
Stoke on Trent Art Gallery.
Scunthorpe Art Gallery.
Texaco Collection.
Westfield State College, Mass. USA.
Yale Centre for British Art, New Haven, USA

BIBLIOGRAPHY

BOOKS

Woods, Alan, and Runkel, Claus, *Will Maclean: Sculptures and Box Constructions, 1974-1987* with a Catalogue Raisonné, Claus Runkel Fine Art Ltd (London 1987)

BOOKS ILLUSTRATED

Gillies, Valerie, *The Chanter's Tune*, (Edinburgh 1990) with pen drawings and cover by the artist

CATALOGUES: SINGLE ARTIST

McGrath, Tom and Maclean, Will, *Ring-Net Herring Fishing on the West Coast of Scotland:* a documentary exhibition by Will Maclean, Third Eye Centre (Glasgow 1978)

Macmillan, Duncan, *Will Maclean: New Work*, Runkel-Hue-Williams (London 1990)

Neat, Tim, *Will Maclean: Constructions and Small Sculptures*, Richard Demarco Gallery (Edinburgh, April 1983)

Oliver, Cordelia, *Will Maclean: Constructions and Drawings*, Kirkcaldy Museum (1984)

CATALOGUES: SHARED

Woods, Alan, *The Artist as Voyager* (Will Maclean and Richard Demarco), Peacock Printmakers (Aberdeen 1991)

Lucie-Smith, Edward, 'Will Maclean and Barbara Rae', *Scottish Contemporary Art in Washington and London*, Leinster Fine Art (1984)

CATALOGUES: GROUP AND THEMATIC EXHIBITIONS

Hartley, Keith, for Scottish National Gallery of Modern Art, *Scottish Art since 1900* (London 1990), p93 and colour illustration pl48 of *Bard MacIntyre's Box*

Kaplan, Wendy, ed., for Glasgow Art Gallery and Museums, *Scotland Creates: 5000 Years of Scottish Art and Design* (London 1990), ppl78-180, colour illustrations of *Leviathan Elegy* and *Memories of a Northern Childhood*

Klepal, Jean, 'Boîtes et Reliefs', *Cahiers de la Gare*, No.15, Galerie de la Gare, Bonnieu(1990), including colour illustration of *No Man's Land*

MacLean, Malcolm, ed. for An Lanntair, Stornoway, *As an Fhearann; From the Land* (Edinburgh 1986), pp68-9, black and white illustration of *Memorial to the Glendale Martyrs* and colour illustrations of *Sabbath of the Dead* and *Memorial for a Clearance Village*

REFERENCES AND ILLUSTRATIONS IN BOOKS

Block, Jonathan and Leisure, Gerry, *Understanding Three Dimensions* (1987), p60, black and white illustration of *Museum for a Seer*

Gage, Edward, *The Eye in the Wind: Contemporary Scottish Painting Since 1945* (London 1977), pp74-5, black and white illustration of *Trap Image No. 3*

Hardie, William, *Scottish Painting from 1837 to the Present* (London 1990), ppl96-206

Macmillan, Duncan, *Scottish Art 1460-1990* (Edinburgh l990), pp396-8, colour illustration of *Skye Fisherman: In Memoriam*

O'Driscoll, Robert, ed., *The Celtic Consciousness* (Edinburgh 1981), pp306-8, black and white illustration of *The Elders*

Orel, Harold, Snyder, Henry, and Stokstad, Marilyn, *The Scottish World* (London 1981), pp306-8, black and white reproduction of *Plate Rack*

Spalding, Frances, *A Dictionary of Twentieth Century British Art* (London 1991), p306

Wishart, Anne, ed. and Oliver, Cordelia, *The Society of Scottish Artists: the First 100 Years* (Edinburgh l990), p60, black and white illustration of *Window Visitation North Uist*

SELECTED ARTICLES AND REVIEWS

Beaumont, Mary-Rose, 'Will Maclean at Runkel Fine Art', *Arts Review* (12 Sept 1987)

Beaumont, Mary-Rose, 'Will Maclean at Runkel-Hue-Williams', *Arts Review* (5 June l990)

Carr, Richard, 'Memorabilia of a Box Maker', *Craftwork* (May 1980)

Carr, Richard, 'The Work of Will Maclean', *Glasgow Herald* (13 April 1983)

Carr, Richard, 'Constructions that Disturb', *The Scotsman* (20 March 1990)

Clough, Juliet, 'Elegy for Fish', *The Times* Educational Supplement (23 August 1974)

Gage, Edward, 'Painting by Will Maclean at the New 57 Gallery', *The Scotsman* (19 April 1968)

Gillies, Valerie, 'Will Maclean: Symbols of Survival', *The Green Book*, Vol.VIII, no. 9 (1991) with black and white illustrations of *Hallaig No. 4, Nantucket Front and Back* and *Pole Marker Triptych*

Henry, Clare, 'Will Maclean at the Richard Demarco Gallery', *Glasgow Herald* (13 April 1983)

Henry, Clare, 'Will Maclean' (The *Ring-Net* at the Scottish National Gallery of Modern Art) *Glasgow Herald* (8 May 1986)

Henry, Clare, 'The Rise and Rise of the Scots', *Glasgow Herald* (7 May 1991)

Keller, Victoria, 'The Work of Will Maclean', *Scottish Life*, Volume 4, No.l (1989) including colour illustrations of *Memorial for a Clearance Village, Memories of a Northern Childhood, Abigail's Apron* and *Leviathan Elegy*

Michie, Eileen, 'Will Maclean RSA', *Royal Scottish Academy Publication* No. l9 (1991)

Oliver, Cordelia, 'Will Maclean at the Richard Demarco Gallery', *The Guardian* (20 April 1984)

Oliver, Cordelia, 'Will Maclean at the Third Eye Centre', *Artscribe*, No. II (1978)

Smith, W. Gordon, 'Poetry in Motion', *Scotland on Sunday* (7 June 1991)

Stevenson, Sylvia, 'Will Maclean at Claus Runkel Fine Art', *Galleries Magazine*, Vol.V, No. 4 (1987)

Stevenson, Sylvia, 'Will Maclean', *Apollo* (March 1990) including black and white illustrations of *Kyles of Little Bernera* and *Red Ley Marker*

Vaizey, Marina, 'Scottish Contemporary Art in Washington and London', *Arts Review* (November 1984)

Woods, Alan, 'Interview with Will Maclean', *Alba*, No.9 (1988) with colour illustrations of *Pole Marker Triptych, Leviathan Elegy* and *Landscape and Totems*

DISSERTATIONS

Allerston, Patricia, *The Ring-Net* by Will Maclean, University of St Andrews (1990)

Payne, Judith, *Individual Constructs of Cultural Identity*, South West Polytechnic, Plymouth (1991)

FILM AND TELEVISION

Will Maclean, produced by Nigel Finch, *Arena Fine Art*, BBC2 (1978)

Will Maclean, produced by Michael Paterson, *The Scottish Picture Show*, STV (1987)

Will Maclean, Grampian Television (1990)

A Night of Islands: Will Maclean, N.B. Arts Programme, STV, 1992

FOOTNOTES

1. Ian Finlay, *Art in Scotland* (Oxford 1948)
2. Sir Archibald Geikie, *Scottish Reminiscences* (Glasgow 1908) p226
3. Ibid., p227
4. Neil Gunn, *Highland River* (London 1960) p121
5. Sorley MacLean, *From Wood to Ridge: Collected Poems in English & Gaelic* (London 1991) p111
6. Ibid., pxvi
7. Angus Martin, *The Larch Plantation* (Edinburgh 1990) p53
8. MacLean, 'Hallaig', *Collected Poems*, p229
9. *Ken Dingwall*, Scottish Arts Council (1977) p14
10. *Sunday Times*, March 9, 1975
11. In *Inner Worlds* (ACGB) 1982
12. 'The Antique Scene', *Scots Hairst* (London 1967) p124
13. Ibid., p75
14. Jessie Weston, *From Ritual to Romance* (New York 1957) p124
15. *Highland River*, p255
16. Ibid., p55
17. *A Drunk Man Looks at the Thistle, Complete Poems of Hugh MacDiarmid* (London 1978) I, p139
18. MacLean, 'The Selling of a Soul', *Collected Poems*, p15
19. MacDiarmid, *To Circumjack Cencrastus, Complete Poems*, I, p281
20. *Comus*, lines 115-6
21. *Highland River*, p215
22. Weston, *From Ritual to Romance*, p125
23. Ibid., p124
24. MacDiarmid, *To Circumjack Cencrastus, Complete Poems*, I, p289
25. John Gregorson Campbell, *Superstitions of the Highlands and Islands of Scotland* (Glasgow 1900)
26. John Gregorson Campbell, *Witchcraft and Second Sight in the Highlands and Islands of Scotland: Tales and Traditions collected entirely from oral sources* (Glasgow 1902) p172
27. *Scottish Gaelic Texts*, Vol. I, *Scottish Verse from the book of the Dean of Lismore*, edited by William J. Watson (Edinburgh 1937) p219
28. MacLean, *Collected Poems*, pp308-9
29. MacLean, *Collected Poems*, p227
30. *Highland River*, p125
31. MacLean, *The Cuillin, Collected Poems*, p121
32. George Campbell Hay, *Fuaran Sleibh* (Glasgow 1947) p20